NORAD

AND THE SOVIET NUCLEAR THREAT

NORAD
AND THE SOVIET NUCLEAR THREAT
CANADA'S SECRET ELECTRONIC AIR WAR

GORDON A. A. WILSON

DUNDURN
TORONTO

TO MY FAMILY

Emily

My True Love

The airspeed slower than me
The altitude below me
The fuel in my tanks
The wind beneath my wings

Mark, Jennifer, Cameron & Emmett

The welcoming runway lights
On a dark and stormy night

Copyright © Gordon A.A. Wilson, 2011

Library and Archives Canada Cataloguing in Publication

Wilson, Gordon A. A.
        NORAD and the Soviet nuclear threat : Canada's secret
        electronic air war / Gordon A.A. Wilson.

Includes bibliographical references and index.
Also issued in electronic formats.
ISBN 978-1-4597-0410-7

        1. Air defenses--Canada--History. 2. Cold War. I. Title.

UG735.C3W54 2011   358.4'030971   C2011-906072-8

1 2 3 4 5   15 14 13 12 11

Conseil des Arts du Canada Canada Council for the Arts

ONTARIO ARTS COUNCIL
CONSEIL DES ARTS DE L'ONTARIO

We acknowledge the support of the **Canada Council for the Arts** and the **Ontario Arts Council** for our publishing program. We also acknowledge the financial support of the **Government of Canada** through the **Canada Book Fund** and Livres Canada Books, and the **Government of Ontario** through the **Ontario Book Publishing Tax Credit** and the Ontario Media Development Corporation.

Care has been taken to trace the ownership of copyright material used in this book. The author and the publisher welcome any information enabling them to rectify any references or credits in subsequent editions.

J. Kirk Howard, President

www.dundurn.com

Dundurn
3 Church Street, Suite 500
Toronto, Ontario, Canada
M5E 1M2

CONTENTS

Acknowledgements

My wife Emily for her continued total support and encouragement, without reservation, from the very beginning to the last words. Without her moral support this book would not have been completed

My daughter Jennifer, the librarian, for her invaluable professional editing services and guidance. My son-in-law Cameron, who looked after their newborn son Emmett while Jennifer wielded her pencil.

My son Mark, a pilot, who gave me the inspiration to write about my era as he lives his own flying adventures.

Joan and Chuck Gauld who were continually amazed of the progress of Joan's 'little brother'.

Our friends, in alphabetical order, who supported me through words and gesture in my fight against multiple sclerosis which at times interfered with my writing progress: Jean and Ted Andrew, Tamara and David Douglas, Chrissie and Colm Egan, Dorothy and Bill Glendinning, Jette and Terje Hartvigsen, Angela and Rick Hovey, Mayling and Barrie Laycock, Judy and Geoff Pickard, Lynn and Harold Pratsides, Wayne Ralph, Anne and Peter Tilbury.

Congregation of St John's Presbyterian Church, White Rock, British Columbia, whose Sunday enquiries as to my progress were very supportive.

Lois Peterson, author, my creative writing course instructor, who opened my eyes to a new endeavour, writing, and gave me the tools to complete it.

Wayne Ralph, author, for his professional advice during the whole process.

Nicola Pierce, author, for compiling the comprehensive index.

Mansel Robinson, Surrey writer in residence 2009, for allowing me to read my work at a public forum.

Nelle Oosterom, assistant editor, *Canada's History* magazine, who schooled me in my first writing project for the magazine, which subsequently became this book's foundation.

Colm Egan, who looked after/sorted/salvaged/altered the images for this book.

Ron Bell, who captured the very essence of the book and what I wanted to say in his Foreword.

Rick Hovey, former Voodoo pilot, artist, for his continued enthusiastic support and contributing the chapter sketches.

Rob Dunlop, who tried to get classified material released from the library and public archives and found out that NORAD 'Secret' information is still 'Secret' after forty years.

The interviewees for their time and anecdotes, many of which I did not use due to publishing constraints – all the stories are suitable for another book: Ron Bell, Roger Blais, Bill Bland, Sydney Burrows, Lowell Butters, Nick Chester, Malcolm Dewar, Jack Donnelly, Rob Dunlop, Dan Farrell, Randy Faulkner, Doug Fitzpatrick, Richard Girouard, Jim Graham, Maurice Hanberg, Rick Hovey, Bob Keith, Dennis Kelleher, Barrie Laycock, Gene Lukan, Larry Lundquist, Peter Maunsell, George McAffer, Andy McGraw, Robert Merrick, Bob Moore, Gordon Moore, Ron Neeve, Grant Nicholls, Pierre Parent, Ken Peacock, Ken Penny, Jim Pocklington, Wayne Ralph, Roy Roch, Marty Schlosser, Wayne Scott, Richard Sopczak, John Stuart, David Trotter, Lew Twambley, Jerry Vernon, Gary Wiffen, and John Wiggin.

Jerry Vernon, for verifying/supplying specific aircraft history and images and being 'one of the most knowledgeable historical aviation authorities around'.

Janet Lacroix, Department of National Defence, Canadian Forces Joint Imagery Center, Ottawa, for researching/duplicating images.

Dr Stephen Harris, Sabrina Fairchild and Valerie Cosbourn, Directorate of History and Heritage, Ottawa, for help accessing/researching military files.

Sydney Burrows, John Stuart, Book of Remembrance, Ottawa.

Library and Archives Canada, Ottawa.

Surrey Public Library, Semiahmoo Branch and Inter Library Loans Dept., British Columbia.

University of British Columbia, Library and Continuing Education, Vancouver.

Aviation Museums: Bob Moore at Western Canada Aviation Museum, Winnipeg, Manitoba; Canadian Warplane Heritage Museum, Hamilton; Calgary Aero Space Museum, Alberta; Nanton Air Museum, Alberta; Terry Brunner, Bob Fowles (prepared CF-100 for crew images), Canadian Museum of Flight, Langley, British Columbia; Ian Leslie, Library, Canada Aviation and Space Museum, Ottawa; British Columbia Aviation Museum, North Saanich; Alberta Aviation Museum, Edmonton.

Randall Brooks, Canada Science and Technology Museum, Ottawa, for access to Air Weapons Controller's scope.

Bruce Grayson, modeller, for assembling the CF-100 Canuck and CF-101 Voodoo models for my book signing table.

John Kimberley, Malcolm Nason and Bill Powderly for keeping the romantic vision of 'Airspotting' and aircraft photography alive for fifty years.

Joseph Pettican, Project Editor, Amberley Publishing, for checking the manuscript and making sure it made the required standard. We are still talking!

For those of you who I have not mentioned, due my own oversight, rest assured that your contribution was greatly appreciated and added to the success of this book, my apologies.

Foreword

Tally-Ho. Two TU-Ninety Five, Bear H, heading zero nine zero, speed four hundred, angels two nine.

5 February 1988. An actual radio transmission from one of a pair of Canadian Air Force CF-18 Hornets flying out of Inuvik, NWT, shortly after taking a handover from two Alaska, based USAF F-15 Eagles about 160 kilometres north of Alaska's northern shore. A superb example of cooperation between Canada and the United States made possible by the NORAD treaty.

My last assignment in the Canadian Forces was as Deputy Commander of the Alaskan NORAD Region at Elmendorf AFB, just outside Anchorage. Lt-Gen. David Nichols USAF, the American military commander of all Alaskan forces, made me responsible for operations required to intercept, identify and, if necessary, destroy Soviet Union aircraft entering Alaskan airspace. To accomplish this task the NORAD Region had use of two squadrons of F-15s, two AWACS aircraft, SAC refuelling tankers, ground-based long-range radars and a very large supporting network.

This was 1986. Few in the Region expected much activity from the Soviet Strategic Aviation force, most of whose incursions had been on the east coast of North America en route to Cuba. To our great surprise, over the next twenty-four months the Soviets conducted more combat patrol missions in the Arctic airspace contiguous to the North American mainland than at any other period of the Cold War. These missions were not flown by high-speed jets, but TU-95 Bear turboprop bombers. Although considered obsolete, they could fly vast distances without refuelling and the Bear H carried a load of AS-15 Long Range Cruise Missiles, nuclear tipped, which could be deployed a long way from their intended targets. Between 1986 and 1988 the Alaskan NORAD combat team of air and ground supporting units intercepted and indentified more than fifty Bear H and Bear G bombers. F-15s and sometimes CF-18s controlled by the 22nd NORAD Region accompanied them throughout their patrols, some for as long as seven hours. The message NORAD sent was clear. We know you are coming; we will intercept you far away from North American territory and will escort you with armed fighter aircraft until you depart our airspace. Make a hostile move and you can be destroyed!

This was the kind of air defence envisaged for NORAD at its inception more than fifty years ago. Long-range radars, intercept controllers and fighters from the United States and Canada against the air-breathing bomber. This aspect of NORAD still has relevance today, despite the emphasis on intercontinental ballistic missiles. Starting in 2007, the Russians are again flexing their muscles and F-22 Raptors and CF-18s have intercepted Bear bombers on patrols in the high arctic.

The author of this book, Gordon Wilson, fully understands the importance of the many elements which comprise NORAD. From a Canadian perspective he leads us through the historical background essential to understanding the framework for the NORAD treaty. He discusses, in considerable detail, the technical and equipment requirements for such a huge undertaking, but does not swamp the reader with facts and figures. He uses the prism of a single NORAD air defence exercise to look at the full spectrum of participating ground radars, interceptor squadrons, and use of electronic warfare, communications networks and command elements in a NORAD-wide exercise and shows how the component parts work together. But most important of all, he gives the reader a living history through anecdotes, interviews and reminiscences from people with real identities – I recognise many of their names – who worked tirelessly to make NORAD an effective bulwark against Soviet incursions into the airspace of North America during the height of the Cold War years.

Gordon covers the history and employment of the CF 100-Canuck and the CF 101-Voodoo in exquisite detail, which brought back vivid memories for someone like myself, who flew as a Navigator in both these aircraft. There is much to enjoy here as the author induces some of the visceral excitement of flying in a fighter aircraft.

Gordon understands this feeling well, having flown for four years on missions in the NORAD system, including time piloting electronic-warfare aircraft with 414 EW Squadron. He reminds us frequently of the vulnerability of the interceptor aircraft and ground radar systems to electronic counter measures which could nullify their operational capability. He stresses this theme of counter measures, counter-counter measures and so on, which were significant in the preparation of the NORAD units for operations against a Soviet attack.

He finally brings it all together in the form of an actual NORAD-wide flying exercise where all components of the air defence system are tested by a target force simulating an attack by Soviet bombers. There is a sense of anticipation and tension in his description of unfolding events in this aerial chess game played out on a board of continental dimensions.

Those who worked in NORAD at some time in their careers will enjoy this well-researched book for the insights it brings and the memories it will evoke. For those not so enlightened, the book provides a very readable history of a remarkable treaty, NORAD, of the enduring benefit to Canada and the United States, and the equally remarkable components and people which made it, and continues to make it, so effective.

Brigadier General (retired) Ron Bell
RCAF and CAF 1954–1988

Prologue

Canada was not at peace for long in the years following the Second World War, as it became involved, once again, in an overseas war. This time it was as a member of the United Nations in the Korean conflict. On the home front it also maintained a quiet but continuous alert to protect Canadian sovereignty; of particular importance were the Cold War and the growing threat of Soviet bombers armed with nuclear weapons. The Canadian Armed Forces (CAF), in partnership with American forces under the auspices of the North American Air Defence Command (NORAD) agreement, conducted secret exercises designed to test their ability to detect and intercept Soviet bombers. What follows is the account of all the Canadian men and women in their various military capacities who took part in these exercises in the 1970s to protect us as we slept. The book will describe the part played by all the different occupations in the defence of North America. The relationship between these professions during these exercises will be examined to explain why NORAD was such a formidable force.

Canada emerged triumphant from the Second World War and realised the need to maintain its territorial sovereignty. This was not an easy task given the physical size of the country. In the aftermath of the Second World War, political and military alliances were an important part of international relations. Canada had long-standing ties with Britain and formed new alliances as a member of the North Atlantic Treaty Organisation and a signatory of the 1958 NORAD agreement, with its neighbour, the United States of America (USA). The NORAD agreement was designed to protect North America from air attack by constructing an extensive radar defence network in conjunction with fighter interceptor squadrons from both countries. The CAF provided three squadrons of fighter interceptors to NORAD in 1973, the time of our narrative, to protect Canadian airspace. Technological developments in aircraft performance meant that long-range Union of Socialist Soviet Republics (USSR) bombers, initially developed during the 1950s and capable of carrying nuclear bombs and cruise missiles, could easily reach North America. As a result, Canadians were under the threat of possible annihilation as they went about their daily lives.

The CAF maintained dedicated crews and aircraft 'on alert' for twenty-four hours every day of the year. 'On alert' meant that crews and armed aircraft held in readiness would be airborne within five minutes of a command from the NORAD system to intercept possible intruders. In the 1970s CAF Squadrons were held on alert at Comox, British Columbia, Bagotville, Quebec, Val d'Or, Quebec and Chatham, New Brunswick, to cover the possible flight approaches to Canada.

NORAD developed an extensive training system designed to maintain the proficiency of the agreement between Canada and the USA. Failure was not an option. These missions often disrupted daily family lives, as the most suitable time for these exercises was in the early hours of the morning, to avoid interfering with civilian air traffic. 'I knew that my husband, a member of a fighter interceptor crew, was involved in the defence of Canada but he spoke mostly of the Voodoo aircraft, his love of flying and not of the details of the actual job. I never enquired further as I knew there were many things that he could not tell me – better not to ask!' related Pamela Bland, a supportive wife.

CAF CF-18 and a Russian Bear bomber, 5 September 2007. (Courtesy of Canada's Air Force)

These 1970s exercises have become only personal memories now. Recent events, however, indicate that the vigilance of our twenty-first-century interceptor crews is as vital as ever. Once again Russia is flexing its military muscle. For example, the Russian Victory Day parade held on the 9 May 2008, to commemorate the 1945 victory over Nazi Germany, was particularly remarkable because Red Square in Moscow, for the first time in seventeen years, since the collapse of the Soviet Union, felt the tread of thousands of troops, the rumble of massive tanks and the roar overhead of jet fighters and bombers. Mark Colvin, presenter for the Australia Broadcasting Corporation's current affairs programme *PM*, attended the parade and remarked, 'There are heavy echoes of the Cold War in Moscow's Red Square today.' History will be the judge of whether David H. Wilkins, ambassador of the United States to Canada, is correct in his letter published on 12 May 2008 in *The National Post*. He stated, on the fiftieth anniversary of NORAD, that 'their valiant [US and Canadian] heroes of the Second World War ... determined to keep the homeland secure ... would become the most successful and unique peacekeeping agreement the world has ever known.'

Today, the global political and military situation is echoing Cold War tensions, fuelled by the economic recovery of Russia and the diminishing international influence of the USA. The passing of time has allowed some previously unknown and secret information to become available. The public has a right to know these facts that will help people understand what really went on during those years.

This book will give the reader an insight into all aspects of NORAD exercises never before gathered in one source. Extensive background information on radar, electronic warfare, air weapons controllers, fighter aircraft and aircrew has been collected to provide top secret details of NORAD defence. Archival research and interviews with RCAF and CAF personnel provide the facts and anecdotes presented in *NORAD and the Soviet Nuclear Threat*.

In the following chapters you will:

- Discover what it is like to be the hunter or the hunted as you fly with fighter aircrew struggling for electronic supremacy with fictitious 'Soviet' targets.
- Meet the pilot who became the first Canadian ever to win the coveted NORAD 'Top Gun' award in 1972.
- Read a CAF Navigator's personal account of the first intercept of a Soviet bomber as it threatened our Canadian shores in the 1960s.

- Relive the exercises with the Air Weapons Controllers and Air Surveillance Officers seated at their radar screens deep underground in 'The Hole' at North Bay, Ontario.
- Comprehend the daily struggle to maintain and prepare a fighter interceptor response that was at the ready 24/365.
- Understand how nuclear weapons came to be on Canadian soil while the Canadian government denied possession of such weapons.

This is the story of Canada's secret electronic air war during the Cold War as told by the many participants, the author included, who stood 'on guard' in the effort to preserve Canadian sovereignty. Those who were a part of the Canadian Air Defence system share their experiences with those who want to learn more about our Canadian political and military history.

From far and wide
O Canada, we stand on guard for thee.
God keep our land glorious and free!
O Canada, we stand on guard for thee.

Quotation from the Canadian National Anthem.

CHAPTER ONE

The Cold War

Cold War tension was born in the race to capture Berlin. The Second World War was drawing to a close and the triumphant combatants realised that, while they were united in battle which would soon be over, they were divided by ideology. What would happen when all the victorious countries had no common enemy? They would look to their own future. Canada, the USA and Britain were looking to a very different future than the one that the USSR envisioned. The cooling off had begun.

The Cold War can be defined as an extended period of tension between capitalism and communism that manifested itself in military skirmishes of varying seriousness, political manoeuvring and influencing of world economics which changed the very way we lived. The different ideologies were centred in the USA and the USSR, but affected the entire globe. What side are you on, the good guys or the bad guys? If you could not make up your mind to join the Communist side or tended to the other side then you risked being invaded to toe the party line; Hungary in 1956 is a clear example of this.

It would be a long, cool period, forty-two years from 1947 until 1989, until reason prevailed. In 1945, the Second World War ended and the USA and the USSR found themselves as powerful nations with large armies. The difference between the two countries was that the USA had retained its industrial might as its mainland had been remote from the war. The army of the USSR had been beaten back and their country ravaged, all the way to Stalingrad, before the tide of war reversed. It had been a long fightback to recover the territory lost and the Soviet countryside and industrial heartland had been devastated. Both countries were determined to have their political and economic systems survive and prevail during the years ahead.

The Cold War superpowers, the USA and the USSR, played an ideological chess game and countries were the chess board. It ranged from local border skirmishes in Germany and the Korean War to the near cataclysmic stand off during the 1962 Cuban Crisis, when the USSR was shipping missiles to Cuba. Simultaneously there was a race to develop bigger and better weapons that would act as deterrence to the other superpower to keep it in check.

The Korean War involved all three Canadian armed services. The Royal Canadian Air Force 426 Transport Squadron ferried goods and supplies from the USA for the war in Korea. Many missions were flown in support of the war effort. A documented report indicated 599 missions that required 34,000 flying hours. Captain Dan Farrell, whom the author had flown with on 414 Electronic Warfare Squadron, recounted the long flight in the Canadair C-54GM North Star from Washington to Japan with 426 Transport Squadron. The aircraft was unpressurised and had an extremely noisy exhaust from the four Rolls-Royce Merlin engines. This contributed to a very long, exhausting, and uncomfortable flight that was repeated throughout the war.

A typical supply mission for Dan was a flight from McChord Air Force Base (AFB), Washington, to Elmendorf AFB (Anchorage), Alaska, to Shemya AFB, Alaska, to Haneda (Tokyo), Japan. His log book showed 38:00 flying hours from 8 to 11 December 1950. The return trip he mentioned was bringing back the wounded by way of Wake Island to Honolulu, Hawaii, to San Francisco to Elmendorf AFB, Alaska. His

Captain Dan Farrell in 2010. (Courtesy of Author)

log book showed 35:05 flying hours from 13 to 16 December 1950. The wounded, the sick and the dying on that flight remind us today that a combative war, not a Cold War, is indeed brutal.

Although Canada did not send any fighter squadrons to Korea, it did send pilots there on 'exchange' with the USAF. A total of twenty-two pilots served on Sabre squadrons and one RCN pilot served with a US Navy Panther fighter squadron. They accounted for a total of nine Mikoyan-Gurevich Mig-15s confirmed downed, two probably downed and ten damaged. RCAF pilots were awarded seven US Distinguished Flying Crosses, one Commonwealth Distinguished Flying Cross and four US Air Medals. Canadians flew a total of 1,036 sorties in Korea. One pilot, S/L A. MacKenzie, was shot down accidentally by friendly fire and became a prisoner of war. Canada, in war-effort support, supplied the USAF with sixty F-86 Sabre Mk 2s (USAF F-86 E-6s).

In discussions with Colonel G. (Grant) W. Nicholls regarding his responsibilities as the Commanding Officer of CFB Comox, home of 409 All Weather Fighter Squadron, he mentioned that he had served overseas in Korea. Grant was on exchange tour with the USAF 16th Fighter Interceptor Squadron (FIS), flying the North American Sabre from Suwon, South Korea, on fighter sweeps and bomber escort duties over North Korea. Grant recalled that, 'The Migs were not very active, it was difficult to get any action so you had to be very very aggressive to get any action most of the time. It was an interesting tour.' The tour was to give RCAF pilots actual combat experience. The duty was for fifty missions or six months, whichever came first. The Cold War was certainly hot for some Canadians, Grant included.

On 16 October 1962, a Lockheed U2, nicknamed '*Dragon Lady*', on a high altitude surveillance flight discovered, thanks to initial information from the US spy Oleg Penkovsky, the presence of Soviet missile sites under construction in the pro-Soviet island country of Cuba. The island is a mere 150 kilometres from the USA. After careful and extensive deliberation, the line was drawn in the sand. President Kennedy addressed his nation on the 22 October 1962 and he indicated that missiles had been discovered in Cuba and announced a blockade of the island nation. The entire world waited with baited breath to see who, if anyone, would blink first, President Kennedy or Premier Khrushchev? The world was on the brink of a war which probably would be fought with nuclear weapons. Would this be the Third World War? Would it be the final war of the twentieth century or even the last war that the world would ever see – total annihilation?

Tensions were extremely high in the USA for the next three days as the Soviet missile supply ships continued to steam towards the blockade. The RCAF was on high alert due to Canada's NATO commitments in Europe and NORAD commitments at home. What would Khrushchev do? He, thank goodness for world peace, decided to withdraw the missiles from Cuba and negotiated terms that included a promise that the USA would not invade Cuba. Another Cold War crisis had passed peacefully into history. What happened in the post-war years leading up to the Cuban Crisis, and the subsequent years until the Amalgam Mute exercise in 1973?

To further understand the global history prior to our mission of 1973, a chronological list of world and Canadian events follows. Some events are well known and some are not; they all contributed to the political tensions of their time, which was reflected in the varying degrees of military preparedness. The preparedness of the military could be judged by the budget, the level of training of the troops and the amount of military assets available. Military budgets are directly connected to the mental state of the politicians, when détente prevailed the budget was decreased, when tensions existed the budget was increased!

Cold War World Events during the 1940s

Canadian events in italics

April 1945	United Nations founded in San Francisco.
May 1945	Germany surrendered.
July 1945	First USA atomic bomb tested in New Mexico.
August 1945	Two atomic bombs dropped on Japan.
2 September 1945	Japan signed surrender documents.
September 1945	*Igor Gouzenko defected from the Soviet embassy in Ottawa, Ontario. A cipher clerk, he had proof of an espionage network in Canada. He took some time convincing authorities of the significance of his information before he was spirited away into hiding for extensive debriefing. Counter-intelligence officers from Britain and the USA interviewed him in the hope of getting information of spy rings in their countries.*
February 1946	*The news finally broke about the Gouzenko defection and the twelve spy suspects named by his testimony were taken into custody for interrogation. The news was sensational around the world and proof that the Soviets were indeed 'an evil empire' spying on their former allies.*

March 1946	Winston Churchill's 'Iron Curtain' speech at Westminster College in Fulton, Missouri; he used the term 'iron curtain' in the context of Soviet-dominated Eastern Europe. 'From Stettin in the Baltic to Trieste in the Adriatic an 'iron curtain' has descended across the Continent. Behind that line lie all the capitals of the ancient states of Central and Eastern Europe. Warsaw, Berlin, Prague, Vienna, Budapest, Belgrade, Bucharest and Sofia; all these famous cities and the populations around them lie in the what I must call the Soviet sphere, and all are subject, in one form or another, not only to Soviet influence but to a very high and in some cases increasing measure of control from Moscow.'
May 1946	*Canada established a Security Panel in great secrecy to administer government internal security in the background, away from the politically damaging public eye. The Gouzenko defection had triggered an awareness of the possibility of Soviet spies that worked within the Federal Government. The Panel members were senior members of the Department of Defence, the Royal Canadian Mounted Police and the Department of External Affairs.*
June 1946	*Fred Rose, the only elected Communist member of Canadian Parliament, 1943, until arrest, was sentenced to six years for espionage. Deported to Poland, he was refused reentry to Canada.*
July 1946	First US peaceful atomic bomb test.
March 1947	President Harry S. Truman disclosed containment document NSC-68, a top secret policy plan against Communist aggression. The plan shifted foreign policy from passive to active containment of Soviet expansion. It explicitly stated that the Communists planned for world domination.
September 1947	Communist Information Bureau (COMINFORM) formed.
February 1948	Moscow denounced Tito's independent Yugoslavian Communist regime.
February 1948	*The Province of Quebec reinstated the infamous 'Padlock Law' of Maurice Duplessis' Union Nationale Party. The party and the Roman Catholic Church would not tolerate any interference in the running of*

the Province, especially from the Communist Party or sympathisers. The law 'permitted the Quebec authorities to close any premises deemed to be used for the propagation of communism or bolshevism by any means whatever; to prohibit the publication of any ideas propagating Communism or Bolshevism; and to destroy any such material seized'. This law was used indiscriminately 'to crush strikes and labour organizers'.

March 1948   Czechoslovakia became a Communist regime. The USSR started pushing the central party Communist boundaries outwards from Moscow.

March 1948   *Secret Cabinet directive on the security screening of Canadian civil servants.*

May 1948   West German state proclaimed.

June 1948   A major political and military event in Europe: Stalin blockaded Berlin in the hope that the Allies would relinquish the city to the surrounding Soviet sector. Instead it triggered a massive airlift of previously unknown proportions from 24 June 1948 that kept the city alive until Stalin relented, nearly a year later in defeat, on 12 May 1949.

October 1948   East German state proclaimed.

March 1949   *A strike by the Canadian Seamen's Union (CSU) was brutally put down under the guise of routing out Communists in the Union. A notorious labour racketeer, Hal Banks, was brought in from the USA. He worked for the opposing Seafarers International Union and destroyed the CSU.*

April 1949   North Atlantic Treaty Organisation (NATO) founded.

August 1949   The Soviets exploded their first atomic bomb, surprising the Americans, who had forecasted many years of weapon superiority.

September 1949 Germany divided, East (Communist) and West (capitalist).

October 1949   Chinese Communists took control of mainland China. The Chinese Communists showed no interest in aligning themselves with the Soviet Communists. Nationalist forces and supporters retreated to the island of Formosa, now called Taiwan.

November 1949   *The National Film Board (NFB) purged of all left-wingers and the Commissioner, Ross McLean, was dismissed. No perceived Communist propaganda was going to be published by the NFB in Canada.*

Cold War World Events during the 1950s

1950   *The most draconian of peacetime national security programmes was devised by the RCMP Commissioner, Stuart Taylor Wood. It was called PROFUNC, which stood for PROminent FUNCtionaries of the Communist Party. PROFUNC listed suspected Communists and sympathisers who would have to be watched and interned in the event of a Federal emergency. The identities of individuals on the list were kept hidden in sealed envelopes at RCMP detachments throughout the country; the files were regularly updated with photos and personal details. The programme was finally scrapped in the 1980s and contained in excess of 60,000 names; it included some prominent Canadian public figures. Thomas (Tommy) C. Douglas, former Canadian National Democratic Party, was rumoured to be on the watch list.*

January 1950   The USA planned the hydrogen (thermonuclear) bomb to take deterrence to a higher status. This did not bode well for world stability as each side probed and manoeuvred within the context of 'world peace'.

February 1950   US Senator Joseph McCarthy gave his first major anti-Communist speech in Virginia, USA.

June 1950   The fragile peace broke; North Korea invaded South Korea with Communist support, either directly or indirectly, from China and Russia. The first military engagement of the Cold War began.

August 1950   *Canada deployed all three components of the military. Of note is that the RCAF had twenty-two pilots on exchange with the United States Air Force (USAF) who flew North American-built Sabres in the conflict. The arrangement was for the Canadian pilots to get combat experience by serving six months in Korea or fifty missions, whichever came first.*

October 1950	*Bruno Pontecorvo, an atomic scientist working at the Chalk River, Ontario nuclear plant, defects to the Soviet Union.*
January 1951	*Canada deployed army and air force units to Europe. NATO built its forces, positioned to face the Soviet Union. It had only been six years since the end of the Second World War, when the USA and USSR had been Allies.*
May 1951	British diplomats Guy Burgess and Donald Maclean defected to the Soviet Union.
May 1952	*Reverend James Endicott, leader of the Canadian Peace Congress, avoided treason charges. He had been born in China and believed '[the Communists] represented the forces of progress in an impoverished land'. He had sympathy for the Chinese Communists, but was never a Communist Party member himself. A political 'hot potato' at that time, if he had been found guilty of the treason charge the penalty was death. The government wisely considered its options and did not bring charges.*
September 1952	First television broadcast in Canada.
October 1952	Britain exploded its first atomic bomb.
November 1952	USA exploded its first hydrogen bomb. It was now leading the arms race, but no one could predict how long it would take the USSR to catch up.
June 1953	The Rosenbergs executed in the USA for atomic espionage activities.
July 1953	Korean War ended in stalemate. No nuclear weapons used.
August 1953	Nine months behind! The Soviet Union exploded its first hydrogen bomb.
January 1954	The Cold War is gathering momentum; the USA announced the doctrine of massive retaliation. American Cold War advocates proclaimed 'better dead than Red'.
May 1954	Vietnam divided in two – Communist North and non-Communist South. Asia was very much affected by the spread of communism. It was not only Europe that felt the geographical/political boundaries being expanded.
May 1955	The Warsaw Pact formed in opposition to NATO. The chess game of the superpower alliances continued.

July 1956	First USAF Lockheed U-2 spy plane mission flights over the Soviet Union.
October 1956	The free world watched the Soviet army suppress the revolt against communism in Hungary.
March 1957	*The Supreme Court of Canada ruled the Quebec 'Padlock Law' as unconstitutional.*
April 1957	*The Canadian Communist Party in disorder. It lacked leadership and direction and suffered from members leaving the organisation.*
April 1957	*The Canadian ambassador to Egypt, the distinguished scholar and diplomat Herbert Norman, took his own life after being hounded shamelessly by the USA. The Americans had pushed the Cold War too far according to Canadian politicians and media.*
August 1957	*The creation of NORAD announced.*
August 1957	USSR launched first intercontinental ballistic missile (ICBM).
October 1957	Soviet Union launched the first Earth orbit satellite (Sputnik 1). The author remembers standing at night in the streets of Dublin, Ireland, watching the small white light travelling overhead among the stars. There was no doubt who was leading the race now: the Soviet Union. It had taken the race into outer space, the new frontier.
November 1957	Britain exploded its first hydrogen bomb.
November 1957	Soviets orbited a dog, Laika, in outer space. The Soviet Union had the attention of the world media as Communist prowess was demonstrated.
December 1957	*Prime Minister Lester B. Pearson was awarded the Nobel Peace Prize for establishing the United Nations peacekeeping force during the Suez Crisis of 1956. He was an avid supporter of NORAD and NATO but also had a passionate commitment to peace and negotiation of political deadlocks. It was because of this passion for peace that he had been on an American watch list for subversive behaviour.*
January 1958	The USA finally had its first successful satellite launch.
Early 1958	*The RCMP Operation Feather Bed initiated. The file contained information on 'suspected or known Communist sympathizers employed by the Federal*

Government'. It lasted until the mid-1970s as a separate file from the public PROFUNC list.

November 1958   Khrushchev issued first Berlin ultimatum, giving the Western powers six months to agree to withdraw from Berlin and make it a free, demilitarised city: the Cold War was heating up with this first ultimatum. The Allies, USA, France and Great Britain replied that they would remain in Berlin. The ultimatum was withdrawn and a conference was held by Premier Khrushchev and President Eisenhower to discuss the situation.

1959   *Work secretly began on the Emergency Government Headquarters outside Ottawa, Ontario. It was known officially as Canadian Forces Station Carp and unofficially as the 'Diefenbunker', named for Prime Minister John G. Diefenbaker, who authorised the construction. It was an underground, four-storey, 2,832-cubic-metre building with 1.5-metre-thick walls, which could support 535 people for 30 days. In 1998 it was declared a Cold War National Historic Site and opened to the public.*

Conference Room, Diefenbunker. (Courtesy of Author)

January 1959   Fidel Castro assumed power in Cuba – where would his loyalties lie?

February 1959   *Avro Arrow fighter production cancelled. A very significant event in Canadian aviation. The subject is examined in Chapter Five.*

Cold War World Events during the 1960s

February 1960   France joined the nuclear club and exploded its first atomic bomb.

August 1960   First satellite reconnaissance photos viewed.

January 1961   First US ICBM test.

May 1960   USAF U-2 spy plane shot down over the USSR, which had now demonstrated its ability to protect its territory. The USA no longer enjoyed the advantage of undetected surveillance by high flying aircraft.

April 1961   The USSR put the first man in earth orbit, a new dimension for the USA to cope with – manned space flight.

May 1961   The USA caught up fast and put the first US astronaut in space.

August 1961   The Berlin Wall constructed to stop the flow of citizens from the eastern Communist sector to the western sectors. The two sides faced off with each other and, at one time, armed tanks were separated by 200 metres at the Brandenburg Gate. President Kennedy ordered troops to West Germany and the mobilisation of reserve troops in the USA. The two sides paused.

September 1961   *The 'Continuity of (National Canadian) Government' site, the Diefenbunker, revealed by newspaper as being at Carp, Ontario.*

October 1961   USSR flexed its muscles by conducting the largest ever atmospheric nuclear test. When was this escalation going to end? The situation was building to an event of epic proportions – what and where in the world would it be?

September 1962   *Canada's first satellite, Alouette 1, orbited.*

October 1962   The Cuban Missile Crisis was the event that brought the world to the brink of nuclear holocaust. A holocaust is defined as a huge slaughter or destruction of life and a nuclear holocaust is one that could cause the complete annihilation of human civilisation by nuclear warfare. With the discovery of a Soviet-supplied missile site in Cuba, Fidel Castro had obviously decided what 'team' he was on. President John F. Kennedy established a blockade around Cuba and it was up to Premier Khrushchev to decide what to do as his ships steamed towards the blockade. To blink or not to blink? That was the question. Seventeen years after the second of two World Wars had ended, the world was on the brink of total destruction by nuclear forces. Premier Khrushchev turned the ships back and the world's population collectively breathed easier – the crisis had been averted. Vasily Kuznetsov, Soviet First Deputy Foreign Minister, negotiated the end of the crisis at the UN and he remarked, 'Well, Mr McCloy (John J. McCloy, Presidential advisor and chief negotiator on the Presidential Disarmament Committee), you got away with it this time, but you will never get away with it again.' The Soviets vigorously pursued nuclear parity with the USA and essentially achieved it, at great cost, around 1970.

February 1963   *The beginning of the end of the minority Diefenbaker Conservative Government. Minister of Defence Douglas Harkness resigned from the government over the policy not to accept nuclear warheads from the USA for defence purposes.*

April 1963   *The minority Pearson Liberal government assumed power, largely due to the indecision to accept nuclear weapons on Canadian soil.*

May 1963   The US spy Oleg Penkovsky was executed by the Soviets. He was instrumental in supplying vital information to President Kennedy before the Cuban Crisis.

June 1963   President Kennedy gave a famous speech to Berliners to say that the USA, through NATO, was committed to preserving Berlin in the 'West'. His oft-quoted line of 'Ich bin ein Berliner' was received with tumultuous applause.

June 1963   A USSR–USA hotline was established, the famous red phone. In view of the near catastrophe of six months ago it was felt that a strong communication link between the superpowers was absolutely essential to diffuse any future confrontations, Premier to President.

August 1963   The Soviet Union and the USA signed the test ban treaty.

November 1963   Kennedy assassinated.

December 1963   *The Bomarc missiles are equipped with nuclear warheads. The significance of the Bomarc is explained in Chapter Five.*

October 1964   China explodes first nuclear bomb.

October 1964   Khrushchev lost leadership less than one year after the death of Kennedy. The Soviet Politburo thought that Khrushchev was weak in backing down during the 'Caribbean Crisis', but he had in fact prevented the invasion of Cuba and it was learnt, after his death, that he was instrumental in preventing NATO missiles being installed in Turkey.

October 1964   *The former Canadian ambassador to the USSR, John Watkins, died from a heart attack while under questioning by the RCMP. There had been information that he may have been 'honey trapped' – sexually entrapped – while in Moscow. He admitted to being a homosexual and the RCMP security service were concerned that he may have been blackmailed. No 'smoking gun' was ever found to suggest that Watkins was ever influenced by the Soviets.*

October 1964   The first Chinese atomic bomb test. A new member for the group of nuclear nations.

February 1965   *Canada unveiled new national maple leaf flag, an event connected to the repatriation of the constitution from Great Britain in 1982.*

March 1965   The US bombings of Communist North Vietnam began.

July 1965   US troops deployed to South Vietnam. Prior to this time there had been 23,000 'military advisors' in the country.

March 1966   *The name of Gerda Munsinger was mentioned in the House of Commons. She was an alleged East German spy and prostitute living in Ottawa who freely admitted having had a relationship with several politicians, including the Associate Minister of Defence. She was deported in 1961.*

April 1967	*Canada's three armed services (Army, Navy and Air Force) unified as the Canadian Armed Forces (CAF).*
June 1967	The Middle East was embroiled in Six Day War. Both the Cold War superpowers had a vested interest in the conflict. The USA supported Israel and the USSR supported Egypt. The war caused global tension as the superpowers observed and prepared for possible intervention.
June 1967	In Glassboro, New Jersey, USA, at the Arms Control Talks, Premier Kosygin of the USSR said to President Johnson of the USA that 'defence is moral, offence is immoral' when asked about the new Moscow defence system.
June 1967	China takes its weapons to the next nuclear level; it explodes its first hydrogen bomb.
December 1967	In thirteen years the US went from a doctrine of massive retaliation at the time of the Korean War, to the brink of an escalating nuclear war during the Cuban Crisis, to a doctrine of flexible response during the Vietnam war. The USSR and US wondered about the aims and ambitions of China and a brand of communism which showed no desire to align itself with Moscow.
January 1968	US offensive began in Vietnam.
July 1968	Nuclear Non Proliferation Treaty signed by Britain, USSR and USA, in order to curb the availability of nuclear weapons to other states.
August 1968	Warsaw Pact countries invaded Czechoslovakia to stop a reforming movement within the Communist government.
August 1968	France tested its hydrogen bomb.
March 1969	China and the USSR engaged in border clashes. The USA watched with interest as its Cold War foe turned its attention to its eastern borders.
July 1969	USA landed astronauts on the moon.
November 1969	The start of the very important Strategic Arms Limitations Talks began. The Treaty froze the number of strategic ballistic missile launchers at existing levels. How many times did you have to obliterate your enemy? Once should be enough. The USA had 1,700 missiles! Presumably the Soviet Union could match or exceed that number?

Cold War World Events during the 1970s

1970	USA taps into underwater cables used by the Soviet Pacific Fleet.
August 1970	USSR signed Non Aggression Treaty with West Germany, twenty-two years after the start of the Berlin blockade. The warming of the Cold War was gaining momentum as the superpowers devoted their political and military attention elsewhere. The USA continued its involvement in Vietnam.
October 1970	*Canada recognises the People's Republic of China as the 'real China'. Taiwan diplomats leave Ottawa in protest.*
May 1971	US Congress voted to keep troops in Europe, reluctant to abandon its foothold.
September 1971	*The Greenpeace ship sailed from Vancouver to protest a nuclear bomb test in Amchitka, Alaska. The old fishing boat, the* Phyllis Cormack, *was prevented from reaching Amchitka, but it did draw public attention to the underground nuclear testing facility in an earthquake prone zone. The testing ended that year and the island was subsequently declared a bird sanctuary. Sometimes peaceful civic action works.*
February 1972	Nixon visited China; the political triangle is established with the Soviet and Chinese Communists not on good terms.
May 1972	US bombing campaign escalated in Vietnam.
May 1972	Nixon visited the Soviet Union and signed SALT1 Limitation Treaties after two and half years of negotiations.
September 1972	*The first Cold War ice hockey series, Canada versus the USSR, ended in a Canadian victory with Paul Henderson's game and series winning goal.*
December 1972	USA commenced the second phase of Vietnam bombing campaign.
January 1973	Vietnam ceasefire agreement.
1973	SALT 2 talks continue between the USA and USSR.
May 1973	*Amalgam Mute exercise to test the NORAD response capability to a Soviet bomber threat. This book was written to allow the reader to understand the inside account of what went on in the secret world of NORAD.*

11 November 2010

I stood at the cenotaph in White Rock, British Columbia, Canada, and observed the Ceremony of Remembrance for those who had given the ultimate sacrifice for their country.

> They shall not grow old, as we that are left grow old;
> Age shall not weary them, nor the years condemn.
> At the going down of the sun and in the morning
> we will remember them.

I could not help reflecting on the futility of war. Some of our former enemies are now our friends and allies. Prime Minister Pearson got it right – diplomacy and deterrence is the only answer.

These world events were the historical and political military background leading up to our narrative of the Amalgam Mute exercise on 10 May 1973. The USSR bombers existed then, as they do today, 2011, and were a part of the aerial aircraft threat. This threat has diminished with time as missiles became the preferred weapon of choice.

There was one major cooling off period in détente during the early 1980s under President Ronald Reagan, partially due to the previous Soviet invasion of Afghanistan. President Reagan said, in January 1981, during his inaugural address, 'They [the Soviets] reserve unto themselves the right to commit any crime, to lie, to cheat in order to attain [their goals].'

The Cold War continued to warm up for the sixteen years following the training exercise detailed in this book, until the generally agreed end in 1989, with the breach of the Berlin Wall. However, there are many other plausible dates suggested for the end of hostilities. Some historians suggest it was 1985, the year that President Gorbachev came to power, while others suggest it was 1990, the year that the four Allied powers signed the German Reunification Treaty. Another suggested date was when the Soviet Union ceased to exist on 31 December 1991; it was subsequently called Russia. Still others maintain that it was when the last ultimate symbol of the Cold War, the USAF Strategic Air Command, closed operations in 1992. A sign in the SAC museum states: 'The Cold War just didn't end ... it was won.'

It would seem that in recent years, under the guidance of Vladimir Putin, former President and presently Prime Minister, that Russia wants to re-establish itself as a world superpower. Keep in mind that Putin was a former employee of the KGB, the Soviet spy agency, and in 1998 was head of the FSB, a successor agency to the KGB. In order to regain influence, Russia will have to re-establish an effective, wide ranging network for intelligence gathering. That will affect us all, the global family, and Canadian citizens must be aware of Russian manoeuvring; Cold War-like tactics have already started. The planting of the Russian flag by submarine on the seabed at the North Pole on 2 August 2007 and the increase in the number of Tupolev Bear International Arctic airspace bomber training flights during the latter half of 2007 are just two examples. On 17 August 2007, President Putin announced that long-distance patrol flights of strategic bombers would resume after a 1992 suspension. On 20 September 2007, two Tupolev TU-95MS Bear-H bombers carried out a flight along the Alaska and Canadian coasts in international airspace. They were airborne for seventeen hours and the mission included mid-air refuelling by Ilyushin IL-78 Midas tankers.

President Putin made sure that he set the tone for the future Russia before he stepped down and assumed the title of Prime Minister in March 2008. He is often quoted as having said, 'The breakup of the Soviet Union was the greatest geopolitical catastrophe of the twentieth century'. 'The Americans are circling Russia with radars and installing antiballistic missiles close to our borders' said the defence commentator Viktor Litovkin in a 2007 interview. 'It's a matter of serious concern. We are being provoked into a new arms race.' Sergei Ivanov, First Deputy Prime Minister of the Russian Federation, has announced a major rearmament programme, which included new intercontinental missiles and a fleet of supersonic bombers by 2015. To meet this new supersonic bomber threat, Canada must consider it in future defence plans, in light of Russia's reinvestment in intelligence and military equipment.

A blatant provocation was the Russian Bear bomber flight which approached Canadian airspace on 18 February 2009. This coincided with the first time that the newly elected US President Barack Obama was scheduled to leave American soil for a visit to Canada. Was it a coincidence? Not a chance. The new Russian regime is determined to be observed on the world stage.

In addition to its military manoeuvres and political commentary, Russia has taken steps to position intelligence operatives in the West. In June 2010, eleven members of an alleged spy ring were apprehended in the USA after a lengthy surveillance. Four of the members used documents which identified them as Canadians. One member used the name of a deceased Canadian infant. The members, alleged agents, were instructed to seek out information on the new generation of top secret nuclear warheads, attempt to learn the US arms control position and follow White House rumours.

The CAF must examine or reaffirm the decision to purchase the new proposed fighter, the Lockheed Martin F-35 Lightning, as the most suitable for the interceptor role. It is admirable that Canada is on the

Tupolev TU-95 Bear bomber.

world military stage as a combat force, training force and peacekeeping force. It does require the necessary air superiority to carry out its various roles. Furthermore, it is paramount that all these tasks emanate from an environment which can be kept free from enemy interference. The primary roll, consequently, should be the protection of Canadian territory. Deterrence, rather than the more expensive conflict scenario, is the most desirable option in financial and human cost to keep Canada safe. The new fighter must provide reliable air superiority in Canadian climatic conditions found during the winter in the far north. The new fighter interceptor must be able to protect our populated areas by carrying the air war to the sparsely and unpopulated areas of northern Canada. The men and women of the CAF must be given the best aircraft available for the job.

The first ten years of the Cold War, 1947 to 1957, saw an increase in the cooperation between Canada and the USA in fighting 'Communist aggression'. Canada was firmly on the side of the 'West', the democratic capitalistic countries. It had sent its forces overseas with NATO to protect democracy in general, and specifically in Europe, against Communist expansionism. But what about protecting the home front in the late 1950s? Canada's closest neighbour, and possible enemy, to the north was the USSR. It was the making of an Arctic threat. If Canadians were prepared to go to Europe with our allies to protect our way of life, what were they prepared to do at home? The answer took longer to discover: it was called NORAD.

CHAPTER TWO

North American Air Defence Command (NORAD)

The success of NORAD is due to the thousands of men and women over the past 50 years who dedicated themselves to the service of defending Canada and the United States.

Mike Perini, NORAD public affairs director, on the fiftieth anniversary of NORAD in 2008

The commuter bus slowly proceeded down the road to the terminus. It came to a halt and Kelleher, Keith, Graham and Schlosser, and the rest of the occupants, exited the bus and entered the nearby three-level building. Nothing unusual about this scene except that most of the commuters wore a military uniform and the building was deep underground. It had been a cool, cloudy day with rain showers in the city but down here, in this building filled with immense heat-generating vacuum-tube computers, the problem was how to keep the environment cool. It was May 1973 and another shift change was taking place at the 22nd North American Air Defence Region Headquarters in North Bay, Ontario.

The NORAD early warning radar system had covered North America like a huge umbrella from 1957 until the present, 2011. This immense defence network extended from the frozen wastes of the Arctic to the tumbleweed-strewn Mexican border, from the Pacific Ocean to the Atlantic Ocean, from the inhospitable frozen Bering Strait separating Alaska and Russia to the warm waters of the Gulf of Mexico and the Caribbean. NORAD, always at the ready, protected Canada and the USA from foreign threats. Its very existence was the comprehension by the two nations that the synergy of cooperation gives the greatest security reward.

The Cold War prompted Canada and the USA to develop a sophisticated defence system to guard against the Soviet threat. The primary focus of this book, an airborne electronic warfare exercise, took place in 1973.

NORAD had been in existence for sixteen years by 1973 and continued to evolve as the threat changed from primarily bomber aircraft to the intercontinental ballistic missile. To counter the bomber threat NORAD adopted, in the 1960s, an improved radar system called Semi-Automatic Ground Environment (SAGE). SAGE replaced the operation of the individual radar sites with a central controlling agency. The radar sites now fed all their information to their NORAD Region headquarters.

The Years Leading to NORAD, 1945–1958

The United States has already a Permanent Defence Agreement with the Dominion of Canada, which is so devotedly attached to the British Commonwealth and Empire. This agreement is more effective than many of those which have often been made under formal alliances.

Sir Winston Churchill's 'Iron Curtain' speech, 5 March 1946

The Royal Canadian Air Force (RCAF), after the Second World War ended, took a few years to adjust to a peacetime role and a vastly reduced budget. Now it was constrained by tight budgets which necessitated the reduction of the workforce and, hard to believe, the decision to have no active separate squadrons for 1946 and 1947. All the aircraft were in the Air Force pool. The once-mighty RCAF, which was a major part of the British Commonwealth Air Training Plan, which trained in excess of

120,000 aircrew in Canada, was reduced to a caretaker force, mainly to satisfy meaningless bomber reconnaissance requirements. Who were they going to bomb or observe? During 1946 and 1947, Canada watched the manoeuvring in Europe as the former allies, the Soviets, the British and the Americans, struggled to hold on to war spoils and exert their influence accordingly.

The Americans were surprised that the Soviets embarked on an aggressive posture so quickly after the demise of Hitler's Germany, as they really thought that it would be many years before the Soviets would be a threat to the USA. The USA had the atomic bomb and the military did not expect the war-torn economy of the Soviet Union to be able to develop any atomic bomb for quite some time. The American military philosophy subsequent to the Second World War was to develop their strategic bombers and tactical capability primarily, with cursory consideration on defence considerations. The Berlin Crisis, as it came to be known, and the detonation of the first Soviet atomic bomb in August 1949 caused the USA to address the home defence situation. The Berlin Crisis of 1948 heightened the awareness of North America's vulnerability to attack. The Americans finally realised that emphasis must be put on protection of the homeland to guarantee a retaliatory strike against an attack by the enemy. In 1949, the USA funded a permanent air defence system, based on a 1947 US Air Force Chief of Staff's model, which established military bases in Iceland, Greenland and Newfoundland. Newfoundland, however, was now a part of Canada, raising the possibility of a political obstacle.

This obstacle, foreseen in 1940, by the Prime Minister of Canada, William Lyon Mackenzie King, and the President of the USA, Franklin Delano Roosevelt, no longer presented any problem as the two countries had established the Canada–United States Permanent Joint Board on Defense to address such political issues. The board surprisingly organised the countries as equal partners in spite of the difference in military capability. The Permanent Joint Board on Defense was a senior advisory board and did not have any planning responsibility. It focused on the policy, finance and logistics of the defence of North America. It was very effective as it provided an alternative avenue of communication between the Canadian and American diplomats on difficult political issues.

The next important mutual agreement was the decision to establish a Canada–United States Military Co-Operation Committee, in May 1946. This sanctioned the Joint Chiefs of Staff of the United States and the Canadian Chief of Air Staff to meet and coordinate military activity. This committee immediately established the joint Canada–United States Basic Security Plan. This plan proposed establishing a wide range of defensive measures, which included comprehensive facilities to provide a warning, of approaching hostile aircraft, meteorological warning, communication, and fighter aircraft bases.

By November 1946, the Basic Security Plan had identified the need for a radar network to surround North America. The security plan established a chain of radar sites from the Mexican border north to Alaska, across northern Canada just south of the Arctic islands, down the Labrador coast to Newfoundland, and continued southward to the Mexican border. This air warning system required a further chain of radar sites on the 50th parallel of latitude from Manitoba to Nova Scotia and a large force of Canadian and American fighter interceptors to ensure the battle area was as far as possible from the cities and strategically important areas.

The time had arrived to consider a combined American and Canadian air defence headquarters with operational control over all forces available. Thus, the seeds were sown of the future development of such an agreement, namely NORAD. Certain events hastened this process. In May 1947, the world became aware of the Tupolev TU-4 long-range bomber, codenamed BULL. It had an uncanny resemblance to the American Boeing B-29, a copy perhaps. The USSR now had the ability to deliver bombs to North America, a frightening prospect. Two years after the Second World War had ended Canada now had to consider a growing threat again, this time from its polar neighbour the USSR.

The National Security Act of 1946 had created the United States Air Force (USAF) in 1947. The Army Air Corps had done the flying up until this time. In 1948, it was still an inexperienced air force. The RCAF, established much earlier on 1 April 1924, already had war-experienced personnel in its ranks. Canada responded to the threat posed by the USSR in December 1948, when it equipped 410 Squadron, stationed at St-Hubert, Quebec, with the first RCAF operational turbine engine aircraft, the De Havilland F3 Vampire day jet fighter, equipped with four 20-mm cannon as armament. In September 1949 a second squadron, 420, was also equipped with the Vampire and became operational at Chatham, New Brunswick.

Canada also realised at this time that it had a requirement for a unique, tailor-made fighter due to the unique Canadian meteorological and geographical conditions. The harsh winter flying conditions, extreme cold, ice and snow, required a unique type of aircraft. The widely scattered airports demanded an aircraft that carried a sufficiently large fuel load to complete the mission and perhaps recover at another base. The successful Avro (Canada) CF-100 would be the result of this thought process and it eventually took over fighter duties from the Vampire and Canadair Sabre.

In April 1949, the USA decided on a large 'temporary' radar system called LASHUP. This system concentrated on protecting certain strategic areas: the north-western approaches to the USA, California, the Los Alamos secret testing area, the Atomic Energy Commission facilities of the Tennessee Valley, and the north-eastern approaches to the USA. Then, the history of North American defence took an immediate change of direction. In September 1949, the Soviets exploded their first atomic bomb. The immediate fear of the American military, in October 1949, influenced the US Congress; it reacted quickly and allocated funds for a 'permanent' radar system to be constructed.

In June 1950, the Korean War commenced and communism expanded as a threat, and changed from subversive means to engaging in war to achieve its global ambitions. The USA reacted domestically and established 24-hour air defence operations. Canada planned the establishment of four or five radar sites supporting the two Vampire squadrons. The Vampire aircraft were at the end of the 'fighter pilot's eyeballs' era of searching out threat aircraft, as the emphasis now shifted to two-man-crew, pilot and Airborne Intercept (AI) Navigator, fighters with onboard radar. In June 1950, the Canadian air defence system further expanded to five RCAF squadrons and in 1951 changed the name to Air Defence Command, headquartered at St-Hubert, Quebec.

The lack of depth and coverage of the Canadian radar system concerned the Americans. The present air warning, being so close to the Canada–USA border, would not give the USAF fighters time to prevent the Soviet bombers reaching their assigned targets. The USAF grew impatient with their RCAF counterparts regarding the improvement to the defence system. The RCAF did not have the necessary budget allocated by their political masters. Something had to change. The question was how?

The Military Cooperation Committee submitted their extensive plan to their respective governments. The RCAF and USAF recommended sharing the cost of radar site construction on Canadian territory by both countries, as both Canada and the USA would mutually benefit. The planners proposed thirty-one radar stations in Canada and one in Greenland. The proposed Canadian sites would be manned by the RCAF, an important sovereignty issue for Canada, and the three sites in Newfoundland by the USAF on their previously established pre-war bases. The radar data would be shared, for the first time, between the RCAF and USAF Defence Commands. That was the plan, but the RCAF did not have the trained personnel to operate the Canadian sites.

The issue of sovereignty arose among the Canadian politicians of the Permanent Joint Board on Defense. American nationals staffed radar sites on Canadian soil. To allay the fears of Canadians, a Canadian crown corporation, Defence Construction Limited, assumed the leadership role. The legal land title of the radar site, regardless of who controlled it, remained with the Canadian government. In July 1951, Mr C. D. Howe, Minister of Defence Production, when acting-Prime Minister, instructed External Affairs to exchange diplomatic notes with the USA and initiate the planned construction. This action guaranteed the funding by the USAF. The US and Canada agreed to register the agreement later with the UN – unusual, but it was a legal arrangement.

The radar sites would shift the area of the air battle northwards, away from the north-eastern USA, to over Ontario and Quebec – not an ideal Canadian scenario. The USA also pushed hard for an eventual agreement to allow the USAF to shoot down hostile aircraft in Canadian airspace. The timely coordination of this act, foreign aircraft crossing the border, would be very hard to achieve with the independent operational situation of the respective air forces. In his book, *No Boundaries Upstairs*, Joseph Jockel commented that, 'A Canadian suggested the remedy; Air Vice Marshall A. L. James wrote to his counterpart Major General R. L. Walsh, "The RCAF believes that the air defence of these Canada-US vital areas which are contiguous is a common problem and should be taken care of by an integrated Canada-US air defence system." In 1951, RCAF liaison officers quietly assumed duties with the USAF Air Defense Command Headquarters at Colorado Springs, Colorado, USA.' These Canadian officers quickly realised that there was a requirement for all of the defence system to be under one commander. The starting point of NORAD had now become a seedling.

Further operational integration of the two air forces occurred without much fanfare. The fighter aircraft, agreed to by USAF General H. S. Vandenberg and RCAF Air Marshall W. A. Curtis, would be under the control of the nearest Air Defence Control Center, American or Canadian, regardless of their nationality. Finally, the Cabinet Defence Committee authorised the RCAF Air Defence Commander to force hostile aircraft to land or shoot them down. The circle was now complete, except that it was still a basic manual radar system.

No history of the defence of Canada would be complete without mentioning the Ground Observer Corps, formed in 1951 to supplement the Aircraft Control & Warning system. It consisted of 50,000 civilian volunteers from every occupation, whose slogan was 'The Eyes and Ears of Air Defence Command'. The volunteer corps was a network of manned observation posts, operating twenty-four hours a day, which reported all aircraft movements to a filter centre, which verified the information and passed it onto Air Defence Command. Observation towers, built by the volunteers at their own initiative and expense, sprang up from coast to coast. Master Corporal R. (Bob) Keith, who described his radar site operational experience in Chapter Four, worked at the 20 RCAF Ground Observer Corps Squadron from 1959 to 1961 in Edmonton, Alberta.

At the radar sites many plotters marked tracks on large rectangular plotting boards and wore their communication headsets with long, cumbersome cords. Metal plotting arrows and thousands of grease pencils completed the functioning of this antiquated, but effective in its time, system. Furthermore, continuous reports from all sources required a large amount of paper. The system needed an upgrade. It was time for the radar sites to join the computer age.

The US Department of Defense contracted, with the Massachusetts Institute of Technology, Lincoln Laboratory, for a study on the defence of North America. The Project Charles study agreed that the radar system was a simple solution, but that the US Permanent and the Canadian Pinetree chain of radar sites needed to give more warning time of an impending attack and required a system extension. The study also urged the development of the plotting and tracking capability. The result was the Lincoln Transition System, released in 1953. It was renamed Semi-Automatic Ground Environment (SAGE) system prior to operational use. A SAGE computer handled the massive amounts of input information and created a radar display that allowed the tactical decisions of an air battle to be made through human input.

Simultaneously, the US Civil Defense Project East River recommended an outer warning system at least 3,219 kilometres from the continental USA – in other words, the Canadian Arctic. In 1952, the Lincoln Summer Study Group proposed two Distant Early Warning (DEW) lines of radar sites. DEW Line number 1 stretched from the Mackenzie Delta to Thule, Greenland, and down the Greenland coast. DEW Line number 2 ran south-east from the Mackenzie Delta to Great Bear Lake to join up with the Pinetree Line in Labrador.

In Canada, scientists working at McGill University in Montreal developed a major breakthrough in the theory of Doppler shift caused by an aircraft passing over ground sensors and giving an aural presentation, which indicated the speed and direction of the target. The DEW Line in the Arctic could only report that targets were on their way, but could not predict where they were going. It was proposed that the McGill Fence, as it became known, would be constructed further south, at the 55th Parallel of latitude. This proposal would give the fighters two hours warning and was a lot cheaper addition to the existing system than the Arctic DEW Line. However, the Lincoln Study Group would not accept the Fence as a substitute for the DEW Line, only as a suitable addition to it.

The American Joint Chiefs of Staff were concerned that too much emphasis on defence would take away from the resources available to develop strategic special weapons for retaliatory strikes. However, President Harry Truman was persuaded by persistent USAF lobbying, to back the DEW Line proposal to be completed by December 1955. In February 1953, the Canadian government authorised the construction of one radar site in the Canadian Arctic. Then an event occurred which altered the thinking and speed at which the military and politicians considered the defence situation: the Soviets took their offensive weapons to a higher level of destruction and exploded their first thermonuclear device in August 1953.

Jockel included an excerpt from a Canadian External Affairs Top Secret memo, dated 8 December 1954, stating that:

> The most important conclusion to be drawn from all the discussions on the threat is that responsible United States officials are firmly of the opinion that the Soviet Union has now, or will have shortly, the capability of launching an atomic attack on North America on a scale sufficient to eliminate this continent as an effective source of resistance to the achievement of Soviet objectives. For this reason, the United States officials assert that, even to provide a margin of protection sufficient only to keep our losses to the point where we would have the ability to recuperate and retaliate, the North American air defence system must be greatly expanded and that it is necessary that this be done rapidly.

Canada decided to build the McGill Fence, renamed the Mid-Canada Line, at its own expense. The cost would be shared if the USA did not build the DEW Line. The Americans commenced construction of the Arctic DEW Line and the issue of sovereignty seemed to fade into the background as required by the more important issue of North American defence. Military thinking of the time concluded that even if a small percentage of bombers got through, the result would be economically devastating and destroy North American free society. USAF Lt-Col. John J. Lombardo, office of the deputy chief of staff, stated that 'at best, a 50% kill rate, the 540 bombers with 2 Megaton bombs would result in 117 million deaths.'

By 1954, the US Permanent radar system and the Canadian Pinetree, later called the Continental Air Defense Integration-North (CADIN)/Pinetree Line radar system, became fully operational. The two systems alerted the RCAF and USAF simultaneously and national boundaries were no longer an impediment to the air defence of North America. The USAF had seventy-five squadrons available and the RCAF now had nine squadrons. The RCAF assumed responsibility for the St Lawrence Valley and north of the Great Lakes. The USAF Alaskan Air Command and the RCAF Air Command base at Comox on Vancouver Island in British Columbia took care of the western approaches.

The Americans still struggled to unify and coordinate all the components of the defence system. The US Army had control of the Nike surface-to-air missile. The US army and USAF argued over whether the missiles were very long-range artillery or unmanned aircraft. In 1947, the US Army had lost control of their aircraft to the USAF and it did not want to lose the funding and control of the missiles. The USAF wanted to unify all aerial vehicles, missiles and aircraft under its jurisdiction.

In 1954, the Americans created the Continental Air Defense Command (CONAD) to unify the defence efforts of the Army, Navy and Air Force. CONAD tried to solve the American defence problem, control versus command. The American Air Defense Command and the Canadian Air Defence Command continued to work as separate entities but closely together. This way the Canadian sovereignty issue – loss of control of the defence of Canada, a political dilemma – did not interfere with the day-to-day defence operations.

During the winter of 1954/55, the RCAF and USAF became even more convinced of the need for a single Air Defence Command to coordinate the resources of both countries. It was important that the resources of both countries could be activated quickly to respond to any aerial threat. In September 1955, the Director of Plans in USAF headquarters, General Earle E. Partridge, Commander-in-Chief CONAD, and Commander USAF Air Defense Command, drafted a proposal for a joint Canada–US Air Defence Command. The Canadian Chiefs of Staff were all in favour of the idea, but once again, the sovereignty issue caused caution and the reluctance to approach their political masters. The word Command had connotations of complete loss of control of the military to a foreign power, namely the USA.

The solution was to create a position, not a command, to unify the structure. A single commander would be in operational control over all the defence resources of both countries for the benefit and protection of both countries. The RCAF and USAF would retain command of their respective forces, a very important issue for the Canadians and their sovereignty concerns. The position of Commander-in-Chief Air Defence Canada United States (CINCADCANUS) was created; the CINCADCANUS reported to the Canadian Chiefs of Staff and the American Joint Chiefs of Staff. A headquarters, staff, and a Canadian as a deputy would support the CINCADCANUS. This arrangement built on the Commander-in-Chief CONAD (CINCCONAD), who had authority over all three US services and his Colorado staff already in place. The Colorado staff importantly included a Canadian liaison staff.

In February 1957, the American Joint Chiefs of Staff and the Canadian Chief of Staff approved the concept for submission to their respective governments. The Canadian government delayed approval as it was in the middle of a general election, which, as it turned out, the Liberal party in power lost. The Progressive Conservatives, under Prime Minister John Diefenbaker, took over and were encouraged, by Lt-Gen. Charles Foulkes, to approve the process started by the previous government to minimise political fallout. The agreement, subsequently approved by the government on 24 July 1957, went into operation on 12 September 1957.

The seed had now grown into a plant! General Earle E. Partridge, the first commander of the new agreement, found the name CINCADCANUS, too awkward, and changed the title to North American Air Defence and himself to Commander-in-Chief NORAD (CINCNORAD). The deputy commander (DCINCNORAD), as per the agreement, was a Canadian, Air Marshall C. Roy Slemon, RCAF. He had full authority to take what action was necessary in event of a threat with the CINCNORAD absent. NORAD was given operational control of the air defence commands, called component commands, of Canada and USA, their assigned forces, and the air defence forces in Alaska. The component commands were the RCAF Air Defence Command, the US Army Air Defense Command, the US Naval Forces CONAD and the USAF Air Defense Command.

There still was a grey area of the use of nuclear weapons, alluded to by Joseph T. Jockel in his book, *Canada in NORAD*. He observed that, 'There was a legal restriction on the books concerning the access to nuclear information to non-US citizens, which included the deputy commander Air Marshall Slemon. President Eisenhower had pre-delegated the use of nuclear weapons to CONAD, but NORAD had no pre-delegation until 1964 when continuing US fears of a surprise attack prompted the change. General Partridge dealt with the situation in house when he acknowledged that as his deputy Air Marshall Slemon had to know all about the nuclear weapons at his disposal.' General Partridge could have lost his commission and been imprisoned for that act, but he felt it a necessary step to preserve the defence of North America in his occasional absence. For Canada, this was an amazing military/political agreement with the USA, the most powerful country on earth.

The Liberal Party, now the official opposition, made a hot issue of an American general in charge of Canadian forces. The governing Conservatives avoided the word 'command' and instead emphasised 'headquarters' and the ability of the CINCNORAD to summon US forces to assist Canadians. They also pointed out that the Liberals had all but approved the agreement prior to loosing the election. The signing of the agreement, an exchange of diplomatic notes on 12 May 1958, officially created NORAD. NORAD now legally existed with, surprisingly, the Canadians being equal partners in spite of the difference of operational contribution.

NORAD Mission Statement:
DETER DETECT DEFEND

The mission statement implied three main responsibilities of the organisation. The first responsibility was to deter the USSR by showing that a unified North American defence network was in place and would respond immediately to any threat by informing the Canadian and US governments of that threat. The USA then had the full force of the Strategic Air Command at its disposal to respond as necessary. SAC was a major USAF command consisting of a nuclear arsenal of missiles and bomber aircraft from 1946 until 1992. Its motto was 'Peace is our Profession'. The old adage applied: 'a best defence is a good offence'. A very brave foe, indeed, that would risk facing the resulting armada of nuclear-armed US bomber aircraft. The second responsibility was to construct and maintain a radar network to detect any airborne threat approaching North America. The third responsibility was to have a force, always at the ready, to deal effectively with that threat.

The First Fifteen Years from 1958 to 1973

On 25 March 1958 the famous, and infamous in some circles, Avro Arrow completed its first flight in the capable hands of the test pilot Jan Zurakowski. The RCAF now had a jet fighter that was capable of replacing the Avro CF-100. The Arrow would meet the need for a supersonic fighter interceptor as the speed of bombers increased. The second post-war Canadian designed jet fighter took to the skies and proved the capability of Canada's aviation industry to maintain its position as a world leader in aircraft development and production.

The Arrow proved to NORAD that Canada was a full partner and was contributing to the fighter defence of North America. However, there was one very important drawback: Canada had been unable to get orders for the Arrow and the cost had spiralled so much that the military Chiefs of Staff felt that they could get a comparable aircraft for a quarter of the price from the USA. The demise of the Arrow had started and in September 1958, Diefenbaker announced that the radar site upgrade to the SAGE system would proceed, along with the addition of the Bomarc missile – there was no mention of the Arrow. The matter of the supersonic fighter faded into the background, for now, as the Canadian public assumed the new systems met the defence requirements. However, the CF-100 was too slow for the new Soviet bombers and the Bomarc missile was only effective against bombers, not missiles.

The announcement came on 20 February 1959 – the Arrow programme was cancelled due to high costs and the thought that the aerial war was now shifting to missile defence. The ageing CF-100 was about to leave Canada without any significant fighter interceptor defence, bringing up the question: was Canada still a full contributing member of NORAD? The US proposed diverting a new batch of McDonnell F-101 Voodoos on the assembly line to the RCAF. This aircraft, possibly inferior to the uncompleted Arrow, met the requirements for an interceptor, but the purchase certainly would be an embarrassment to the government, after cancelling the Arrow programme.

The USA, now under the new government, John F. Kennedy had to find a way to make Canada a full NORAD player again and keep the 'action' as far away from the north-eastern USA as possible. A new 1961 American proposal was threefold: that Canada would be given the sixty-six Voodoo aircraft at no cost, that Canada would assume the cost of and operate twenty-one radar sites, and that it would manufacture the Lockheed 104 Starfighter for NATO allies at a shared cost with the USA. Canada could not refuse this offer for three reasons: it solved the problem of the supersonic interceptor, it decreased US personnel on Canadian soil, and it gave some work to an ailing military aviation industry.

NORAD, in anticipation of the new Voodoo fighters in Canada, the new Semi Automatic Ground Environment radar site information and command network, and the Bomarc missile, redefined the operational boundaries and established the vast 'Northern NORAD Region'. The region headquarters opened in 1963 in the new SAGE complex, built underground in North Bay, Ontario. The importance of this region was vital to NORAD as it lay on the anticipated route of the Soviet bomber threat. The region had four squadrons of Voodoos, the other squadron being on the west coast at Comox, British Columbia. It also had the two bases of Bomarc missiles at North Bay, Ontario, and La Macaza, Quebec. The USAF now also had a presence in Newfoundland with nuclear-armed fighter aircraft. The American Harmon Air Force Base at Stephenville, previously negotiated with Great Britain under the 'Destroyers for Bases' programme prior to Newfoundland joining Canada, had created a political dilemma as Canada debated the nuclear weapon issue.

A dichotomy existed between military and political thinking on nuclear weapons. The USAF NORAD fighters in Newfoundland had nuclear weapons in the legal custody and protection of US forces stationed at Stephenville. Eisenhower had great faith in the Canadian NORAD connection and wanted to provide nuclear armaments for Voodoos and Bomarc missiles. Canada, having quickly reached an agreement about the

Voodoos, SAGE and Bomarc missiles, had impressed Eisenhower with the attitude of the St Laurent and Diefenbaker governments. Cooperation between the two countries was at an all-time high. The military of both countries fully agreed with his decision; however, the government of Canada did not.

The Diefenbaker government drew the line in February 1959 at owning nuclear weapons. It said 'No' to nuclear proliferation by indicating that Canada would not own any nuclear weapons. Canada worried about the escalation of tension in the Cold War. However, it continued to work with the Americans on how to solve the problem of having nuclear weapons available, if necessary, on Canadian soil. Due to the technology of the times, the Bomarc missiles would not be very effective without a nuclear warhead. Did the Diefenbaker government realise this fact before agreeing to the Bomarc deployment?

The debate raged within the government. Howard Green, Secretary of State for External Affairs, did not want to antagonise the USSR and he was sceptical about nuclear deterrence while also committed to nuclear disarmament. Green was a good friend of Diefenbaker and had a personal avenue of communication. George Pearkes and later Douglas Harkness, as Minister of Defence championed the other side of the argument for arming the defence forces with nuclear weapons. The Conservative government remained deadlocked in debate. It declared that the Newfoundland nuclear weapon arrangement for USAF fighters was in abeyance until all bilateral nuclear agreements were settled.

The Liberal party, under opposition leader Lester B. Pearson, suggested that Canada was wasting its resources in 'active air defence', because it was no use against the ICBMs. It suggested, basically, no nuclear weapons for the RCAF, limit the Voodoos to an identification role, and scrap the Bomarcs. The Conservatives scoffed at these suggestions and accused the Liberals of reducing the defence of Canada to 'bird watching'.

In 1961, the US Chiefs of Staff added a Space Detection and Tracking System to the NORAD responsibilities. Canada installed a surplus Baker-Nunn space surveillance camera at Cold Lake, Alberta. The Defence Research Board operated a radar laboratory, in conjunction with SPADATS, at Prince Albert, Saskatchewan. Canada was now in the space age.

Let every nation know, whether it wishes us well or ill, that we shall pay any price, bear any burden, meet any hardship, support any friend, oppose any foe, in order to ensure the survival and success of liberty.

President John F. Kennedy's inaugural address, 20 January 1961.

The election of John F. Kennedy in November 1960 did not lead to a change in Canada's position. Canada remained nuclear-free and the Bomarcs remained virtually useless without nuclear warheads. The NORAD partnership strained as the government of Canada resisted the entreaties of the USA to equip the RCAF with nuclear weapons. The Cuban Missile Crisis further fuelled the distrust and mutual dislike of both the leaders. Diefenbaker wanted an independent team sent to Cuba to verify Kennedy's claim of 22 October 1962 that the Soviets had installed nuclear-armed missiles in Cuba. In defence of Diefenbaker's reaction, Kennedy did not consult him as per the initial NORAD agreement.

The political masters had discovered, certainly from the Canadian side, that in time of crisis, the agreements took a back seat to national reaction. Should this have been a surprise to Canada? The military functioned very well, with both the headquarters of NORAD and CONAD under the one roof at Colorado Springs. CONAD went to a heightened level of alert, DEFCON 3, and put US forces at that level. The RCAF remained at the normal level, DEFCON 5. NORAD was the coordinating organisation that kept the channels of communication open and preserved the defence of North America.

Jockel commented that, 'Air Marshall Slemon phoned the RCAF headquarters and requested that the RCAF upgrade to the same alert level. To every one's surprise Diefenbaker referred the decision to a cabinet meeting the next day and subsequently to 24 October. The cabinet split with Prime Minister Diefenbaker and Secretary of State for Foreign Affairs Green firmly blocking the permission to heighten the alert level. Harkness, the defence minister, quietly upgraded the RCAF alert status on his own initiative and with minimum fuss and public awareness.' Subsequently, when the government learnt of Soviet preparations and that the US Navy and Strategic Air Command had gone to DEFCON 2, Diefenbaker, convinced now of imminent danger, authorised NORAD to bring the Canadian Forces up to DEFCON 3. An equal partner? I do not think so. It was admirable in the eyes of some to limit escalation. However, had Canada let the agreement down? Not really – Canadian forces were still available to NORAD for the defence of North America.

Opposition leader Lester Pearson now changed his tactic to humiliate Diefenbaker over the Cuban Missile Crisis. He took the position, despite not agreeing with nuclear weapons, that Canada was obligated to honour its commitments. Defence Minister Douglas Harkness once again tried to get the government to accept the acquisition of nuclear weapons. Only when he threatened to resign did the cabinet endorse the proposal. The last obstacle was Prime Minister Diefenbaker and he would address the House of Commons on the subject.

In his speech on 25 January 1963, PM Diefenbaker acknowledged that Canada had nuclear commitments, but argued that because of ICBMs the air defence of North America was becoming obsolete. Harkness called for clarification of his remarks, but Diefenbaker refused to endorse Harkness' statement that Canada was obligated to acquire nuclear weapons. The opposition immediately called for Harkness' resignation. He, along with two ministers, resigned, which resulted in the defeat of the Diefenbaker government by a non-confidence motion and subsequent election. The outcome was a minority Liberal government under PM Pearson in April 1963.

Finally, in August 1963, the USA and Canada reached an agreement for nuclear weapons on Canadian soil. The US retained legal and physical custody of the weapons stored at Canadian bases. The authorisation of both governments was required before their use. The Bomarcs were the first to achieve nuclear operational status, followed by the Voodoos in 1965. The US had a pre-delegation agreement and Canada had a prior authorisation agreement. Jockel observed that: 'This meant that in the event of the following three conditions, an attack, imminent attack or defined emergency circumstances, NORAD had prior authorization to arm the defences of both countries under the direction of CINCNORAD or the Canadian DCINCNORAD as necessitated by circumstances.' This agreement remained secret as long as the weapons were on Canadian soil.

The 1965 agreement excluded the use of NORAD nuclear weapons against single aircraft intrusions of North American airspace. However, the US CONAD reserved the right to use whatever force necessary, even nuclear, to protect its own airspace even against single intruders. An interesting situation arose in that the USAF interceptors had two military obligations, NORAD and CONAD, as the situation dictated. This exact situation occurred during President Kennedy's address on 22 October 1962 regarding the Cuban Missile Crisis. CONAD forces, the USAF included, went to DEFCON 3 status and NORAD remained at the normal DEFCON 5 level.

The government decided to reduce the air-defence resources during the early 1960s. The Voodoo squadrons were reduced to three, some Pinetree radar stations were closed and, due to SAGE making the Pinetree Radar Line more effective, the Mid-Canada Radar Line, along roughly the 55th parallel of latitude, was closed. The USA also planned a gradual reduction in interceptors of approximately one half. The subtle move to missile defence, or more accurately assured retaliation, took place. NORAD had previously planned to deploy Nike-Zeus ballistic missile defences to Ottawa and Toronto in 1965 and Montreal in the following year. Five years previously in 1960, it had established the foundation of an operational Ballistic Missile Early Warning System; missile defence assumed a greater importance as the decade progressed. In 1967, the US announced a limited missile defence system called 'Sentinel' using the Nike-X missile. This shield protected southern Canada at no cost. The entire system, based on US soil, avoided the politically sensitive issue of US missiles on Canadian soil.

In March 1967, the RCAF *Sentinel* magazine reported that NORAD had 170,000 personnel involved in the defence of North America. Canada contributed 15,000 personnel stationed from the east coast to the west coast and from the 49th parallel of latitude (the US border) to the high Arctic. In spite of the movement towards missile defence, there still existed a need to counter the existing USSR bomber arsenal. The fighter interceptor was a required part of the defence network.

In 1968, the USA announced a four-part defence focus. First, there would be civilian radar cooperation of data for the peripheral of the USA. Second, Over-the-Horizon Backscatter radar was to be constructed with a 3,219-kilometre range; this radar used ionospheric reflection to send and receive its signals. Third, Airborne Warning and Control System aircraft would be deployed to the far north. These aircraft would orbit in position, monitoring all aerial traffic activity with their airborne radar – in effect, an airborne onsite command centre. Fourth, the USA would develop an improved interceptor. The changes affected Canada in a number of ways. The Bomarcs could be dispensed with in the mid-1970s and the DEW Line could be closed, bringing the political sensitive issue of Americans on Canadian soil to an end. Now the concern was the possible basing of the Airborne Warning and Control System aircraft in Canada and the unknown capability of the Over-the-Horizon radar system.

The NORAD agreement expired in 1968 and, in addition to the basic 1958 agreement, efforts centred on changing the name of the agreement to 'North American Aerospace Defence replacing Air'. Canada opted out of any anti-ballistic missile system and renewal of the agreement for five years with a one-year termination clause. The face of NORAD was constantly changing at this time as a result of thoughts on defence and offence by the USA. Canada did not have any offensive capability in North America to respond to the USSR threat. The name change did not happen and the NORAD agreement signed on 12 May 1968 included a clause to exclude Canada from any ballistic missile defence.

The new agreement coincided with the election of Liberal Pierre E. Trudeau as the Prime Minister of Canada. It took Trudeau a year to review and establish a new Canadian defence policy. His government established four priorities. The first was to protect Canadian sovereignty with Canadian forces on Canadian soil. This would require the need to improve the identification capabilities of the Canadian NORAD forces. The second was to cooperate with the USA through NORAD. The third was to support NATO and the fourth was to support international peacekeeping efforts. Furthermore, he initiated cuts to Canadian support of the North Atlantic Treaty Organisation in Europe.

In continuing with the thought that 'the best defence is offence', Richard M. Nixon, now US President, scrapped the Sentinel defensive missile system and established the Safeguard missile system. The Safeguard missile system would not protect cities, but would protect the US inter-continental ballistic missiles for an assured retaliatory attack. Trudeau subscribed to this thought as 'stable mutual deterrence'. The assured mutual destruction theory was described as 'do not try anything, as after your attack we will still have the capability of destroying you.'

Since 1968, the USSR had tested North American defences by flying long-range bombers along the coast of North America on their 'training' missions to Cuba. Occasionally, they would stray into Canadian and US airspace, probing the radar defences and interceptor response time. NORAD had responded by putting Canadian Voodoo aircraft at Chatham, New Brunswick, and US interceptors at Loring Air Force Base, Maine. On 26 June 1968, the first successful interception and identification of a Soviet bomber by a Canadian crew occurred off the east coast of Newfoundland. A full account of this event occurs later in this chapter.

In Canada, the Ministry of Transport, which operated the civil radar network and controlled civil aviation in Canadian airspace, showed no interest in establishing a joint radar system with NORAD to help in the identification of aircraft that strayed off course, hijacked aircraft and aircraft that were flying outside of controlled airspace. A curious stance, as the complete opposite occurred in the USA. The US equivalent, the Federal Aviation Authority, worked closely with the USAF and established a Joint Surveillance System in 1973, replacing the Permanent radar system, the US equivalent of the Canadian Pinetree Line.

The establishment of the Joint Surveillance System allowed Canada to redefine regional boundaries and plan to build facilities to control all Canadian airspace from North Bay, Ontario. Centres in the US controlled some NORAD regions that extended into Canada. The new technology centres built on the surface would eventually replace the obsolete underground SAGE centre. This confidence to build command centres on the surface would seem to be the result of a philosophy of assured mutual destruction. The massive destructive potential of US forces available ensured that the USSR would not dare destroy these command centres.

The early 1970s turned into a great stalemate, luckily for humankind, as the two nuclear superpowers faced each other in the deadly chess game of the Cold War. Finally, after seventeen years of political suspicion and various serious skirmishes, such as the Berlin Blockade, the Korean War and the Cuban crisis, representatives from the USA and the USSR sat down to diffuse the volatile situation that existed between them. President Richard Nixon gets full credit for breaking the standoff by previously offering the hand of friendship to China, causing the USSR to be the 'odd man out'. Nixon used a brilliant tactical political move that resulted in the Strategic Arms Limitations Talks. In 1972, Nixon and L. I. Brezhnev, General Secretary of the Central Committee of the Communist Party of the Soviet Union, signed the SALT 1 agreement, limiting the amount and type of ICBMs that each country should have in its arsenal.

The increase in dialogue and limiting agreements between the superpowers agreed with the Canadian policy of preventing nuclear war by promoting reconciliation and arms control, while contributing, through NORAD, to stable mutual deterrence. Five years had passed and new negotiations ensued for an updated NORAD agreement. The USA brought up the 'Aerospace' name change again and wanted to remove the Canadian anti-ballistic missile opt-out clause. The May 1973 agreement retained the original 1958 agreement as well as the Canadian anti-ballistic missile opt-out clause and a two-year renewal period. The USA had made better progress for change with the USSR than with the Canadian defence policy. The USA and Canada did acknowledge the commitment to the secret 1965 accord of consultation and authorisation of the use of nuclear weapons.

Such was the atmosphere of cooperation that existed at the time of the NORAD training exercise, the focus of this book and described in detail in a later chapter, which took place in the early morning hours of 10 May 1973. In 1968, the RCAF ceased to exist, due to unification of the Canadian forces, which were training very hard to be the very best with the resources that were available at the time. In 1972, an interceptor Voodoo crew of 425 Squadron, based at Canadian Forces Base (CFB) Bagotville, Quebec, won the NORAD Top Gun Award, truly reflecting the dedication and expertise of the personnel of the Canadian Air Defence Command and their commitment to NORAD.

NORAD Headquarters

Cheyenne Mountain, Colorado Springs

The agreement reached in 1951 to integrate the defence of North America resulted in the RCAF sending Air Defence Command liaison personnel to Ent Air Force Base (AFB) in Colorado Springs, Colorado, USA. The United States Air Defense Command had established their headquarters there as part of Continental Air Defense Command. Ent AFB is situated in the central United States, approximately 4,400 kilometres, or greater than four hours flying time for a Soviet bomber, from Gander, Newfoundland. The expected route of the Soviet bombers coming through 'The Gap' between Iceland and Greenland would continue westward to enter Canadian airspace over Newfoundland or Labrador. The bombers would have to fly through many lines of defence to get to NORAD headquarters; a no chance and slim at best proposition. In 1954, the two national air defence commanders set up a joint planning group to draw up a plan for the air defence of the entire continent. By 1958, Canada contributed twenty-nine officers, ten other ranks and four civilians to the NORAD headquarters staff at Ent AFB.

Ent AFB was an unusual kind of air force base as it did not have a runway. Instead, for air movements, it used Peterson AFB nearby. Ent AFB hosted NORAD, including the Canadians at no expense, and provided all the support facilities. These included transportation, messes (dining facilities), a hospital, a dentist, a library, a commissary, etc. A very fortunate position for Canada as its personnel were an integral part of the headquarters staff. Air Marshall C. Roy Slemon RCAF was Deputy Commander in Chief NORAD (DCINCNORAD) to General Partridge. General Partridge became concerned about the possibility of an attack on the vulnerable above-ground Ent AFB and construction started on an underground Combat Operations Center in nearby Cheyenne Mountain in May 1961.

The NORAD Combat Operations Center in Cheyenne Mountain became operational on 20 April 1966. The original requirement was to provide command and control of Canadian and US forces in the event of a Soviet-manned-bomber attack. However, changing technology and threat altered that role through the years. In the mid-1970s, it also briefly became the Ballistic Missile Defense Center. At the time of the NORAD exercise on 10 May 1973, it was a fully operational command centre, very much involved in monitoring the North American threat assessment. Colonel Grant Nicholls was a Command Director at that time in NORAD headquarters and could have been monitoring the status screens that night in the command centre. NORAD headquarters had control and command of the various regions, which, over the years, have changed names and geographical responsibility.

In the early 1960s, NORAD was comprised of six regions, each with its own divisions. These six regions and respective divisions covered the entire area of North America from the Mexican border to the North Pole. This bi-national agreement served a gargantuan area. The Central Region had headquarters at Richards Gebaur AFB, Mississippi; the Western Region had headquarters at Hamilton AFB, California; the Southern Region had headquarters at Gunter AFB, Alabama; the Eastern Region had headquarters at Stewart AFB, New York; the Alaska Region had headquarters at Elmendorf AFB, Alaska.

The Northern Region had its headquarters at North Bay, Ontario, Canada. It was the largest geographical area, 20 per cent of North America, and faced any Soviet threat coming over the North Pole and approaching North America. The area extended within a line from the North Pole down the Alaska/Canadian border to the 60th north parallel of latitude, east to the Saskatchewan/Manitoba border, south to the 55th north latitude, east to the western shore of Hudson Bay, down south to the north shore of Lake Huron, east to the Atlantic Ocean and north again to the North Pole, remaining clear of Greenland. It consisted of the Hudson Bay, Ottawa, Bangor and Goose NORAD sectors or numbered divisions. The Canadian forces' base at North Bay had four major responsibilities. First was to maintain the base and to provide support to all resident units. Second was as the HQ of the Canadian Air Defence Command. Third was as the HQ of the 41st Division of the Northern NORAD Region. Fourth was as the HQ of the Northern NORAD Region. A very busy place indeed, together with the SAGE underground complex commonly called 'The Hole'.

In 1969, NORAD realignment took place to abolish the old regions and divisions and establish eight new regions, numbered twenty to twenty-six inclusive plus Alaska, to cover the air-defence requirements of North America. The 20th Region covered south-eastern USA. The 21st Region the covered north-eastern USA and the southern tip of Nova Scotia. The old Northern NORAD Region became the 22nd NORAD Region, with very little change in area; it remained the largest region with 5,180,000 square kilometres and the HQ remained at CFB North Bay, Ontario, Canada. 'The Hole' offered the same underground protection to the 22nd Region HQ as Cheyenne Mountain protected the NORAD HQ. The 23rd Region covered the states south of Minnesota and north into Ontario. The 24th Region covered the states south of Montana and north into central Alberta, Saskatchewan and Manitoba. The 25th Region covered the west coast of the USA and British Columbia and western Alberta. The 26th Region covered south-west and south central USA. The Alaskan

NORAD Region covered all of Alaska, including the Aleutian Island chain to the very tip at Shemya. It is interesting to note that the fighters that protected the Canadian Prairies flew out of US bases. However, it was NORAD policy that the deputy commanders of these US regions would be Canadian. The reverse situation was also true. The deputy commander of the 22nd NORAD Canadian Region was an American. This enforced the bi-national aspect of the NORAD agreement. Lt-Col. George McAffer, experienced in many NORAD roles throughout the organisation, said 'that NORAD had a lot of bureaucracy but by and large (Canada) almost always an equal partner'.

North Bay, Ontario

North Bay, Ontario, Canada, was a very suitable site for the 22nd NORAD Region HQ and underground SAGE site. It is close to government and industrial areas, less than 400 km, and easily accessible by air, highway and rail. The airport, opened in 1938, is situated north-east of the city at the top of 'airport hill', and provided an important link in opening up northern Ontario to air travel. During the Second World War, it was associated with both the Royal Air Force and RCAF in training and ferry flight capacities.

In 1951, due to the build up of Canadian air defence systems, a RCAF station was formed at the airport. Various RCAF operational and training squadrons, using the Canadair Sabre and Avro CF-100 aircraft, were resident until 1962. In 1954, the station assumed the role of 24-hour alert readiness and the resident CF-100 Squadron provided the '5 minute' response interceptors. In 1962, the interceptors became supersonic as the CF-100 was replaced with the McDonnell CF-101 Voodoo fighter. These fighters were housed in special Quick Reaction Area hangars at the east end of the main runway, fully armed and ready to go at a moment's notice, day or night.

Coincidental with the formal formation in 1958 of NORAD, the government decided to build the first, and only, Canadian underground nuclear hardened SAGE complex at North Bay. The Northern NORAD Region would be the first region to face the incoming Soviet bombers/missiles and would need maximum protection to continue functioning. The site selected, just south of, and adjacent to, the RCAF station at North Bay, commenced construction in August 1959 after an extensive test-hole programme to verify the competent granitic gneiss of the two-billion-year-old rock of the Pre-Cambrian shield. The Swedish 'smooth wall' blasting technique was used to give remarkable clean rock faces.

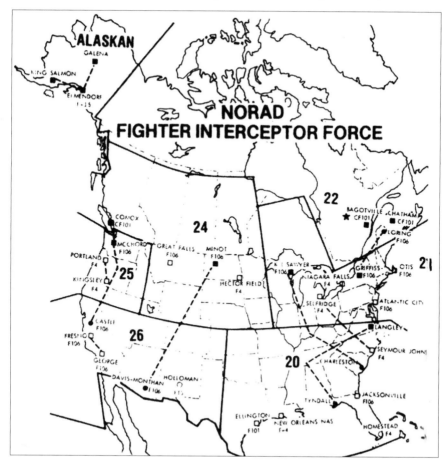

NORAD Regions, 1982. (Courtesy of DND, Directorate of History and Heritage)

The face was further stabilised as necessary by long bolts and steel wire mesh.

The building is in the shape of a squared off number eight, giving two long sections with three cross sections, all joined together, but constructed in five caverns. There was also a separate cavern for the emergency power supply. Two separate caverns were used for domestic and cooling water reservoirs. The building was totally independent of the surrounding rock and sat on seismic designed pillars to absorb any shock from earthquakes or nuclear bomb blasts. The whole complex was accessible by three entrance tunnels, each sealed with a 17,000-kg blast door.

Shuttle buses moved the SAGE complex personnel from Canadian Forces Base North Bay, situated at the north end of the tunnel, south to the underground complex. The north tunnel did not allow pedestrian traffic.

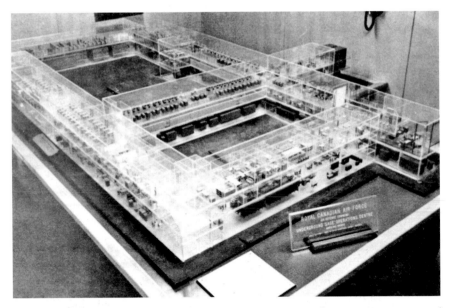

Underground Complex, North Bay, Ontario. (Courtesy of DND, Directorate of History and Heritage)

The buses continued driving further south to the South Portal, above Trout Lake, to turn around before proceeding north again. There were a few passing areas designated by coloured lights to indicate what vehicles had the required dimensions to safely pass. The bus speed limit was 25 km/hr, which had an illusion of a far greater speed because of the proximity of the tunnel walls. Approximately 700 people used the transport each workday in the round-the-clock operation.

22nd NORAD Region HQ Underground Complex, 'The Hole'

Alighting from the bus, the personnel featured in this book passed through the open blast door and along a short cavern before coming to the front steps of the building. The blast doors closed in the event of hostilities and the building was sealed off; in the early 1970s, they closed only for maintenance purposes and even remained open during exercises. Lt Dennis Kelleher, later Lt-Col., remembered that 'you always knew what was cooking for supper as the smell hung in the air outside the building'. Approaching the steps to enter the building, the giant pilings supporting the structure were clearly visible, as was the surrounding rock of the cavern. Captain Peter Maunsell,

Blast door. (Courtesy of Canadian Forces Joint Imagery Centre, Department of National Defence)

who worked in the exercise planning area, remembered hearing at times 'the noise of hammering followed by the sound of rock hitting the outside of the building'. He stated that 'there was a crew of hard rock miners whose job was to look after and maintain the caverns'.

The bottom of the three-storey building housed two giant AN/FSQ-7 IBM computers, nicknamed 'Bonnie' and 'Clyde', and a massive communications network which was the heart of the SAGE system. These computers were 1960s technology comprised of 58,000 vacuum tubes that generated massive amounts of heat. A water-based cooling system dissipated all the heat energy. All incoming information was stored in core devices, tapes and magnetic drums. The computer-generated results were displayed graphically on a visual display scope. The computers continuously analysed past movements and positions and projected the future information on to the screens.

A water-based cooling system was a very important part of the complex to keep the working temperature of the building at a normal level. The building was like any other structure of that era, except it was 183-metres (600-feet) underground and did not have any windows. The lights were on 24 hours a day. A building maintenance crew looked after the building as they would any major complex on the surface.

The building housed a myriad of offices, some small and some big, to facilitate the daily business of protecting this region of Canada from aerial threats. The number of personnel would vary depending on whether it was a normal day or if it was during an exercise, when the numbers would increase substantially. These exercises were run regularly to simulate heightened world tension or actual wartime conditions to test the system. Thus the 22nd NORAD Region maintained its competency at the leading geographical edge of NORAD against the Soviet threat.

The complex housed all the amenities to allow it to function in the event of it being sealed off from the world above: a vast reservoir of water, a cafeteria, food storage, medical facilities, a fire-fighting team, washroom and shower facilities, and an independent power supply. Walking down the brightly lit corridor to their workstations, the five personnel interviewed for this project could have been in any office building in Canada. Dennis Kelleher remarked that 'he found the air quality good except sometimes when they were closed up for exercises there was a smell of cooking'.

All the people mentioned in this part of the chapter and Chapter Nine, the actual mission, worked in CFB North Bay on 10 May 1973. During my interview with them they recalled the events that occurred during an exercise and their part in it. They were exciting times and they recalled their time in NORAD and the importance of their job with fondness.

Their remarks reflect the memories of the actual people involved nearly forty years later.

Halfway down the long corridor of the squared off figure-eight-shaped building Lt Marty Schlosser, later Lt-Col., entered the air surveillance section. Maunsell headed for his exercise monitoring office on the second floor. Kelleher, Capt Jim Graham and MCpl Bob Keith headed the other direction to the dimly lit 'Blue Room' of the weapons section; this room was full of radar screens positioned down each wall. The other occupants of the bus all disappeared into various offices. Some of the personnel were civilians, such as the IBM computer and Bell Telephone employees. Security demanded rigorous screening of all personnel, civilian and military, prior to working in the highly secure area of the Underground Complex.

The military personnel working there were all highly experienced people. Peter Maunsell had been an AI Navigator on the CF-100 and CF-101 fighter interceptors. He had also done a tour as a Weapons Controller, so he was fully qualified in all aspects of the roles in ADC. He was an ideal candidate to plot the devious details of the NORAD exercises. He knew the strengths and weaknesses of the entire system and could use them to his advantage to test the NORAD preparedness.

This was truly a 24/7 operation, complete with bus schedules and shift changes. Like any commuter it was possible to miss the bus! Using the south tunnel, it was feasible to walk out to the South Portal if your car was parked there. The south tunnel was used for all the excavating activity and as a result was larger than the north tunnel, to accommodate all the tunnelling equipment and the removal of the rock. The sidewalk was only delineated by a yellow line from the roadway. The north tunnel was restricted to vehicles only. It felt quite daunting to some people as Kelleher figured 'it had about a 20 degree down-slope'.

The 'Deter, Detect, Defend' of the NORAD mission statement describes in general terms what the whole Underground Complex, or 'The Hole' as it was known as affectionately in North Bay, represented. Its existence demonstrated to the USSR that 'we are prepared at any time to see you coming and deal effectively and immediately with anything that you may try militarily to gain advantage over North America'. That is the 'Deter' factor; the fact that NORAD will 'Detect' any threat and 'Defend' against it completes the NORAD motto. Kelleher, Keith, Schlosser, Graham and Maunsell, amongst hundreds of others, were part of this formidable NORAD organisation down 'The Hole' during 1973 in North Bay, Ontario.

In the early 1960s, there were three lines of radar sites which provided coverage for the 22nd NORAD Region. The CADIN (Continental Air Defense Integration-North)/Pinetree Line was located at 50 degrees north latitude; this line was the closest to the US border. The Mid-Canada Line was at 55 degrees north latitude and the DEW Line was at 70 degrees north latitude. These radar systems will be explained in depth in a subsequent chapter. These lines, except the Mid-Canada Line, which closed in 1965, provided radar data to the SAGE system at North Bay during the time of our exercise in 1973. All displayed radar air traffic entering Canadian airspace would either be identified and confirmed 'friendly' or declared 'unknown.'

One way of thinking about the system was that the 22nd NORAD Region HQ was the central gathering location for all the technology and human effort that had gone into producing a clear, accurate and concise radar display on which decisions regarding the security of North America depended. The technological contribution consisted of the radar sites installed in the Canadian Arctic and remote areas of Canada that created a defensive radar wall. The sites were positioned on mountains, or hills at the very least, to give better 'line of sight coverage'. The human contribution consisted of the army of personnel that kept the network functioning to its highest level of efficiency, sometimes in appalling weather conditions. The Canadian winter can be a very unforgiving environment; frostbite and hypothermia are common complaints. The summer has its own challenges of black flies and thunderstorms. The isolation of the radar site added an important additional consideration. This is where the dedication comes in.

The Air Surveillance Officer was responsible for providing a clear radar picture, a composite from various sources, to the tracking, identification and weapons teams. This was the technical section of the 22nd NORAD Region HQ and coordinated the effort to achieve the best presentation of the incoming technical data. The Air Surveillance Officer's team consisted of three people working with him: a Radar Input Counter Measures Officer, Schlosser's position in 1973, and two Radar Input Counter Measures Technicians.

Marty Schlosser had worked as an Intercept Director and then decided to specialise in the Surveillance section. This was a more technically challenging position that dealt with the quality of the radar information provided to the Intercept Director. He attended a radar theory course conducted by the USAF at their largest training facility in Biloxi, Mississippi. He mentioned that 'there were over forty nations represented which in 1972 included Iraq and Iran'.

These radar systems were 'primitive' in comparison to the present-day radar systems and required a team to make them function properly. They needed constant adjustment and maintenance. The Air Defence Technicians at the radar sites worked with the Radar Input Counter Measures Technicians down 'The Hole' at North Bay to tweak the radar picture to give the best available data. The 'Common Digitiser' processed the radar signal from the radar sites before transmission to the SAGE computer in the Underground Complex.

The Air Surveillance Officer was also responsible for three other teams. The Manual Input Team processed teletype data and converted it to displayed radar data. This displayed data would show up on the radar screen as symbols to allow the operator to examine all the details. This data could come from the DEW Line or Air Traffic Control. The incoming message was typed on to eighty-hole punch cards and then loaded in a hopper that would read the information into the computer. The resulting data was incorporated in the computer's memory and become part of the radar display.

The Tracker Team watched every radar contact coming into Canadian airspace and passed on any 'unknown' contact, called a track, to the third team, the Identification Team. On one occasion, Kelleher was walking by one of the tracker scopes in the middle of the night and noticed the tracker had his eyes closed. It was a tough job at the best of times but particularly challenging in the night. The tracker normally worked one hour on and one hour off. 'Are you okay,' said Kelleher. 'Yes Sir, just checking my eyes for holes.'

The Identification Team had two minutes to identify the unknown track, now called a 'pending' track. The team compared the track and the information received from the Air Traffic Control centres. The acceptable geographical difference between the radar track and the flight plan position decreased or increased as per the conditions, depending on whether it was wartime or peacetime. In peacetime, the aircraft had to be within 20 nautical miles of position and five minutes of estimated time of arrival at the position. There was constant dialogue between the Identification Team and Air Traffic Control to identify all unknown tracks. The Identification Team had to identify the track or, if classified as hostile, the Senior Director, Jim Graham in 1973, took action and assigned it to a Weapons Control Team to deploy, 'scramble' in Air Force jargon, the interceptor aircraft to perform a visual identification.

The Senior Director was like an orchestra leader; he even sat up on a dais above floor level. He had all the information displayed at hand regarding serviceable interceptors, aircraft on Alert Status, weapons available, airborne aircraft, aircraft fuel states, meteorological reports and forecasts for the 22nd Region, status of all radar sites and lines of communication. Based on all this information he would conduct the air battle to identify and destroy, if necessary, all hostile aircraft. In day-to-day operations he reported to the Director of Operations.

In the event of war or exercises he would work closely with, and under the guidance of, the assembled Battle Staff. The Battle Staff consisted of the Region Commander and many senior officer advisors and experts in the field of air defence. Captain Rob Dunlop, later Lt-Col., related that, 'the [Battle Staff] personnel had day jobs as Staff Officers in 22nd NORAD Region. For example, my position was as Senior Staff [Officer] Intelligence, Plans and Requirements. My position in the Battle Staff was as Fighter, Officer Interceptor.' His boss was Lt-Col. 'Tiny' McDonald featured, by coincidence, in Chapter Nine. The Battle Staff observed the ongoing exercise, or battle, on a tall three-storey screen. The screen 'displayed information such as a map, targets, fighters, weapons status, fighter status, weather and battle damage', according to Dunlop.

Jim Graham had many years with NORAD in the USA and Canada. His previous posting had been at the very busy manual site in Goose Bay, Labrador. The Soviet Bear bombers were always testing the response to possible Canadian Air Defence Identification Zone incursions as they routinely flew down the coast en route to Cuba. This Amalgam Mute exercise should have been routine for Jim, but there was always the chance of a surprise created by Peter Maunsell.

The four weapons control teams all sat at radar screens and each team consisted of many personnel. The Weapons Director led the team with the Weapons Director Technician, Bob Keith in 1973. The Weapons Director had five Intercept Directors, each with their technician. The Intercept Director, Kelleher in 1973, with his technician performed the vectoring

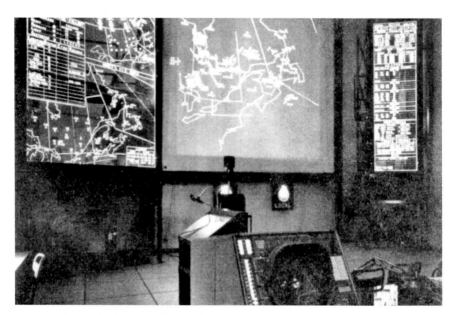

Combat Centre, Underground Complex. (Courtesy of Canadian Forces Joint Imagery Centre, Department of National Defence)

of the interceptor to identify the 'unknown' aircraft and destroy it if necessary. The 'buck stopped here', as the well known phrase goes. All the personnel featured worked at their positions down 'The Hole' in May 1973, but it was not possible to ascertain if they worked the night of 10 May 1973. For the sake of illustration we will assume that they were all at their posts that night.

Jim's assistant that night was Bob Keith. Bob was a very experienced NORAD Fighter Control Operator, later called Air Defence Technician, who had controlled in the USA at Duluth, Minnesota, with the 23rd NORAD Region. It was there that he worked with the Mach 2 Convair B-58 Hustler bomber and a wide variety of USAF fighters, including the F-101, F-102 and F-106, that gave him irreplaceable training.

There were three complete crews to cover the 24/365 operation. Kelleher remembered the work cycle was twenty-one days with three shifts. The Day shift was from 0700 hrs to 1500 hrs, the Swing shift was from 1500 hrs to 2300 hrs and finally the Mids (midnights) was from 2300 hrs to 0700 hrs. He mentioned that: 'The exercises were manned separately with your best people. So you could work periods where you never got your days off. This was always a source of complaint, however God forbid that you were not chosen to be part of the exercise team. Every exercise for us was some sort of evaluation or lead up to an evaluation and you wanted to be there.'

Weapons Director, 1978. (Courtesy of Canadian Forces Joint Imagery Centre, Department of National Defence)

Dennis Kelleher started his career as a Meteorology Technician and re-mustered to become an Air Weapons Controller. In 1971, a third-stage blade problem in the Pratt & Whitney J-57 engine grounded all the Canadian CF-101 Voodoos. This caused Dennis to certify in Duluth, Minnesota, USA, with the 23rd Region. He was determined to be involved in all the exercises available and worked the Amalgam Mute exercise.

Keith, the Weapons Director Technician, who handled the communication duties for the Weapons Director, was responsible for contacting the Quick Reaction Area at one of the interceptor bases. He would speak to the Operations Officer and give the order to scramble the interceptors on Alert. At each interceptor base there was always two aircraft, the McDonnell CF-101 Voodoo in 1973, armed with two Falcon infra red heat-seeking missiles, kept in a Quick Reaction Area hangar at the end of the runway ready to go airborne, or scramble, within 5 minutes of the call from 'the Hole'. The two aircraft, called the '5 minute birds', were ready to go anytime of the day or night, 365 days a year.

Weather was not a factor in the defence of North America. The aircraft belonged to the RCAF all-weather fighter squadrons. The aircraft always scrambled in pairs so that the lead aircraft could do the visual identification on the unknown aircraft, while the other interceptor remained on guard some distance away. This allowed the second Voodoo to destroy the unknown aircraft if the first Voodoo was destroyed.

Getting the Voodoos into position for the visual identification or within range to lock their weapons control radar on to a hostile target was the job of the Intercept Director. The Intercept Director was the geometry expert, as he worked out intercepting tracks at closing speeds of 1,900 km/h for two subsonic aircraft. Can you imagine the thought process involving controlling four supersonic interceptors on two widely separated targets at the bewitching hour of 0300 hrs? Welcome to the world of the highly-trained Intercept Director. Now do that for long shifts over many days and nights during an exercise; dedication and hard work was required.

This operational environment developed a language of its own. It comprised of brevity code words originating with the more senior RAF service. The officers of the original RAF generally came from an upper-class background and they naturally brought the language of the foxhunt into the world of air fighting. The interceptor, when it had visual contact of the target, called 'tallyho', which was the same cry as when the hunt spotted the fox. The homing pigeon kept on many country estates gave the code 'pigeons', meaning the range and bearing to home base.

All this action in 'The Hole' was the result of the personnel and equipment out on the isolated radar sites on the frozen tundra. It required the expertise of the surveillance section to tweak the radars to present the best picture, the dedication of the communications section, the technicians who maintained the two gigantic computers, the experience of the air weapons controllers, and let us not forget the attending support staff. Who wants to use a dirty washroom or eat cold food? This entire NORAD organisation's purpose was to get the Voodoo interceptors of the Canadian Armed Forces to the right place in plenty of time to take care of Soviet bombers intent on destroying our way of life.

CAF Fighter Squadrons

In 1973, the accepted theory of the time was that the Soviet bombers would attack the political, military and industrial areas of the north-eastern USA. They would have to cross Canadian territory, namely the Maritimes, Ontario and Quebec, to get to their targets. On the west coast of Canada the attacking route would be close to, or over, British Columbia. The interceptor squadrons were located to cover these areas, using the normal Voodoo combat radius of approximately 850 km. No doubt politics entered into the equation somewhere. A fighter interceptor base would put a lot of money into the local economy.

In 1973, the Operational Training Unit for the Voodoo aircraft was in Bagotville, Quebec. CFB Bagotville is 200 km north of Quebec City. All crews on the two-crew aircraft, pilots and AI Navigators, went through their training with 410 Operational Training Unit Squadron at CFB Bagotville. The graduating crews assumed combat-ready positions at one of three operational squadrons, which operated out of four bases. The bases were CFB Comox, Bagotville, Chatham and Val d'Or. All the squadrons were formed during the Second World War and had a long and distinguished record.

Based at CFB Comox on Vancouver Island, British Columbia, 409 Squadron was in the 25th NORAD Region. Based at CFB Bagotville, Quebec, the 425 Squadron was in the 22nd NORAD Region. This Squadron also deployed to hold alert at CFB Val d'Or, Quebec, which is nearly 600 km west of Bagotville. This would give interceptor coverage right up to the border of the 23rd NORAD Region headquartered at Duluth, Minnesota, USA. Based in Chatham, New Brunswick, 416 Squadron was in the 22nd NORAD Region. The Operational Training Unit, 410 Squadron, had a unique operational commitment. Not only was the squadron responsible for training, but its crews were combat-ready and supported the 22nd Region. These were the CAF Squadrons in Air Defence Command that, in 1973, supported NORAD.

Each of the four bases had Quick Reaction Area Hangars where the '5-minute birds' would be scrambled and controlled from the 22nd NORAD Region HQ in North Bay. Kelleher mentioned 'that no one liked to be woken from a deep sleep in the middle of the night, so if I knew something was brewing I would phone the Quick Reaction Area Ops Officer and give him a heads up to wake the crews'. Also available were two interceptor aircraft at each base on one-hour alert to provide backup for the '5-minute' aircraft. These crews were on call in the immediate area and ready to go airborne within one hour.

During an exercise like the Amalgam Mute of 10 May 1973, as many of the squadron aircraft would be made available for interception duty as possible. The squadron and some base personnel would be recalled to the base and all hands would be on deck for the duration of the exercise. It was a source of pride that all training-mission hostile aircraft were intercepted and 'shot down' electronically. Mission Accomplished 'MA', – as the interceptor crew would say. That proved to NORAD that the 22nd Region Fighter Interceptor Squadrons ruled its skies for this exercise and were ready for when the threat was real.

USAF Fighter Squadrons

Other NORAD regions exhibited similar pride of accomplishment. The peripheral of the USA was ringed with fighter interceptor bases providing a wall of coverage against any unknown aircraft penetrating the continental USA. Indeed, each of the NORAD regions were held on alert and had interceptors on '5-minute' alert. The Region squadron aircraft could also be deployed to other locations if the area of enemy activity was elsewhere. The NORAD structure allowed total flexibility under the command of Cheyenne Mountain.

For example, the Convair F-106 Delta Darts of the USAF 27th Fighter Interceptor Squadron at Loring AFB, Maine, came under the control of the 22nd NORAD Region in CFB North Bay. This existed until the squadron left Air Defense Command on 1 July 1971 and was transferred to another location. The reverse situation was true on the west coast of Canada. The McDonnell CF-101 Voodoos of the CAF 409 Squadron at CFB Comox, Vancouver Island, British Columbia, came under the control of the 25th NORAD Region in McChord AFB, Tacoma, Washington.

Missiles/Bomarcs

So far we have just talked about the use of fighter interceptors to face the incoming Soviet manned bombers, but NORAD had another weapon in its arsenal: the missile. The USA had various types and capabilities of missiles in its defence system throughout the Cold War years. However, Canada did not become involved with a missile system until September 1958, just prior to the cancellation of the Avro Arrow on 20 February 1959, when it announced the order of Bomarc missiles. The decision to purchase the Bomarcs, no doubt under American encouragement, hastened the demise of the Arrow.

Two missile squadrons were formed in the early 1960s: 446 Squadron at North Bay, Ontario, and 447 Squadron at La Macaza, Quebec. Each squadron had twenty-eight missiles that eventually became operational and nuclear armed. More information about this can be found in Chapter Five, devoted to the Bomarc and Arrow. They were part of the SAGE system of the 22nd NORAD Region in North Bay, Ontario. The Air Weapons Controllers had the ability to use the Bomarc missiles to destroy incoming bombers until the Bomarc squadrons were totally disbanded by 1 September 1972.

Exercises

How do you keep such an organisation at a high level of efficiency? Failure of NORAD to perform as expected was not an option. The answer was training, training and more training. NORAD was continually re-evaluating its performance to improve areas that were weak. The method of evaluation was to run exercises to test the system. There were two kinds of exercises-simulated or live. The first North America-wide exercise, called Sky Shield, was conducted in September 1960. The exercise grounded all non-exercise air traffic throughout the continent. The exercise proved to be so disruptive that it never occurred on such a large scale again.

The synthetic exercises used the computer to simulate unknown tracks that required interception. Computer programmers would create war-game scenarios that seemed very real to the radar scope operators. The live exercises used real aircraft and real interceptors and took a lot of organisation to conduct safely. The exercises varied in complexity and scope. There could be one target aircraft going back and forth on a 'Towline' exercise for a squadron. There could be a sector, region or NORAD-wide exercise held during the quiet air traffic hours. The chapter entitled 'Sparks in the Night Sky' will recount all the details about a typical

NORAD mission and its varied participants, including the five persons identified previously in this chapter.

The 1973-era CAF target aircraft was the Avro CF-100 'Canuck' of 414 Electronic Warfare Squadron, supplemented by the Canadair T-33. The USAF equivalents in those years were the Martin EB-57 'Canberra' and Lockheed T-33. The venerable Boeing B-52 occasionally provided electronic jamming experience for the interceptor crews. Keith also mentioned 'he had worked with the B-58 Hustler', the USAF Mach 2 bomber in the 1960s. In subsequent chapters, we will examine the target aircraft in detail and their place in the electronic warfare battle.

This vast network, at an astronomical cost, was trained, ready and waiting. NORAD had been legally operational since 1958 and the SAGE network at the 22nd NORAD Region headquarters had been operational since 1963. So where were the Soviets? The deterrence had obviously been a factor in world politics as up to this date no air activity had been observed. Alternatively, was the system not good enough? Finally, in June 1968 it happened. Probably, with the combination of human intelligence and the Ballistic Missile Early Warning System site at Fylingdales Moor, Yorkshire, England, the controllers at NORAD noticed the Soviet long-range bomber activity. It is more than likely that the aircraft also showed up on radar as it proceeded through the gap between Iceland and Greenland. This was a common route for Soviet aircraft entering the western Atlantic Ocean region. This was the route taken by the Soviet aircraft on their way to Cuba, but NORAD never had positively identified any target, track, outside the Canadian Air Defence Identification Zone off the east or west coast.

The Day I Met a Soviet Bear

Captain Ron Neeve was glad to be driving out to work at the military base at Chatham, New Brunswick. It was June 1968 and he had just rejoined the Air Force after years as a civilian Air Traffic Controller. The career interruption had not been his choice. He was one of the names on the infamous 'Five Hundred List' of 1964 that saw 500 aircrew released from the Air Force as Canada adjusted to the post-Korean War era and the political manoeuvring to unify the Armed Forces.

Neeve and his wife Nicole were settling in again to the military life they both enjoyed. Although Neeve had adjusted to civilian life, he still missed the excitement of flying as part of an interceptor crew. When the Air Force had a shortage of aircrew, he did not hesitate to enlist again and resume his career. Neeve had taken his refresher training as an AI Navigator with 410 Squadron in Bagotville, Quebec, and now was combat- ready. He had previously been an AI Navigator on the Avro CF-100 and the McDonnell CF-101 and as a result he was very familiar with the world of airborne intercepts. He had taken part in a 'weapons rocket meet' with 413 Squadron at Bagotville, Quebec, and had fired live rockets at airborne towed targets.

A couple of tours of duty with the ground radar stations had given him an appreciation for the work of the very valuable Air Weapons Controllers. He had been stationed at CFS Sylvestre, just south of Quebec City, which was part of the Pinetree Line of radar sites. His most isolated posting was at Cape Dyer on Baffin Island. This radar site was part of the Distant Early Warning Line that stretched across the Canadian Arctic to warn of Soviet aircraft coming across the Polar regions.

Neeve was happy to be back flying and looked forward to today's flight as a member of 416 All Weather Fighter Squadron. Wing Commander Sam Miller commanded the squadron and Neeve's Flight Commander was 'Ping' Green. His lead AI Navigator was Squadron Leader John Houghton. At this time, 26 June 1968, he was assigned to fly with Ron 'Pat' Pattison as one of the two 'one-hour alert' birds. NORAD held them in reserve and assigned them to two dedicated aircraft, 'birds', to hold alert as backup to the two '5-minute' aircraft. They had one hour to get airborne if needed and the call came from NORAD. They were to fly a local mission in the afternoon. Little did they know that their flight would make aviation history.

The daily briefing commenced in the Operations Center with a detailed weather briefing on the area of squadron responsibility; this included the eastern seaboard of Nova Scotia and Newfoundland and Labrador. The assignment of aircraft and aircrew duties followed. Pattison and Neeve headed for their aircraft, a McDonnell CF-101 Voodoo number 101441, parked on the flight line. They installed their parachutes and flying helmets in their cockpits and prepared for a quick takeoff if needed. They returned to the squadron to get a cup of coffee and attend to some administrative matters. Then they heard it, about 0900, the two 'five-minute' birds takeoff in full afterburner roar and climb away on their secret mission. The 'five-minute' birds were held alert for 24 hours per day, every day of the year. The crews 'lived' in the secure Quick Reaction Hangars alongside their two armed aircraft at the end of the runway. The hangars had full accommodation facilities, including a kitchen.

Neeve and Pattison knew that they were next to go. They realised something different was developing when operations informed them that the 'five-minute' birds were on their way to Gander, Newfoundland. This normally meant that there was some activity, real or anticipated, through intelligence sources, at the Canadian Air Defence Identification Zone out in the Atlantic Ocean east of Newfoundland. Then it happened, they got the call to scramble. Running out of Ops they headed for their aircraft, strapped in and, before Neeve had time to think about the ramifications of this mission, they taxied for the active runway. Neeve's logbook records a takeoff time of 0945 local Chatham time. The morning was taking on a new meaning. After the hours of training and simulation they would now be required to perform their mission with no room for error.

Rapidly accelerating down the runway, they were destined for a new adventure to talk to their squadron mates about – if only they knew! Climbing rapidly, they checked in with their assigned Air Weapons Controller who gave them an easterly heading and confirmed they were going to Gander as backup to the previously departed aircraft, the 'five-minute' birds. As they swiftly climbed through 5,000 feet above sea level, Neeve performed the 5,000 Foot Check.

Neeve followed this up with '5,000 foot check completed,' and they continued their rapid climb to above 30,000 feet. Pattison and Neeve's aircraft was the lead aircraft with the number two aircraft following them in close formation. The normal accepted procedure was for the number one aircraft to close in for visual identification of the target with the number two aircraft remaining close by as a witness and a backup to take whatever action was required.

The two Voodoos streaked across the sea towards Stephenville in south-east Newfoundland. The information becoming available to NORAD was getting more critical. There was a target(s) approaching the Canadian Air Defence Identification Zone to the east of Gander and, according to intelligence reports, there was a good chance that it was (they were) Soviet Tupolev TU-95 Bear bombers on their way to Cuba. The Soviets scheduled these flights for long-range training and intelligence gathering purposes as they flew down the eastern seaboard of North America, just on or outside the Air Defence Identification Zone. The radar sites had seen the aircraft before but, up until now, there never had been a visual identification to confirm the suspicions that they were in fact Soviet Bear aircraft

It was then that Neeve and Pattison received an astonishing order from the air weapons controller: 'Kilo November go gate!' This was an order for the crew to go to maximum speed. 'When we heard that, we thought, what is going on here?' recounted Neeve. Pattison moved the throttles fully forward and outboard to engage the afterburners. The aircraft quickly accelerated through the sound barrier and reached a cruising speed of Mach 1.3, the maximum with external tanks. Now the aircraft burnt fuel at a very fast rate as raw fuel was injected into the exhaust to give the necessary thrust to maintain the supersonic speed. It was shortly thereafter that the number two aircraft, with Captain Tom Campbell as the AI Navigator, indicated a fuel-feed problem and diverted to Gander, Newfoundland.

To conserve fuel Pattison stowed the afterburners and resumed military power cruise as they left the coast and headed for the Atlantic Ocean. Neeve thought it was very strange that 'the control now changed to the Remote mode'. Remote control was verbal instructions to grid positions on a map. During our interview in January 2009, he said, 'I am not sure why they could not give us positive control'. One of the reasons that there was no positive control was that the radar sites at Goose Bay, Labrador and Gander, Newfoundland, were manual control centres and could not upload intercept information using the data link system, and the other could have been that the radar targets were now just out of range of the radar coverage. The actual reason is lost to history. The air weapons controller started to give target information in geographical references. 'That would have been fine,' said Ron, 'except we did not have the proper maps and I had to work off a government airways map which did not have any geographical grid information and only displayed routes and navigation aids. This was corrected and later all aircraft carried grid maps.' Neeve stated that he now got very busy, 'working out the position of the target, giving heading instructions to Pattison to steer for the intercept, and working the radar to scan for the target'. They both were very aware of how far east of Gander they were flying. They had to have enough fuel to return to Gander regardless of intercepting the unknown target or not. Losing a valuable fighter crew and aircraft was not warranted in peacetime, or was this peacetime?

They truly were on their own now as the three other squadron aircraft were on the ground in Gander – the 'five-minute' birds rapidly refuelling to get airborne again and Neeve and Pattison's wingman, who had the fuel-feed problem. Neeve continued to sweep the skies for the elusive target. He said 'and suddenly I picked him up [on my radar scope], in excess of fifty miles. Being over the sea there was little [no] radar clutter.' The target on Neeve's scope was proceeding left to right, north-east to south-west, and he indicated 'that we were a long way behind a beam attack and ended up in a tail chase'. A beam attack occurs when the attacking aircraft is approaching the target aircraft at 90 degrees, or at right angle to its track or path. 'We had very little cut-off and it took us 15 minutes or so to catch up to the target at our subsonic, to save fuel, cruise speed.' Cut-off is the angle with the target to maintain a beam attack – the greater the cut-off angle the better it is to maintain a beam attack. Conversely, the less the cut-off angle, for example 15 degrees off target, the more you are in a tail chase condition, as Neeve and Pattison found themselves. When Neeve was asked if he knew what the target was, he answered 'we did not know for sure but [we] had a very strong likelihood … kept telling us there was something out there … make natural assumption that what you are going to find when you get there is a Bear aircraft … previous briefings had indicated the same thing.'

'I kept calling our overtake speed, about 40–60 knots, and eventually we were close enough to see that it was a big aircraft. We continued to close up to the target – there was no mistake now – it was a Soviet Bear bomber! It was just like the intelligence pictures – four counter-rotating propellers, plexiglas greenhouse nose, red star on the fin and the tail guns parked in the caged or upright position – thank goodness! It was around thirty thousand feet altitude and cruising along at normal speed in a straight line.' So, on this day, the cry of 'the Soviets are coming, the Soviets are coming' finally came true!

'What were your thoughts at that moment?' I asked Ron.

He answered 'There were a certain amount of, "where is our number two", which was not there to help … oh … oh how close do … and do we really trust that this guy is not going to shoot at us, when we get closer to him – does he think we are going to shoot at him? We stayed a fair distance to the side, about 300 yards – no point in getting any closer, we did not have a camera. We did have the two Falcon missiles clearly visible on the bottom of our aircraft.'

Neeve and Pattison were all alone with the unknown. Neeve figured 'that by now we were out of radio range, about 220 nautical miles (407 km) east of Gander, as I do not remember talking with anyone as we flew off to the side of the Bear. We pulled up abeam the cockpit to make sure the pilots saw us and show the flag.' They had done their duty. NORAD had demonstrated to the Soviets that it was protecting Canadian airspace. It had intercepted their bomber in the vastness of the Atlantic Ocean and sent the message that they were getting close to our sovereign airspace and to stay out of Canadian-restricted territory or there would be consequences – namely two Falcon missiles clearly visible on the Voodoo's armament door. 'What happened next Ron?' I asked. Nonchalantly, he answered: 'Then we turned westward and headed for Gander, Newfoundland, where we landed for refuelling.'

History was made in Canada on 26 June 1968 – after all the planning, training and massive NORAD expenditure, it all came to fruition with the first successful interception and identification of an unfriendly Soviet Tupolev TU-95 Bear bomber as it tested our resolve to defend our shores. Neeve and Pattison were there and lived to tell their story. When asked about the high point of the experience, Neeve indicated 'that the first high point was when the target showed up on radar. We had managed to look through those maps that we were making as we tried to fly and eventually

CAF CF-101 Voodoo and Soviet TU-95 Bear. (Courtesy of Canadian Forces Joint Imagery Centre, Department of National Defence)

get to a position where we could say – hey man, there he is! – because Remote (Control) at the time was a hit or miss affair. Sometimes you find him, sometimes you don't.'

They departed Gander at 1435 and headed home to Chatham. It certainly had been a different day's work. They talked to the commanding officer, Wing Commander Sam Miller, and gave a squadron briefing to those crews who were in the Operations Center. The 'jungle drums' of squadron communication happened before Neeve got a chance to call home. A squadron crew member's wife phoned Nicole at home and said, 'Oh, did you hear that Ron intercepted a Bear?' However, other than being the talk of the squadron, the event passed into history with almost no recognition. There was no mention on the national television. 'Just like as if it had never happened', Neeve recounted. In fact, the only official acknowledgement came from Colonel John Pease, 37 NORAD Division Commander in Goose Bay, Labrador, in the form of a Certificate of Recognition.

So on this particular day, 26 June 1968, our Canadian defences were truly tested and passed with flying colours. Captains Ron Neeve and Ron 'Pat' Pattison of 416 All Weather Fighter Squadron, based in Chatham, New Brunswick, responded to the challenge and intercepted the first Soviet Tupolev TU-95 Bear bomber off the coast of Newfoundland. They found 'the needle in the hay stack' over the Atlantic Ocean, 1,240 km (770 miles) flying distance from their home base.

I wonder what the Soviet crew told their squadron commanders and families when they returned to home base, perhaps 'The day I met a Canadian Voodoo!'

NORAD 1973–2011

The Canadian government renewed the NORAD Agreement for a further two years during the same month as the Amalgam Mute exercise, May 1973. An interesting situation developed on 24 October of that same year. The Yom Kippur War, also known as the 1973 Arab–Israeli War, had broken out two weeks earlier and all attempts at a ceasefire had failed. The Soviets threatened to intervene on behalf of Egypt, which was losing the conflict. The USA put their Continental Air Defense Command and worldwide forces on a heightened Defence Condition (DEFCON) 3 alert as a signal to the Soviets to remain clear of the confrontation.

The NORAD DEFCON level and Canada remained at their normal DEFCON 5 level. The USA did not officially notify Canada of its new level of military alert. An unusual event as the integrated US and Canadian staff still manned the desks in Colorado Springs. Canadian forces personnel relaying instructions to US forces personnel now, due to the circumstances, aligned with CONAD rather than NORAD. Imagine that – Canadian personnel ordering the uploading of nuclear weapons onto American aircraft and dispersing them to their assigned holding bases.

Canadian command of American nuclear armed aircraft, on a CONAD not NORAD higher alert status, did not last very long. The Canadian personnel, quickly relieved of their responsibilities by their American counterparts, went home to watch the events unfold on the TV news. The lack of military intervention by the Soviets resulted in the USA returning to the normal DEFCON 5 level the next morning and the Canadians resuming their duties. NORAD was a bi-national agreement but each participant, USA and Canada, still could operate independently.

Having a Canadian issue commands to the USAF was most likely to happen when the USA responded to perceived threats that affected the USA or components of its foreign policy; the Canadian government responded as it saw fit. In this case an interested observer, Colonel J. L. (Lew) Twambley, former Commanding Officer of CAF 416 Squadron, was on duty in NORAD HQ in Colorado Springs when the DEFCON level was changed to DEFCON 3. He proceeded with his duties associated with the increased DEFCON level by moving armed fighters to staging and holding bases, until 'I was finally noticed, replaced by my American counterpart, and sent home'.

What has happened in nearly forty years since the time of the Amalgam Mute exercise in 1973? NORAD still exists, agreements are still being signed, and NORAD was part of the 2010 Winter Olympics aerial security in Vancouver and surrounding area. However, it is a far different organisation compared to its first fifteen years. In June 1969, it was decided to proceed with the Safeguard anti-ballistic missile system. Canada, as per the NORAD agreement, had opted out of any kind of ballistic missile defence. A very expensive, $760 million dollar, site was created over five years at Grand Forks, North Dakota, in the USA.

The Safeguard system became operational in March 1974, fully operational in October 1975, and closed in February 1976 – a twenty-three month life span! The US approach to defence, expressed in March 1974 by the US Secretary of Defense James Schlesinger, was that the best hope of deterring a Soviet attack was to have an assured retaliatory nuclear strike capability after absorbing a Soviet attack. Offence was in, defence out.

The May 1975 five-year NORAD agreement renewal stressed that ballistic missiles constituted the primary threat to North America and that there was a need to monitor space activities and maintain effective airspace surveillance. Canada constructed a Space Detection and Tracking System site at St Margarets, New Brunswick, and it became operational in August 1976. It consisted of a Baker-Nunn satellite tracking camera and a satellite identification and tracking telescope.

Despite the considerable Canadian investments in NORAD-related technologies, politicians, notably Prime Minister Pierre Trudeau, had suspicions about the effects of the NORAD Agreement on Canada. Canadian Prime Minister Trudeau, 1968–79 and 1980–84, shared many of his thoughts about the USA. He commented that having the USA as a neighbour 'is like sleeping next to an elephant: no matter how friendly and even-tempered the beast, if one can call it that, one is affected by every twitch and grunt'. In 1971, he expressed the opinion, with regards to Cold War policy, 'That the overwhelming American presence posed a danger to our [Canada's] national identity from a cultural, economic and perhaps even military point of view.' In contrast, or in spite of Trudeau's concerns, he was the only incumbent Canadian Prime Minister to visit the NORAD headquarters at Cheyenne Mountain, Colorado Springs.

For all the wrong reasons, 9 November 1979 was a very exciting day for NORAD. A test scenario of a missile attack was inadvertently transmitted to the operational side of the Cheyenne Mountain complex. All the bells and whistles functioned as programmed and the warnings were displayed throughout the system for approximately eight minutes before the assessment was made that there was no strategic attack underway.

Similarly, on 3 and 6 June 1980, false missile warning data was transmitted, this time caused by a faulty computer chip, to Strategic Air Command and other agencies. Once again the correct assessment of no imminent attack was rightly made. What if the wrong assessment had been made and the full US retaliatory force had been unleashed? We would be living, if at all, in a very different world.

The anticipated renewal of the NORAD Agreement required a year of negotiation; in May 1981, the next five-year agreement was signed. This renewal created three major changes. Firstly, Canada dropped the ballistic missile defence caveat. Secondly, NORAD finally changed its name to catch up with the times; it was now the North American *Aerospace* Defence, instead of *Air* Defence. Thirdly, NORAD realigned regional boundaries. This resulted in the 22nd NORAD region changing its name in June 1983 to the Canadian Northern Region, headquartered at North Bay, Ontario, Canada.

NORAD had significantly changed over the years from 1960 to 1982: DEW Line radar sites had been reduced from seventy to thirty-one, the Mid-Canada Line had closed, the Pinetree Line reduced in numbers, surface-to-air missiles had been eliminated and fighter interceptors had been reduced in number from 1,600 to 312. NORAD had become a victim of the changing assessment of threat, from bombers to missiles, détente and the reallocation of military funds.

In 1984, the McDonnell CF-101 Voodoo ended its CAF service and handed over the interceptor role to the McDonnell Douglas CF-18 Hornet. An important side effect of the change was the removal of nuclear weapons from Canadian soil. The US warheads existed in Canada since the mid-1960s. The weapons were under the control of the US military, only to be used under very strict circumstances specified in the 1965 authorisation of nuclear air defence weapons document. The agreement covered the release of the weapons by the President of the USA, agreement on their use by both governments and authorisation for Commander-in-Chief NORAD to use as required. These communications would occur as the DEFCON level increased to level one. In the event of a surprise attack, information on a large bomber or ICBM force heading for North America during a period of heightened tension, or several nuclear bursts of unknown origin occurring in North America, the Commander-in-Chief NORAD was authorised to use immediately, no communication required, all weapons at his disposal. These included the NORAD nuclear arsenal, a tremendous responsibility.

In March 1985, as negotiations commenced once again for the NORAD Agreement renewal, a meeting occurred with Prime Minister Brian Mulroney and President Ronald Reagan in Quebec City. It was dubbed the 'Shamrock Summit' because of the Irish heritage of both leaders and the duet sung by Mulroney and Reagan to the tune, 'When Irish Eyes are Smiling'. It was decided at the summit to modernise the DEW Line and call it the North Warning System. This radar system would track low-flying aircraft and cruise missiles. The first segment was in place in April 1987. It consists of fifty-four new radar-equipped sites.

The primary defence preoccupation continued to be the desire to push the air war further north from the industrial and highly populated areas of the USA and Canada. A survey suggested four possible Forward Operating Locations for the fighter interceptors. The sites examined were at Inuvik, Yellowknife, Rankin Inlet, Iqaluit, and Kuujjuaq in the north of Canada. The original idea was to have caches of fuel, ammunition and missiles at these locations. In the event of hostilities, the CAF CF-18s and USAF F-15s would be deployed to these forward bases to intercept the enemy bombers soon after entering Canadian airspace. The whole concept proposed in 1985 included the use of Airborne Warning and Control System aircraft based at Edmonton, Alberta and Bagotville, Quebec, and the North Warning System and the Over-the-Horizon-Backscatter radar. Once again deterrence was the motivation for these plans; making the USSR believe that their first strike would not go undetected before a massive retaliatory strike would be launched by the USA.

Some exercises took place to the Forward Operating Locations, but NORAD activity was decreasing as Cold War hostilities came to a peaceful understanding in the late 1980s. Forty years of political and military sparring had come to an end without any real punches being thrown. In 1993, probably the greatest acknowledgement of the stable US and Russian relations was the new 'flexible alert' concept, which allowed local Region Commanders to establish the level of alert depending on the perceived threat. The 24/365 alert days were over; they were consigned to history and the memories of the crews who answered the horn and dashed out to their ready aircraft and departed in all weather, at all times of the day and night, to find the elusive 'hostile target'.

During the 1990s, the US Over-the-Horizon-Backscatter radars were phased out and kept in 'warm storage' for possible future use. The 1990s saw a further scaling back of NORAD's activities in line with the plan that 'we will see you coming, retaliation will follow quickly, do not try it!' American forces left the Canadian Arctic which, in itself, was an important change for the Canadian national identity. Canadian military personnel and American civilians, not forces, continued to work together. Sector Air Operations Center, 22 Wing, in North Bay, Ontario, operated NORAD in Canada.

In 1992, the last contribution of Canada to the Space Surveillance Network, the Baker-Nunn camera, closed. The last of the DEW Line sites closed in 1993 and the North Warning System was now in full radar control of the Arctic approaches. CAF CF-18s based in Cold Lake, Alberta, and Bagotville, Quebec, became the Canadian fighter interceptor contribution to NORAD. Annual deployments to Comox, British Columbia, and Goose Bay, Labrador, showed the flag on the west and east coasts respectively.

In 1996, the new agreement stated that the NORAD mission was to provide aerospace warning and control for North America. The Canadian NORAD Region Headquarters moved to Winnipeg in 1997, after nearly forty years in eastern Canada. This was in keeping with the consolidation of air resources with the 1st Canadian Air Division, now established in Winnipeg. The Canadian political struggle of joining or not joining the proposed National Missile Defense programme continued.

The Canadians became concerned that NORAD may not have a future as the USA continued to re-evaluate their defensive requirements involving national defence at Norfolk, Virginia, and the United States Space Command at Colorado Springs, Colorado. To avoid being caught up in the US elections and the National Missile Defence decision, Canada signed a new five-year NORAD agreement, with no major changes and one year early. The defence decisions made were the result of academic thought on what may or could happen. Hypothetic scenarios and conjectured defence 'chess moves' influenced defence thinking of a chess game that never took place. Then everything changed – reality struck.

The infamous aerial terrorist attack of '9/11' on the Twin Towers in New York City and the Pentagon in Washington DC on 11 September 2001 altered the thinking drastically. NORAD went to DEFCON 3 for the third time in its history. Terrorists using hijacked commercial aircraft created havoc in the US by crashing the aircraft into the buildings, causing massive loss of life and resources, not to mention the effect on the psyche of the American people. All this time NORAD had been looking outward and the enemy had come from within. NORAD, after forty-three years, was ineffective in meeting its mandate of North American defence.

Four days after the attack, Operation Noble Eagle became the response to the terrorist attack on 15 September 2001. In Canada, CF-18s were on alert at Cold Lake, Alberta, Bagotville, Quebec, and deployed to Comox, British Columbia, and Goose Bay, Labrador. They also deployed to Trenton, Ontario, to show the flag in southern Ontario, close to the national capital of Ottawa, Ontario, and the commercial centre in Toronto. Operation Noble Eagle became a permanent fixture at special events; NORAD provided protection for the G8 summit in Kananaskis, Alberta, in 2002. It provided aerial protection for the Winter Olympics in Vancouver and surrounding area in February 2010. Basically, NORAD went to a higher level of vigilance, which included orbiting command and fighter aircraft.

In 2002, US President George Bush Jr opted out of the Anti-Ballistic Missile Treaty with the Russians after failing to reach an agreement on limited missile deployment and initiated a missile defence system. The USA was back in to missile defence; Canada was not. In August 2004, Canada indicated by diplomatic note that the Canadian NORAD personnel in the bi-national organisation would provide surveillance, warning and assessment duties only. Prime Minister Paul Martin reiterated that Canada would not have missile interceptors on Canadian soil, participate in space weapons or contribute financially to missile defence.

The NORAD agreement renewal in 2006 was highly unusual compared to previous agreements; it was renewed in perpetuity with the added provision of maritime warning for North America and a review in four years, sooner if requested. This review, some sources suggested, could be the termination of NORAD as both countries go about national security with the NORAD Canada Command and the United States North Command. Canada has become less geographically important to the USA as the age of the missile replaced the Soviet bomber threat.

In 2008, the Fiftieth Anniversary NORAD public affairs statement declared,

NORAD is perhaps one of the best examples of how two countries have worked closely together for so long in a positive, mutually-beneficial relationship that continues today. The longstanding, successful relationship has evolved over the past 50 years to remain as relevant today during these times of terrorist threats as it was half a century ago during the Cold War. NORAD remains a powerful symbol of two countries working together to defend the citizens of both countries from those who would harm us.

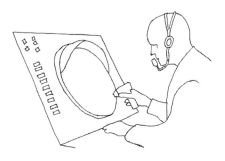

On 24 August 2010, a pair of Russian Bear bombers approached Canadian Arctic airspace on the eve of Prime Minister Stephen Harper's visit to observe a military exercise in the area. NORAD responded to the threat and CAF CF-18s showed the Canadian flag to the intruders and shadowed the Russian bombers. Was it coincidence? Was it a Cold War-type manoeuvre to announce to the West that Russia, the new USSR, is again flexing its muscles to show its status in the global military picture?

What is NORAD today in 2011? It maintains its vigilance for any overseas threat and has the additional responsibility of meeting any domestic aerospace threat from acts of air piracy or terrorist action. Does it have a future? Perhaps it is similar to two longstanding military friends who have written regularly to each other for fifty years and do not want to stop writing for fear that, if they do stop writing, the lines of their effective communication and friendship will never be re-established as closely again.

CHAPTER THREE

Radar and Electronic Warfare

To be prepared for war is one of the first effectual means of preserving peace.

George Washington, 1790

'What speed do you think you were going, Sir/Madam?' said the police officer. That is the first introduction of many people to the phenomenon of radar. It is something that cannot be felt, seen or touched and has no smell. Yet it is such an important part of our day-to-day life on this planet. Not only does it enable more aircraft to fly in the sky safely, but by helping to enforce driving speed limits it makes the roads safer. It makes us safe in North America as we can look far beyond our geographical boundaries to see who or what is coming towards us. Radar is the same idea as the lookout on the castle wall in ancient times.

What is it? Radar, an acronym for Radio Direction and Ranging, is electromagnetic radiation in the radio frequency band of the electromagnetic spectrum that can be manipulated into a beam. The electromagnetic range includes the microwave, where we can feel the heat of warmed food, visible light and the X-ray images of the human body. Technically the electromagnetic spectrum is composed of a range of frequencies from the low frequency, low energy radio wave band through the microwave, infrared, visible region, ultraviolet, and X-rays bands to the high frequency, high energy gamma Ray band. Electromagnetic radiation is the energy created by charged atomic particles being accelerated. Electromagnetic waves travel at the speed of light, 299,247 kilometres per second. When this wave motion beam strikes a solid object, the wave motion, all or some of it, will be reflected back. This reflected information can be processed to give the location of the object.

The common thread of the components that made the vast NORAD made system work was radar. The CF-101 Voodoo Interceptor had a tracking and fire control radar system. The CADIN/Pinetree Line sites had search and height finder radars. The Command and Control Center in North Bay had radar information digitally displayed on the air weapons controller scopes. Radar was the link that enabled the elements to function as one and provide the defence of North America.

The main components of radar are the transmitter, the receiver and the antenna. There are two basic types – continuous wave and pulsed. The continuous wave radar uses two separate antennae for transmission and reception. There is no need for a listening period, so the carrier wave type sends out a continuous stream of radio frequency waves. The pulsed radar uses a single antenna to transmit the radio frequency waves and receive the reflections. It transmits in bursts and listens for the reflected radio frequencies in the interval between the bursts. The bursts are known as pulses. The pulsed radar system is the most common system used, as it only requires one antenna and the switching from transmit to receive can be effectively accomplished electronically.

The pulsed radar timing circuit controls the impulse of a high voltage modulator, which in turn controls the length of time of the radio frequency transmission. The transmitter produces very high amounts of power; high frequency pulsed energy which the waveguide, which looks like a square pipe, contains and sends through a rotating joint to an antenna horn. The shape of the antenna determined the shape of the electromagnetic beam. The search beam was narrow in the horizontal plane and wide (tall) in the vertical plane. MCpl Pierre Parent recalled that 'I did see a [Lockheed] U-2 spy plane at 85,000 feet once over Alsask [Saskatchewan, Canada]'. The timing circuit controls switches the transmitter off at the end of a burst and connects the antenna to the receiver. This is called the duty cycle. The timing circuit controls the number of pulses transmitted per second, which is known as the pulse-repetition frequency. The receiver amplifies the weak returning radio frequency waves and processes them for display. This is normally on a cathode ray tube called the radar scope.

Radar can either be ground-based or airborne. Ground-based radar antenna can be very large heavy units for long-range capability, but the airborne antennae, by necessity, have to fit in the available aircraft fuselage or missile body. The antennae in either case must be able to move mechanically or electronically in azimuth, left to right, and elevation, up and down. The development of radar has continued for the last hundred years and one of the major changes has been digitising the system to display symbology instead of raw radar data. Who first discovered this radar phenomenon and how was it used and improved upon?

A Scotsman, James Clerk Maxwell, published a paper on the dynamical theory of the electromagnetic field in 1864. Maxwell wrote, 'The agreement of the results seems to show that light and magnetism are affections of the same substance, and that light is an electromagnetic disturbance propagated through the field according to electromagnetic laws.' Heinrich Rudolf Hertz was a German physicist who, twenty years later, built laboratory experiments to explain Maxwell's electromagnetic theory of light. Hertz measured Maxwell's waves and proved that the velocity of radio waves was equal to the velocity of light.

Hertz was the first to satisfactorily demonstrate the existence of electromagnetic waves by building an apparatus to produce and detect very high frequency and ultra high frequency radio waves. He also discovered and demonstrated the reflective properties of radio energy. It would be another twenty years, in 1904, before Christian Hulsmeyer demonstrated that by using radio waves he could detect the presence of metallic objects. He used the example of a ship in dense fog. Radar was born and nobody was interested; such is the life of an inventor.

Finally, in 1935, another Scotsman, Robert Watson-Watt, arguably 'The Father of Radar', demonstrated to the British Air Ministry the ability to detect an aircraft by radio methods. The Daventry Experiment proved that it was possible to detect signals from the local BBC radio transmitter reflecting off a circling RAF bomber 13 km away. By the end of 1935, Watson-Watt had a patent for radar, initially called Radio Detection Finding by the British, and he increased the detection range to over 100 km and planned five radars, Chain Home stations, to protect London.

Ken Peacock, a Canadian radar mechanic posted during the war to the Broadbay Chain Home radar site near Stornoway, in the Western Isles of Scotland, recalled, 'the west coast stations were different. We had two 73-metre towers with the MB2 transmitter and RF7 receiver. On my first night there I had to climb the tower. The power amplifiers could put out 650,000 watts. We operated on the twelve metre wavelength. It was fixed direction and we covered the North Minch area. There was also an identification friend or foe transmitter for aircraft, if there was no blip (friendly identification) on the radar return we would phone Stornoway our filter station.'

The basic principle of radar is range measurement by echo timing. A pulse of electromagnetic energy is transmitted at the speed of light and is reflected back from an object. By timing how long the echo takes to return, the distance to the object can be calculated. It takes 6.66 microseconds (one millionth of a second) to go to a target 1 km away and return. By noting the direction of the antenna and the range of the target, the position can be accurately fixed. Modern radar sets amplify the weak return by a factor of several million. The Plan Position Indicator lets the radar system do the plotting of the position, direction and range automatically and displays the results on the scope. The separate height finder radar works in a similar way. The distance to the target is known as well as the angle of the antenna to the horizontal. By using geometry, the distance (height) of the 'opposite' side of the triangle can be calculated and displayed on a scope or numerically.

As with all systems, a variety of factors must be considered in designing radar suitable for the designated application. The two broad categories of system applications are ground-based or airborne, both requiring emphasis on certain design features. Some of these features are:

Ruggedness and simplicity. These are important factors for the military application of radar. The radar could be used in remote areas, under wartime conditions, far from logistical and technical support.

Power output. The power output of the radar determines its effective range. The British invention of the cavity magnetron, small and light, is very popular in airborne power systems. The klystron amplifier, good for large, stable output power and high gain resolution, is more suited to ground installations. The power system used in 1973, at the time of our exercise, meant that the Voodoo fighter interceptor had an effective maximum range of around 80 km (50 miles). The ground based radar range was around 330 km (205 miles), limited by the curvature of the Earth as well as the power available.

Antenna shape and beamwidth. The antenna has two basic functions: to efficiently transmit and receive electromagnetic energy in the atmosphere and to direct that energy in an appropriately shaped beam. The antenna's size in relation to the operating wavelength dictates the beamwidth, which in turn affects the range and accuracy of the system.

Wavelength and operating frequency. The wavelength is one of the major factors in calculating radar performance. Wavelength and frequency are directly related in an inverse way – the longer the wavelength the lower the frequency and the shorter the wavelength the higher the frequency. Radar wavelengths are grouped together by lengths, which also describes their frequency, and given band designations. The band widths used in the Amalgam Mute exercise were the Delta (D) band, 1,000–2,000 MHz, and Echo (E)/Fox (F) band, 2,000–4,000 MHz, for the ground-based search and height finder radar. The India (I) band, 8,000–10,000 MHz, was used for the airborne interceptor (AI) radar.

Pulse size/width. This is the amount of time the transmitter is sending out a radio frequency signal.

Pulse repetition time. This is the interval, time, from the start of one pulse, transmission, to the start of another pulse.

Pulse repetition frequency. This is the number of pulses transmitted per second. The maximum usable range is directly correlated to the pulsed frequency; it must be relatively low in long-range radar to allow the signal to travel to the distant target and back to the listening receiver before the next pulse is transmitted.

Scan patterns. This is the shifting of the beam to provide coverage in the area of interest. It is commonly achieved by mechanical slewing, changing direction, or elevating of the antenna. The search radar uses a circular motion repeating a 360 degree rotation every 12 seconds, 5 rpm. The airborne interceptor radar uses a 'Raster' pattern. This is a horizontal motion, backwards and forwards, shifting up or down in the vertical plane until the limit, the edge of the screen is reached. The movement is then repeated. This not only gives azimuth but relative elevation information for the fighter crew.

Signal to noise ratio. The radar must be able to distinguish true echoes from the ever-present background noise. The signal to noise ratio is the ability of the radar receiver to discriminate between the two.

Receiver gain. This is the ability of the radar receiver's amplifier to increase the signal strength to a usable level. Unfortunately, it also increases the amount of noise or clutter displayed. It necessitates constant adjustment at times as the need to see the target at the maximum distance is balanced with the noise that totally obscures it.

Early radar development in Canada was conducted by the National Research Council which, in 1940, installed a system called 'The Night Watchman' to monitor ship movement in Halifax Harbour. A coastal defence anti-aircraft gun and a radar system specifically designed to determine azimuth, elevation and range to a target, based on secret technical radar information from Britain, was established in 1942. It consisted of a large rotating antenna on top of a 22-metre wooden tower mounted on the cliff tops in Nova Scotia, Canada. This was the beginning of the Canadian radar defence network.

The Canadian ground radar network in 1973 is discussed in detail in the next chapter, included the early warning DEW Line and the ground controlled intercept CADIN/Pinetree Line. Until 1972, the network also included the Fire Control System for the Bomarc surface-to-air missile.

The 1973 Air Defence Command airborne radar comprised the search radar and the fire control system for the Genie and Falcon weapons on the McDonnell CF-101 Voodoo fighter interceptor.

During the Second World War, experiments continued in Britain and Germany, among other countries, to develop radio beam navigation and landing systems. The radio beams were used to direct bomber aircraft to specific targets. The German *Knickebein*, crooked leg, system consisted of one main beam to guide the aircraft to the target and a second beam to create an intersection to indicate that the bomber was over the target. The research of Professor F. A. Lindemann, a British scientist, indicated that the beam could be subtly bent away from overhead the target without the bomber aircraft knowing the beam had been interfered with; the development of electronic countermeasures had begun. In 1940, Winston Churchill referred to this as 'The Battle of the Beams' in the secret war he called 'The Wizard War'. It was a secret war because it went on as a continuous game of technological chess, played out of the public eye by both sides.

Britain continued to build and operate a chain of radar sites on its coast. It was called the Chain Home radar system. It consisted of massive 300-metre metal transmitting towers and 80-metre wooden, to avoid interference, receiving towers. The Chain Home system was capable of providing range and height information of approaching aircraft, which was passed on by phone line to a central command centre. Easily destroyed, but somewhat easily rebuilt, these stations were the backbone of the radar defence of Britain during the Second World War. The initial systems, which were manually operated, were replaced with automatic features as the system constantly improved.

Germany developed a radar system called the Freya. It operated around 2.4 m (125 MHz), and with a peak power output of 15 kW it had a range of 130 km. The Freya was combined in a radar network called the Kammhuber Line by the Allies. Each location cell, *Himmelbett*, had a Freya radar, searchlights, night fighter aircraft, and two Wurzburg radars. One was to pick up the aircraft target from the Freya radar and the other to track the fighter aircraft. The Wurzburg, a 60-cm (500-MHz), 10-kW, pulse-power radar, became the primary gun-laying system used by Germany during the war. The search radars continued to improve as reflected by the Mammut radar; it linked sixteen Freya radars and used phased array beam directing, resulting in a 300-km range. A phased array is a group of radar antennas arranged in such a way as to improve directional control of the radio frequency signal.

The ground radar in Germany and Great Britain provided early warning and ground control intercept capabilities during clear daylight conditions.

To reduce aircraft losses, a campaign of night bombing was initiated. The problem now was for the fighter aircraft to find the bomber aircraft in the night or cloud-filled skies. The solution was for the ground radar command centre to vector, direct, the night fighter into the vicinity of the attacking aircraft and then for the fighter to take over the attack using its own airborne radar.

By 1942, Germany had the FuG 202 Lichtenstein B/C airborne radar operating in the Junkers Ju88R night fighter. It was a 1.5-kW, 62-cms (485-MHz) dipole antenna array, which gave it an approximate operational range of 4 km to 200 metres. The British then designed a radar detection and homing device called Serrate for their night fighters to detect the German night fighters when they used their Lichtenstein radar. When the British fighters used their Air Intercept MkIV radar, the German night fighter detected them using their Naxos ZR radar detection device. So began the aerial electronic war of the radar beams: 'I am looking for you, I know that you know that I am looking for you, but I also know that you are looking for me!'

Radar continued to develop until the end of the Second World War in 1945. Cold War hostilities that started in 1947 and the Korean War caused a renewed interest in the use of ground and airborne radar. By 1973, Canada had progressed from the three lines of radar defence built in the 1950s, and the fighter interceptor, the Avro CF-100 Canuck, by replacing it in the 1960s with the McDonnell CF-101 Voodoo.

Canadian Forces Station Ramore, Ontario, features as one of the Pinetree Line radar sites tracking our target and fighter interceptor aircraft in Chapter Nine, 'Sparks in the Night Sky'. It is fairly typical of radar sites in 1973, having one pulse type search radar, the AN/FPS-27, and two height finder radars, an AN/FPS-6B and AN/FPS-26. The USA set up a military hardware identification system. The AN was originally designated to the Army and Navy, but now designates all military equipment. The F signifies Fixed Ground, the P is Pulse Radar and the S is Detecting, Range and Bearing, Search. The number following the hyphen indicates the version number.

The AN/FPS-27 frequency diverse search radar was built by Westinghouse in the USA and operated in the Echo band on frequencies 2,322 to 2,670 MHz. It had a reported range of 407 km and an altitude capability of 150,000 feet. The AN/FPS-6B frequency diverse height finder radar was built by General Electric in the USA and operated in the Echo band of frequencies, 2,700–2,900 MHz. It had a reported range of 370 km and an altitude capability of 75,000 feet. It had a peak power output of 5 MW and a vertical scanning rate up to 30 cycles per minute. The AN/FPS-26 frequency diverse radar was built by AVCO Manufacturing and operated in the Charlie band of frequencies, 5,400–5,900 MHz.

AN/FPS-6 Height
Finder Radar Antenna.
(Courtesy of Radomes,
Inc.)

These radar systems were 1950s vintage radars. Pierre Parent recounted that, 'A main issue that was a constant factor was the remote tuning capabilities of the FPS-27 Klystron. On the surface, the twitch of a knob in DMCC (Data Management Control Center) would be enough to change the frequency or so the theory went. But, there's always a but, in reality, changing frequency was always a major headache.'

The issues were that the Klystron tuning mechanism was a complex affair that consisted of a servo system hooked up to all three sections of the tube. In theory, when properly aligned, all segments of the tube would move in synch with each other and this movement was zeroed back to the frequency alignment synchro back on the console. If this worked, and it sometimes did, depending on when the last alignment was done, all went well. Now, the other side of the coin was tuning the receiver to the new frequency. A similar situation arose there and again based on the last maintenance performed, the system was supposed to work. Any changes in operating parameters were supposed to be passed on to sector.

It came to pass that due to all the variables I described, these features were seldom used. One of the main reasons was that the operator would

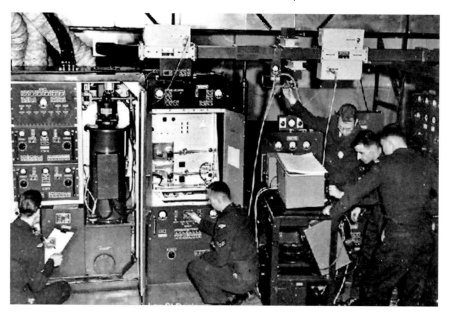

Maintaining Search Radar. (Courtesy of Larry Wilson)

crank the knob to one limit and without waiting, would crank to the other end and so on. The slow-acting mechanisms in the Klystron would not keep up with the rapid changes and would burn up in short order. A replacement of this main tube was a 24-hour affair, requiring a crew of at least eight people, not counting the logistics of getting another one in through the supply system. I changed four of these tubes in a one-month period in Alsask (CFS Alsask, Saskatchewan) and can fondly remember swimming in oil. 'Ahhh ...! Memories!'

They had been improved or were replacements for earlier models, such as the AN/FPS-3 search radar and the AN/TPS-502 height finder radar. They were all part of the SAGE radar network, as mentioned in chapters Two and Four, and had the capability of dealing with electronic countermeasures. Some of the radar sites were upgraded with solid state systems, new technology, in the early 1970s, but unfortunately, CFS Ramore was not and closed in 1974.

In 1973, the only airborne Air Defence Command radar in Canada was the Hughes Aircraft Company MG-13 IIP (Improved Intercept Performance) radar in the CAF McDonnell CF-101 Voodoo. It was a target search, acquire and track radar operating in the India band of frequencies, 8,500–9,250 MHz. It can operate in a frequency agile mode; frequency can change quickly, with a pulse repetition frequency of 416 Hz for a 1.0 microsecond width. The operator puts a range gate, similar to marking, on the target and locks it on. The radar tracks the target and provides steering information for the pilot to fly an interception collision course.

The MG-13 radar package had a Home on Jamming (HOJ) capability and a Counter Angle Deception Jammer (CADJ). The CADJ was used against the USAF Martin EB-57 electronic warfare aircraft as it was equipped with an angle deceiver. All are technical terms and innovations used in the ongoing battle of electronic countermeasures, radars versus jammers. The Voodoo also had a nose/tail switch to keep the MG-13 radar locked on to the target if it was dispensing chaff. It discriminated between the beginning and end of the chaff stream to maintain the fighter radar on the beginning of the stream where the target was located.

Radar is the 'eyes and ears' of air defence, so an attacking force would attempt to 'blind and deafen' the defence radar en route to their target. This is the basic premise of electronic warfare. The following are concepts established from experience during the Second World War. The attacking force could:

- Ignore the defender's electronic sensors and accept the ensuing loss of attacking aircraft.
- Avoid the sensors in the defence network.
- Dilute the defence network with false electronic information and decoys.
- Degrade the defence's electronic sensors with jamming or deception.
- Destroy the defender's sensors and weapons.

In 1969, the US Joint Chiefs of Staff defined electronic warfare as

A military action involving the use of electromagnetic energy to determine, exploit, reduce, or prevent hostile use of the electromagnetic spectrum and action which retains friendly use of the electromagnetic spectrum.

Electronic Counter Measures prevents or reduces an enemy's effective use of the electromagnetic spectrum. It can take the form of jamming reflection of electromagnetic energy to impair the use of electromagnetic devices by the enemy or deception, the deliberate radiation, alteration or reflection to mislead the enemy in the interpretation or use of information received by his electronic systems. This is done by the Electronic Counter Measures of the enemy force, target force in peacetime, which disables the defence and the fighter interceptor's radar. Electronic Counter Measures is in fact a misnomer – there are no electrons involved; it is, in fact, electromagnetic interference of radio waves. Electronic Counter Measures has two basic configurations: electronic or mechanical.

A dictum of Dr Robert Cockburn, a physicist at the Telecommunications Research Establishment at Swanage, England, said that a 'shilling's [British unit of currency] worth of radio-counter-measures will mess up a pound's [twenty shillings] worth of radio equipment'. He was referring to the cost effectiveness of the 'Mandrel' and 'Tinsel' British jamming devices used effectively during the Second World War. Reichsmarschall Göring of the German Luftwaffe complained that the Germans could not jam anything and the British could jam everything.

It was discovered, through a captured system, that the initial version of the German Lichtenstein radar was easily jammed by the use of mechanical jamming, that is chaff or window as it was called in Britain. Originally chaff, metal strips, was approximately half the wavelength of the radar to be countered. When a target dispensed chaff into the atmosphere, it produces a radar echo which obscures the target. Analysis of the action of chaff showed that the length of each metal strip should be a multiple of one half wavelengths of the radar signal to give maximum signal return. The India band radar of the Voodoo interceptor in our story has a wavelength of 2.5 to 3.0 cms. The Delta and Echo bands of the ground radar have a wavelength of 7.5 to 30 cms.

The chaff in the Avro CF-100 Mk 5C Canuck, the target aircraft in our story, was carried in two dispensers, one beneath each wing. The chaff

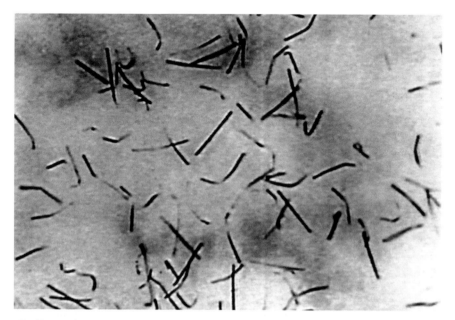

Chaff [Window] Scattering.

weighed 154 pounds. One dispenser carried the Delta/Echo band chaff capable of producing multiple targets on the ground radar sites' scopes and thereby obscuring the actual target. The other dispenser carried India band chaff to confuse the Voodoo airborne intercept radar. Each dispenser had 192 bundles; each bundle contained thousands of pieces of aluminium foil controlled by the Electronic Warfare Officer and could be dispensed into the atmosphere at different rates. Captain W. (Bill) Bland, the Electronic Warfare Officer in this book, mentioned, 'One of the tactics to break lock on the fighter interceptor's radar was to drop bursts of chaff coupled with some evasive action. The idea was to get the fighter's radar to transfer lock on from the actual target to the bundles of chaff which displayed a larger echo than the aircraft.' At the very least this action may cause the fighter's radar tracking ability to become very erratic.

The other chaff techniques used were to drop the bundles in a stream, blanket or random drop pattern. The aim was to fill the radar screen up with so many echoes that the echo of the target aircraft was hard for the operator to see. Another objective could be to screen a second aircraft flying in the chaff echoes. Many millions of pieces of chaff littered the countryside during the years that it was used in training and exercise missions. There was a concern about the effect chaff would have on cattle if digested with their normal feed. The National Research Council investigated and reported that it passed 'through the digestive system with no ill effects'.

The other side of Electronic Counter Measures is the electronic aspect; it is the introduction of artificial noise-like signals to the electronic equipment. An analogy could be that you are listening to one radio station and another radio station is playing simultaneously and is getting louder, making it hard to concentrate and hear the first station. Electronic Counter Measures comes in two configurations: jamming and deception. The jamming Electronic Counter Measures match the transmitted signal head on and try to blank, disturb or overpower the radar returns, while the deception Electronic Counter Measures try to trick the transmitted signal into believing false information.

Dr Malcolm Dewar worked with radio waves during the Second World War in Great Britain, including the standard beam approach landing system. Malcolm spent some time testing equipment with the Telecommunications Research Establishment in Malvern that was so secret that 'I was not allowed to take my own notebook away with me; it was locked in the Operations Unit's safe where I was stationed'. We discussed that one of the early jamming devices was an electro-diathermy device that he had used for cauterising bleeding in hospital operating theatres. It caused high frequency interference. Further research revealed that the units were issued to police stations, which turned them on upon notification of approaching enemy aircraft. Malcolm mentioned that in order for a jammer to be effective it 'must match the jammed signal in frequency and phase'. The phase was the wave form of the signal and could be observed on an oscilloscope.

Noise jammers come in three basic designs: barrage, spot, and a combination of the two called sweep. The barrage jammer is designed to provide noise disruption over a wide range of frequencies. The result is that the barrage jammer only directs a small amount of power at the signals in the range of frequencies covered. An analogy would be a hose set on spray. Conversely, the spot jammer concentrates all its energy on one frequency, a hose set on stream. However, more definitive signals intelligence is required to know what frequency to direct the jamming to.

The sweep jammer combined the barrage and spot jammer. A powerful narrow band output could be tuned over a wide frequency range. This tuning could be done automatically or manually by an operator; in the CF-100 target it was done by the Electronic Warfare Officer. This noise system of jamming was used very successfully from the 1940s to the 1970s. The radar development chess game continued. For example, the original pre-tuned spot jammer was rendered obsolete by radar that could change frequency rapidly in the face of jamming.

By the 1970s, the noise jammers were being replaced and/or supplemented by deception jammers. The deception jammer was made possible by the development of new electronic amplifiers and power sources such as the voltage-tunable magnetrons, carcinotrons and travelling wave tubes. The deception jammer had two main advantages over the noise jammer: less power is needed and, when operated properly, it does not appear as jamming. It provided deception by displaying false targets and false target position and velocity. It also had the new technology to enable 'range gate stealing' and 'velocity gate stealing'. A weakness of the system is that complete signal intelligence is required. If information is not available, or even inaccurate, on the enemy radar then it cannot be mimicked or tricked.

It should be noted that noise jammers are effective against radio communications and can be used to disrupt communications between the fighter interceptors and the ground controlled intercept stations. An interesting aside on wartime communication was the Domino voice countermeasure used by Britain in 1941. The German bombers were guided on FM radio by agents on the ground in Britain. The British intervened with skilled German-speaking linguists and got the German pilots so disoriented that some landed in England. The bombing of Dublin, Ireland, a neutral country, on 29–30 May 1941 by the Luftwaffe may have been an unintended result of Domino.

The Canadian Armed Forces had two marks of the Avro CF-100: the Mk5C and Mk5D, which were used by 414 Electronic Warfare Squadron. The Mk5D had the capability of receiving and jamming both the ground radar sites and airborne interceptors, both mechanically with chaff and electronically with jammers. On an exercise the Electronic Warfare Officer was a very busy person, as he monitored the receiver for ground and airborne radar signals and then responded with electronic and mechanical jamming. The phrase 'one-armed paper hanger' comes to mind.

Now that we have looked at the basics of radar and countermeasures let us look at how they would function in a training exercise. The target aircraft, in this example an Avro CF-100 Mk5D, is coming southbound into ground radar coverage. The Electronic Warfare Officer is looking at the Collins AN/APR-9 radar receiver. The receiver scans the frequencies from 1,000 to 10,750 MHz. These frequencies cover the frequency range for both the Pinetree ground radar sites and the airborne radar of the CF-101 Voodoo fighter interceptor.

The Electronic Warfare Officer notices the radar signal of the CFS Ramore AN/FPS-27 search radar at 2,400 MHz on his APR-9 receiver. He adjusts the AN/ALT-501 jammer to the approximate frequency, then turns the transmitter on and carefully adjusts it so the signal covers, matches, the ground radar signal, setting the jammer to narrow band and alters the power for maximum output. The spot jamming mode is used to give the maximum power back to the distant radar site. The resulting noise obscures the radar target. The jamming would show up as a bright strobe on the radar site scope. The radar Air Defence Tech then contacts the radar technicians to switch to another frequency. Now the Electronic Warfare Officer has to find that frequency on his receiver and retune the ALT 501 transmitters. The Electronic Warfare Officer also has to shut off his jammer periodically to make sure the radar site has not changed frequency. The jammer signal obscures the radar site signal so it is not possible to see if the radar site has moved to another frequency. The cat and mouse radar game continues. The Electronic Warfare Officer changes to wide band mode as he gets closer to the site to cover a wider frequency range and reduce the need to continually monitor for frequency changes. However, he must be careful not to go too wide in the barrage mode as the radar site can 'burn through' the jamming and get a radar target.

The Electronic Warfare Officer also has chaff at his disposal. The ground radar has a set sweep rate and as Bill Bland mentioned, one of the tactics was to 'release a bundle when the sweep went by' to get best results. The sweep rate was every 12 seconds so the chaff dispenser rate could be set at 5 bundles per minute. Now the EWO was really busy – head up against the viewing ring of the APR-9 receiver looking at the green coloured 'D' scope signal display, tuning the ALT-501 radar transmitters and setting up the chaff dispensers. The idea was to prevent the search radar from getting a good radar picture, ensuring that it was unable to set up a track number and get height information from the height finder radars.

As a result of the presence of jamming, the intermittent radar target would be declared hostile and the fighter interceptors would be scrambled. Irradiate Control looked after the target force to ensure safety and advice of fighter activity. The CF-100 target force had no indication of fighter range or direction so it relied upon the controller to give them that information. The order of battle for the Electronic Warfare Officer was tracking radars, search radars and distant search radars. When the approaching fighters became an imminent threat the Electronic Warfare Officer would transfer his attention to the India band AN/ALR 18 receiver and leave the ground radar jammers set with chaff dispensing at a fixed rate. The ALR-18 receiver was capable of seeing the fighter's radar as it approached from the front, rear, above and below the target aircraft. The receiver antenna had to be manually switched from front to rear, or vice versa, by the Electronic Warfare Officer, who concentrated on the blinking red light of the receiver.

The object of all jammer activity is to break the fighter interceptor radar's lock-on. Through manual or automatic interceptor radar antenna operations the target shows up on the AI Navigator's radar scope. The idea is to put the radar tracking gate over the return from the target, which causes a coincidence in the range and tracking circuits of the radar. All parameters being correct, the radar acquires the target and goes into acquisition mode or lock-on. Two symbols now appear on the scope. First is the steering dot to indicate the relative position of the target and second is a range circle whose size is proportional to the distance to the target. The smaller the circle, the closer, the target.

The AN/ALT-6B transmitter would automatically jam the fighter interceptor's search and track radar signal. Judicious use of the chaff dispenser and evasive manoeuvres would make it difficult for the fighter to get good target information and possibly break its radar lock-on. Normally, the CF-101 fighter could break through the CF-100 target aircraft jammers at about 19 to 26 kms and get the radar lock-on that it needed to fire its weapons. The fighter's radar had priority and had been upgraded throughout the years – the target's jammers had not. This made some sense with a limited military budget, but the training value depended on the equipment as well as the operator.

All the foregoing information concerned the primary radar target or 'paint' or 'skin' return as it was called. There was also a secondary radar system: the AN/UPX-14 transponder Identification Friend or Foe/Selective

Identification Feature system. The U signified General Utility, P for Radar and X for Identification and Recognition system. This system used an interrogation signal that was sent out to the aircraft, which responded with a coded reply. This electronic reply appeared as a code on to the Plan Position Indicator console screen. Of course, the enemy would not announce their presence and would have their aircraft transponder turned off.

Exercises such as this were a good practical workout for the ground radar technicians and operators as well as the fighter interceptor crew. The more the personnel worked with the radar sets and displays, the more proficient they became. There was no option; this was the Cold War – the exercises and training would continue.

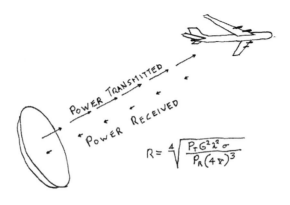

$$R = \sqrt[4]{\frac{P_T G^2 \lambda^2 \sigma}{P_R (4\pi)^3}}$$

CHAPTER FOUR

Canadian Radar Network

The small English car continued its journey through the frozen Canadian bush of Northern Quebec; the temperature was -40 centigrade (-40 fahrenheit). It was Christmas time 1962 and the young aircraftsman 1st Class, L. (Larry) S. Wilson, later Master Warrant Officer, was driving to his first posting at RCAF Station Chibougamau, Quebec, a radar site which was part of the Pinetree Line radar network. He was excited to start his career as a radar technician, but had some trepidation as this was his first posting to an operational station.

When asked about his first experience on the radar site, Larry wrote:

> I believe I arrived on a Sunday so officially reported in the next day. Clearing in and moving in to barracks and preparing my kit took most of the day. Tuesday I caught the bus up the hill and reported to the 'Search' section where I met my bosses and fellow techs for the first time. My immediate boss was a Corporal who was a very hardnosed individual. The first thing he asked me to do was "go align the MTI [moving target indicator]". This petrified me because in trades school we were told never to touch it because "it took a group 3 technician, (and I was a group 1), 4 hours to align", but there was no getting out of it so I found the manual and proceeded to align the MTI. I was either very lucky, or the MTI didn't really need aligning but I succeeded. After that I was just one of the crew.

Larry had joined the vast 'army' of personnel who had planned, constructed and operated the three lines of radar defence that were located in Canada. He subsequently spent his whole military career associated with the radar sites in various capacities. The dichotomy of the lifestyle was part of the job; the continual upgrading of knowledge, working with the latest technical radar developments compared with the remote communities surrounding the sites where hunting and fishing was the norm.

Canada had concentrated its air defences in Ontario and Quebec during the late 1940s. The USA already had a temporary radar system in place in 1949, LASHUP, which consisted of forty-four stations on American soil, but the military commanders felt that they needed more warning time for their fighter interceptors to get airborne. During the 1950s, the Americans wanted to integrate the Canadian and US radar systems and thus improve efficiency and push the air war further north.

This 'extension' of the now permanent US radar network became the sophisticated Continental Air Defence Integration North (CADIN)/ PINETREE Line at 50 degrees north latitude, to provide radar coverage to vector the fighter interceptors for identification or destruction of the target. Next to be constructed was the Arctic DEW Line at approximately 70 degrees north latitude, which could indicate that a target was on its way south. The last to be constructed was the Mid-Canada Line at 55 degrees north latitude, which indicated the target speed and direction. In this way, any incoming targets either from Siberia, over the Polar regions or the North Atlantic, would be tracked by this vast radar network. The construction of these radar sites in such a harsh, isolated environment is a tribute to man's tenacity and ingenuity.

The three Canadian Radar Lines. (Courtesy of Richard Hovey)

The CADIN/PINETREE Line

This line of radar sites was formally agreed to by the USA and Canada in 1951. One line was situated on average on the 52 degrees north latitude in western Canada, dropping southwards to well below 50 degrees latitude in eastern Canada. The other line ran from southern Nova Scotia northwards to Baffin Island. The first phase comprised of thirty-three sites to be completed by 1954. A second phase of eleven sites was constructed to fill in gaps in the coverage between 1957 and 1964. This was done to achieve the new aim of defending the retaliatory Strategic Air Command aircraft rather than the defence of the 'industrial heartland'. Defending the Offence became the new mantra. A total of over 7,000 km was covered from Victoria, British Columbia to St Johns, Newfoundland, and northwards along the Labrador coast to Iqaluit, Nunavut.

The first phase and line of sites is as follows, with the closest major town added (in brackets) as necessary for geographical reference:

Tofino, British Columbia
Comox, British Columbia
Sydney, Nova Scotia
Saskatoon Mountain, Alberta [Beaverlodge]
Baldy Hughes, British Columbia [Prince George]
Puntzi Mountain, British Columbia [Williams Lake]
Holberg, British Columbia [Port Hardy]

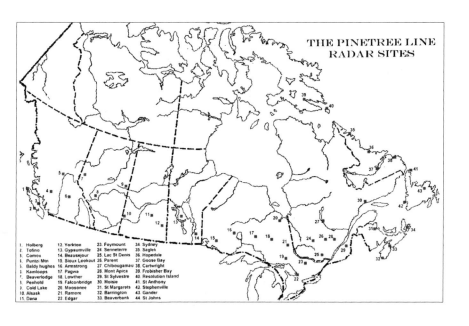

THE PINETREE LINE
RADAR SITES

1. Holberg	12. Yorkton	23. Foymount	34. Sydney
2. Tofino	13. Gypsumville	24. Senneterre	35. Saglek
3. Comox	14. Beausejour	25. Lac St Denis	36. Hopedale
4. Puntzi Mtn	15. Sioux Lookout	26. Parent	37. Goose Bay
5. Baldy hughes	16. Armstrong	27. Chibougamau	38. Cartwright
6. Kamloops	17. Pagwa	28. Mont Apica	39. Frobisher Bay
7. Beaverlodge	18. Lowther	29. St Sylvestre	40. Resolution Island
8. Penhold	19. Falconbridge	30. Moisie	41. St Anthony
9. Cold Lake	20. Moosonee	31. St Margarets	42. Stephenville
10. Alsask	21. Ramore	32. Barrington	43. Gander
11. Dana	22. Edgar	33. Beaverbank	44. St Johns

Beausejour, Manitoba
Sioux Lookout, Ontario
Armstrong, Ontario
Pagwa, Ontario [Hearst]
Halifax, Nova Scotia
Ramore, Ontario [Kirkland Lake]
Falconbridge, Ontario [Sudbury]
Senneterre, Quebec
Parent, Quebec
Sault Ste Marie, Ontario
Chatham (St Margaret's), New Brunswick
Edgar, Ontario [Barrie]
Foymount, Ontario [Pembroke]
Lac St Denis, Quebec [Quebec City]
Mont Apica, Quebec [Chicoutimi]

The other line built/financed by the USAF is:

St John's, Newfoundland
Stephenville, Newfoundland
Goose Bay, Labrador
Gander, Newfoundland
St Anthony, Newfoundland
Cartwright, Labrador
Hopedale, Labrador
Saglek, Labrador
Resolution Island, Former North West Territories [Nunavut]
Clarke City (Moise), Quebec [Sept Iles]
Frobisher Bay, North West Territories [Iqaluit, Nunavut]

The second phase of filler sites built between 1957 and 1964 is as follows:

St Sylvestre, Quebec [Quebec City]
Chibougamau, Quebec
Moosonee, Ontario
Alsask, Saskatchewan [Kindersely]
Dana, Saskatchewan [Humboldt]
Gypsumville, Manitoba [Dauphin]
Penhold, Alberta [Red Deer]
Yorkton, Saskatchewan
Barrington, Nova Scotia

Lowther, Ontario [Kapuskasing]
Kamloops, British Columbia

Gypsumville, Manitoba, situated 200 km north-west of Winnipeg, cost $6.5 million to build this radar site. It is situated in an isolated area between Lake Manitoba and Lake Winnipeg. Some sites were more expensive than others due to remote location and site preparation for radar towers and support facilities. There were forty-four sites constructed for the CADIN/ PINETREE Line.

Some of the original sites were designated as Aircraft Control and Warning sites. The Aircraft Control and Warning site was a self-contained unit and carried out 'manual' interceptions of unknown targets. At the same time, it would 'forward tell to a higher echelon' what was happening. In July 1956, a young Bob Keith, mentioned previously in Chapter Two, stepped off a RCAF Canso flying boat in Holberg Inlet on Vancouver Island to start his first posting at the isolated CFS Holberg radar site. A 8-km drive through the wilderness got him to the domestic site. Bob mentioned that 'getting to the operational site was an adventure in itself. It involved two switch backs up a gravel road on Mt Brandes and the last 50 metres up a 30 per cent grade. The crew was transported in the back of a six by six truck.'

CFS Holberg had a FPS-3 search radar, the antenna of which was huge, 12 metres wide and 5 metres high, and two FPS-507 height finder radars. Bob worked in the operations room and recalled that 'it had a switchboard, the search and height finder scopes, two dais positions and the vertical plexiglas plotting board'. The scope operator had an in-house phone to the plotter. All information from the scopes would be passed to the plotter, who would plot the position on the board map. However, the Fighter Officer Controllers' daises were on the other side of the board. This meant that the plotter had to write all the information on the board backwards! Bob said that 'even now, fifty four years later, I can write backwards, no problem at all'.

Bob remembered that 'the plotter was very busy. Writing and wiping off behind you, all done by grease pencil, every two to three minutes, as the target moved down the plotting board.' The controllers would use the information on the board to vector the fighter aircraft to the target. Nine targets was the maximum that one plotter could handle for a short time. The shift schedule was nine days long, three days each of graveyard, day and evening. Bob mentioned that the 'four to five a.m. period' was the most difficult for him, a blank radar screen refreshing every 12 seconds! He also recalled, fifty years later, that Mt Waddington was a permanent echo on the search scope, '028 degrees for 122 miles'. Impressive – the defence of Canada was in good hands.

On the other side of the country, at Sydney, Nova Scotia, Captain Ken Penny was on duty as a Fighter Controller at the radar site. Ken was a former CF-100 AI Navigator assigned a ground tour. He recalled that, 'One morning at 0400 there was an active cold front interfering with all the returning civilian traffic from Europe. I picked up their radar target about 370 kilometres and vectored them, one after the other, around the thunderstorms. We would provide flight following as our military duties permitted.'

Subsequently, in 1963, the whole Canadian radar network was divided into regions and incorporated into the SAGE network. SAGE did away with manual plotting and controlling. The radar inputs came into the region headquarters from all the CADIN/Pinetree Line sites. The system was now computer based and the whole of the region could now be observed and controlled from one location. This resulted in the radar sites reducing their operations personnel by about a half, to 200 staff or less. The sites consisted of an operations and domestic section. The operations site, always located on the highest point in the vicinity, had a main building with a search and two height finder radars. The antennas were enclosed in radomes to protect them against wind damage. There were two types of radomes: the rigid fibreglass geodesic dome and the blower constant-pressure inflated rubber dome.

Site location and fuel permitting, the author would often perform a high-speed pass over the site to visually check for any radome damage, commonly referred to as a 'bubble check!' CFSs Falconbridge and Mont Apica got more than their fair share as they were close to CFB North Bay and CFB Bagotville respectively. St Margaret's was also regularly examined as it was close to CFB Chatham. The author is proud to add that he did his fair share of checking 'the bubble for leaks!'

Located in the vicinity of the operations site, the domestic site consisted of barracks and all the support buildings. The site was similar to a small town. The housing area at most isolated stations consisted of a mobile trailer park and slabs for double-wide transportable trailers. It had its own power, heating, water treatment and sewage plant. In addition, personnel had access to a recreation centre, fire station, library, administration buildings; some sites had swimming pools, ice rinks and golf courses. A few sites were lucky enough to be next to towns; others were located considerable distance from civilisation.

In 1963 the SAGE system caused some of the sites to be closed. A further upgrade to the radar network in the 1970s caused more site closures. However, performance analysis by Continuous Evaluation flights were flown to ensure the radar sites performed up to specifications. The target would be identified by the search and height finder radars and checked

CF-100 Canucks over radar site. (Courtesy of Canadian Forces Joint Imagery Centre, Department of National Defence)

against actual aircraft position and altitude. The friendly rivalry of the sites caused the 370-km range to be extended as radar technicians and operators tweaked their station radar transmitters, receivers and antennas to the limit. Pierre Parent remembers 'people hunched over the Random Access Plan Position Indicator scopes *wishing* for the target to appear. This was the overall determining factor that generated the max range score of the equipment ... I can remember whoever was on the loop [communication network] with sector declaring a target and arguing with the guy at the other end if he didn't see it.' The competitive nature of the radar sites was very strong – my radar site is better than yours.

The new solid-state technology increased the radar sites capability to cope with environmental factors such as cloud penetration and precipitation. An example of the new equipment is the AN/FYQ-47 Digitizer housed in a 34-cubic-metre room. Previously, the AN/FST-2 Digitizer was housed in a 1,274-cubic-metre air-conditioned room. The radar pulses were now measured in nanoseconds rather than the slower microseconds. 'In many ways, the advent of solid state technology became the death knell of the radar sites we worked on,' lamented Pierre.

The AN/UPX-14 electronic identification, known as Identification Friend or Foe/Selective Identification Feature, and electronic jamming countermeasures further reduced the need for some stations. The fate of the remaining Pinetree Line sites was sealed at the Shamrock Summit in 1985, when President Reagan and Prime Minister Mulroney decided that it had served its usefulness. The change over the years to coverage by four powerful North American perimeter radars finally caused the Pinetree Line to become obsolete in 1988. Thirty-four years of exemplary service in the defence of North America ended – all Soviet Pinetree Line flight encroachments were successfully intercepted.

DEW Line

Minutes were the focus in the 1950s for the defence of North America. Time to get the fighter interceptors airborne and, more importantly, time to get the nuclear Strategic Air Command retaliatory bomber force airborne and on their way to assigned Soviet targets. This, in essence, was the stalemate of deterrence that existed during the Cold War years. The Soviets may attempt the first strike, but they were assured by the American politicians that the response would be immediate, massive and overwhelming. In other words, do not try it.

The response to the threat of a Soviet 'Over the Pole' airborne invasion was a radar system that would immediately notify the Canadian and

American leaders of the situation and enable time for a diplomatic and military response. President Dwight Eisenhower, in consultation with Canada, signed the bill approving construction, in February 1954, of a line of radar sites in Alaska and the Canadian Arctic. It was called the Distant Early Warning Line, commonly referred to as the DEW Line.

The DEW Line ran from Cape Dyer, Baffin Island, Canada, to Lisburne, North Slope, Alaska, USA. It was built on approximately the 70th North parallel of latitude, about 300 km north of the Arctic Circle. The plan included a western segment from Kodiak Island in the Aleutians to Hawaii; this section was to prevent an 'end run' around the defences. The western segment was later modified to run from Umnak, Alaska, to Midway Island in the Pacific Ocean. The eastern segment was eventually extended to include Greenland. A massive sealift, during open ice season, and airlift programme was instituted to construct the line in 1955 to its technological operational opening on 15 May 1957. The DEW Line was planned, built, and largely financed as well as manned by the USA.

The DEW Line consisted of a continuous string of radar sites entirely north of the Arctic Circle. They were situated on pebbly beaches and rocky outcrops in Arctic isolation. The DEW Line had six, four in Canada, 'Main' AN/FPS-19 L band radar stations supported by 'Auxiliary' and 'Intermediate or AN/FPS-124 gap filler' stations. The Main Canadian stations were DYE-Cape Dyer, FOX-Hall Beach, CAM-Cambridge Bay and PIN-Cape Parry. It was a human and technological feat of endurance that the Line was completed in two summers and three typical dark and extremely cold Arctic winters. A total of 25,000 people planned and worked on the project, which used nearly 500,000 tons of material, all of which was transported into this mostly uninhabited area. The material arrived by ship, aircraft, cat train and barges.

The engine that drove this effort was the food: no expense was spared to provide plentiful and good food. Accommodation and facilities could be spartan, but the meals provided would combat the bitter cold and fuel the workforce. The food and the extremely good pay were the 'Good' of the 'Good, Bad and Ugly' of the operation and environment. On occasion during the 1970s, with time permitting during the Pacific Western Airlines schedule flight stop, the author would run up the hill at Cambridge Bay to get a 'piece of pie' from the radar site kitchen for the aircrew!

Buildings, towers, antennas, storage tanks, power plants, water treatment and heating plants, airfields and some hangars were constructed to turn isolated areas into habitable and workable environments. The installation of the radar and communications equipment followed. The Main and Auxiliary sites had the AN/FPS 19 search radar. The Intermediate/gap filler sites had the AN/FPS-23 Doppler radar. The whole DEW Line was tied together with a tropospheric scatter communications system. This system used the phenomena of bouncing radio signals off the troposphere to communicate very long distances. The Main sites used the same system to communicate with Air Defence Command, later NORAD, in the south.

The Main site could have up to 220 personnel at times, the Auxiliary had about 25 and the Intermediate had a lonely 3. The Intermediate site had a Station Chief to look after all the electronics, a chef to cook, bake and keep house, as well as a mechanic to haul water, run the power plant, maintain the road and airfield, and look after all equipment and building maintenance.

There was extensive testing and training for two and a half months prior to the handover to the USAF on 31 July 1957. The military was very confident that no bomber or surveillance aircraft would be able to penetrate the Line without being observed. It is very important to note that ten weeks later, on 4 October 1957, the first Soviet 'Sputnik' was placed into space orbiting the earth. By 1959, both the USA and USSR had inter-continental ballistic missiles in their arsenal. The DEW Line was totally ineffective against the high-flying ICBM. It served out the rest of its years, gradually reducing in size as technology improved, to be finally replaced in 1988 with the North Warning System. The Dew Line provided thirty years of service as a radar fence and deterrent against attacking bombers and an important role of establishing Canadian sovereignty in the isolated areas of the High Arctic.

Mid-Canada Line or McGill Fence

A concern remained, however, that airborne targets could go anywhere after being observed, passing through the DEW Line radar network. A subsonic bomber could take up to three hours to reach the Pinetree Line in eastern Canada before coming on the radar screens again. A military study group conducted in the early 1950s also came to the conclusion that a line of defence north of the Pinetree Line should be established 'at the earliest possible date'. The Canadian Cabinet Defence Committee gave the go-ahead for the project to be engineered, surveyed and planned in November 1953. A Canadian system based on the Doppler radar principle was adopted. It was also called the 'McGill Fence' because of the association with McGill University in Montreal during its development.

The project called for two lines of transmitters and receivers up to 100 km apart and in sight of each other from Hopedale, Labrador, to Dawson Creek, British Columbia, which amounted to over 4,000 km of radar fence. The principle was based on the transmitter sending an un-modulated continuous wave signal to the receiver. This phase of the signal is used for reference. Anything passing between the transmitter and receiver will generate a new signal phase. It is then compared to the original and, if different, it activated a warning signal.

In June 1954, the Canadian Cabinet approved the funding and construction of the Mid-Canada Line. Tractor trains (tractors pulling sleds or wagons) in western Canada and aerial photography in eastern Canada completed the survey of the 55th North parallel of latitude. The construction difficulties were enormous; the climate made areas impassable during the winter freeze-up and the spring thaw. Marshalling areas were established at the end of roads, rail lines, lakes, rivers and sea inlets, and then the material would travel by tractor trailer, aircraft, helicopter, barge, muskeg tractor or any combination necessary. In Hudson Bay it was necessary to use flat-bottomed landing craft.

The Mid-Canada Line became fully operational in January 1958 and had eight manned Sector Control Stations and ninety unmanned Doppler Detection Sites. All ninety-eight stations were linked by a tropospheric communications system, which was also used to communicate to the south. Kempis Mountain near CFS Ramore was part of the relay network. The Sector Control Stations were: Dawson Creek, British Columbia; Stoney Mountain (Waterways), Alberta; Cranberry Portage, Manitoba; Bird, Manitoba; Winisk, Ontario; Great Whale River, Quebec; Knob Lake, Quebec; Hopedale, Labrador.

Inuit camp near Great Whale River Mid-Canada Line Radar Site, 1965. (Courtesy of Dan Farrell)

The Sector Control Station had about 150 personnel, 11 military personnel, and the basic amenities to sustain life in an isolated environment. Connection to the outside world was maintained, although the northern climate played havoc at times. The author had the privilege of working with Captain D. (Dan) Farrell flying the Avro CF-100 with 414 Electronic Warfare Squadron at CFB Uplands, Ottawa, Ontario. Dan mentioned that he had been the titular commanding officer of Great Whale River Sector Control Station in 1962. Farrell recounted that: 'A ship from Quebec City would re-supply the site around the end of August after the ice break-up. The material was brought ashore using landing craft due to the shallow water.' When asked about any roads he said, 'Good grief no, just the airport. Weather permitting we had a flight every few weeks from Ottawa.' The site had a perimeter fence to separate it from the village but in winter, he chuckled, 'The snow drifts were so high the natives would just walk right in. As the Commanding Officer I was responsible for security but what could I do? I tried to keep the Operations building locked. It had a complex key punch padlock on the door. It was ignored and people would come in through the (adjoining) warehouse which should have been locked too!'

Two lines of transmitters and receivers were necessary to determine the direction of the target: north or south. The signal trace could also be interpreted to give an indication of the target speed. Dan commented that, 'The poor Fighter Control Operators watched boards with moving pins, like a seismograph, for hours.' In the event of an aircraft passing through the fence, the change of phase warning signal would be sent to the nearest Sector Control Station. The location and time would be compared to known flight plans provided by Air Traffic Control. Voice communication with the target aircraft could also confirm identity. Unidentified crossings of the radar line would be reported to the Air Defence System in the south. Now it was up to Air Defence Command, and later NORAD, to take the required action.

By the time NORAD reacted to the warning, the unknown target was showing up on the more southern Pinetree Line radar scopes. It was felt that the additional warning time did not justify the expense of keeping the Mid-Canada Line open. The eastern part of the Line was the last to close in April 1965. It had been a tremendously successful learning opportunity for Canada: a $225,000,000 project that moved 200,000 tons of material under the harshest of topographical and meteorological conditions. A total of 370 towers were erected, some, which were over 106 metres high. The mining and hydro-electric industry certainly benefited from the experience gained by the constructors of the Mid-Canada Line.

Radar Site Exercise Activity

There were three of the forty-four radar sites actively involved in tracking our target aircraft during the Amalgam Mute 73-2 exercise on 10 May 1973. There was great rivalry and pride to see who could observe the target at the greatest range and pass the information first to region headquarters at CFB North Bay, Ontario. CFS Ramore in Ontario, as well as Chibougamau and Senneterre in Quebec, all covered the exercise area where our target, Mute 104, was flying. The full story of the exercise is in Chapter Nine, 'Sparks in the Night Sky'.

CFS Ramore is located in Northern Ontario, Canada. The station motto is *Semper Vigilans* (Always Watching). It is close to the village of Ramore and 63 km north of the gold mining city of Kirkland Lake. Some personnel lived in a trailer park on base, but most lived in a trailer park in the nearby

CFS Ramore, Ontario, Domestic Site. (Courtesy of Canadian Forces Joint Imagery Centre, Department of National Defence)

town of Matheson. A few hardy souls braved the winter drive and lived in Kirkland Lake. The radar site was very fortunate to have a spring-fed lake on the property. Through the volunteer efforts of the base personnel a recreational facility lodge was built on the lake called 'The Ponderosa'.

Site C-10 was home to 35 Radar Squadron until forces unification in 1967 changed the name to CFS Ramore. The radars installed in 1953 were gradually improved and replaced throughout the years. Originally a USAF site, it transferred to the RCAF in 1962. It had the FPS-27 search radar and the FPS-6B and FPS-26 height finder radar. CFS Ramore was also unique in that it had a relay station, Kempis Mountain, for the Mid-Canada Line, using tropospheric scatter communication, from 1958 until the mid-1960s. Larry Wilson remembered 'hunting grouse with my wife at the old site'. It was just over a year after the Amalgam Mute exercise that the station was closed on 1 September 1974.

CFS Senneterre is located 70 km north of Val d'Or, Quebec. The station motto is *Silens Exploro* (Exploring in Silence). It is located on the south end of Lac Parent about 3 km from the town of Senneterre. It is an extremely picturesque, if remote, area, which is good for fishing and hunting activities. CFS Senneterre was fortunate to have a swimming pool and curling rink, which compensated somewhat for the isolation.

Site C-8 was home to 34 Radar Squadron until unification in 1967 changed the name to CFS Senneterre. The RCAF-built base was operational on 1 June 1953. It had the FPS-508 search radar and the FPS-6 and FPS-507 height finder radars. It had the additional responsibilities of being a Back Up Interceptor Control site, which meant it could take over control from the 22nd NORAD Region headquarters if ever those computers became unusable. Master Corporal John Donnelly's responsibilities in 1973 were data reduction in the Data Management Control Area, which involved radar pickup and tracking integration; radar site inputs were configured to the Senneterre computers. All the data from the western sector of the region continually updated itself on the CFS Senneterre's AN/GYK-19 computer. It also was designated as an Alternate Command Post, answering, when it assumed this role, directly to NORAD HQ in Colorado Springs, USA, instead of 22nd NORAD HQ in CFB North Bay. The base had 317 personnel in 1970, and because of these added responsibilities the base commander had the rank of lieutenant-colonel. On 1 April 1988, the power switch was turned off and thirty-five years of service in the defence of Canada came to an end.

The CFS Chibougamau domestic site is located in the town of Chibougamau, Quebec. In 1962, Larry Wilson mentioned that 'it had a population of 10,000, a new hospital, two movie theatres and five or six hotels'. The operations site is a 30 minute bus ride away on Bourbeau

Mountain. The station motto is *Intrus Prenez Garde* (Trespassers beware). Like CFS Senneterre, it is in a good area for fishing and hunting activities. Site C-42 was home to 10 Radar Squadron until unification in 1967 changed the name to CFS Chibougamau. It became operational on 1 May 1962, nine years after CFSs Ramore and Senneterre. It was constructed to fill gaps in the initial radar coverage. It had the FPS-93A search radar and two FPS-507A height finders, both much improved with electronic counter-countermeasures, such as the Cascade-Dicke equipment. It suffered the same fate as CFS Senneterre and closed on 1 April 1988. The old height finder could still be found in 1998 in the town, a remnant of the Cold War.

The Amalgam Mute exercise had started the previous day on 9 May 1973 and all the bases were in full operational mode. During the midnight shift, the Air Defence Technicians on the scopes at the three sites in our story were watching the targets fly north and knew what to expect. The

CFS Ramore, Ontario, Operations Site. (Courtesy of Canadian Forces Joint Imagery Centre, Department of National Defence)

targets would continue to fly north until they disappeared off the scopes. Then the waiting began. Where and when would they reappear? The competition was intense to be the first to get the target acquisition and data to the SAGE computer in CFB North Bay.

Mute 104 turned southbound in the early hours of the morning and started its target run. It was relying on the nearby USAF Martin EB-57 Canberra to jam the ground radar sites while it jammed the fighter aircraft radar during the interception. On the ground, Sgt Larry Wilson knew that his radars were operating at peak efficiency: 'burning and turning' as Larry said. He had checked the myriad of electron tubes with a tube checker to make sure they had the optimum gain; only the ones with the highest gain would be used. In preparation for an exercise, Larry wrote that 'all receivers were tweaked, scopes were aligned and the transmitters were checked for maximum power'. Now it was up to the rest of the team. During the exercise, he would work in the Nuclear Defence Section, plotting fallout and determining radiation decay rates.

There it was, finally, the target dot on the Random Access Plan Position Indicator. The Air Defence Technician, working with the Senior Telecom Officer at CFS Ramore, had been waiting for this moment. A quick call followed to the Identification Sector in North Bay declaring the target: 'Do you see it?' Sometimes an argument would ensue on whether or not it was a target. This was at the maximum range of the system and the radar station pride was at stake. The search radar was producing the raw data and the AN/FST-2 turned it into digital data to be sent to the sector.

Shortly thereafter, the target appeared on the scopes of CFSs Senneterre and Chibougamau. Mute 104 became apparent in the system like a 'deer in the headlights'. There were three search radars, six height finders and three IFF/SIF secondary radars looking at Mute 104. The radar sites were doing their job, providing the radar target to sector. It was up to sector to identify the target and take the appropriate action.

The Random Access Plan Position Indicator was the centre of activity; operational personnel huddled around the scope, as the Air Defence Technicians coped with the jamming of the USAF EB-57 and tried to provide the best picture to sector. Pierre Parent, a radar technician, said during our interview, tongue in cheek, 'I seem to remember this as a big 'Scope' surrounded by a whole bunch of very pretty lights and switches and stuff.' This was another friendly rivalry and the radar technicians referred to the Air Defence technicians as 'Scope Dopes'. Larry recalled that, 'The AD techs referred to us radar technicians as plumbers, because of the transmitter waveguides which were like square pipes!'

Now that Mute 104 was on the radar screen the sector would initiate a height request. The request would pass through the AN/FST-2 and through

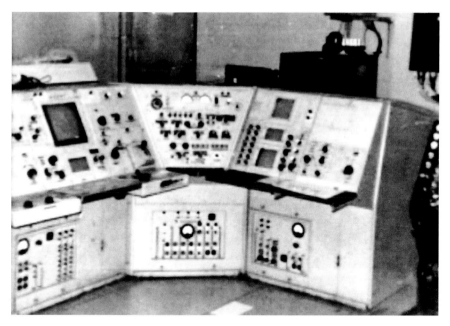

Radar Console at Pinetree Radar Site. (Courtesy of Larry Wilson)

servo systems to the ever-nodding height antenna. Pierre exclaimed that 'the 2.5-ton antenna could swing 180 degrees inside 2 seconds and I have the scars to prove it'. The Air Defence Technician would run the height cursor to where he figured was the centre of the sweep and then press a send button to transmit the target height back to sector.

When I asked Pierre how it all worked he wrote,

> So during your Anti-Jamming exercise, an officer, (STELLO)[*sic*], advised by an NCO would be the link between the site and the sector, the AD techs would respond to Height requests, the techs would make sure the machinery ran as it should, the cooks down the hill would feed us, the MSE (Mobile Support Equipment) section would transport us, the power plant guys would make sure the lights were on, the Air Conditioning guys would make sure that the equipment didn't fry, the Supply section would action any requests usually at a code 1 level and last but not least the military police would bring us coffee and doughnuts [joking]! Bottom line ... there were lots of people involved.

It cannot be overemphasised that the success of the radar site in a hostile geographical and technological environment depended entirely on teamwork. One of the team members at CFS Ramore in 1972 was Corporal

J. R. (Roger) N. Blais. He was working in the Administrative Section when he became aware of a problem with tracking and recording the radiation levels on the site, which could affect its operational status. On his own initiative, he devised a solution to the problem with very little time available before a tactical evaluation deadline. Roger also devised many administrative procedures at the site and as part of the recommendation the Commanding Officer wrote, 'The system (checking in) devised has virtually eliminated the confusion and chaos that used to occur during the early stages of an exercise and it now gives me, in my capacity as Battle Commander, an up-to-the-minute account of all unit personnel by trade, name and section.' On 20 October 1972, Blais was awarded an 'Outstanding Non-Commissioned Officer Award' by General Seth J. McKee, USAF, Commander-in-Chief NORAD, for his work. A chain is as good as its weakest link and it takes all personnel on a radar site to maintain the integrity of the link.

Life on Site

One of the main things that the interviewed Radar Technicians wanted emphasised was the tremendous positive effect of having the families together with the military personnel at the radar sites. The isolation, irregular hours and hardships imposed by a military life were made tolerable by the cohesion of the family unit. This was an effective decision made by the military and Canadian government at the time to maintain morale. They opted for the extra expense of constructing a domestic site with the operations site based on the premise that a happier workforce is a more productive workforce.

The small town concept was not possible at all sites. Pierre Parent mentioned that 'CFS Armstrong, site C-15, was accessed by 142 miles (228 km) on a seasonal road from Hurkett, Ontario, and did not have any school facilities in 1962. The housing consisted of trailers that had been moved to the radar site when the road was passable. The posting was restricted, because of the isolation, to 1 year for married personnel, wife and pre-school children only.'

Parent also alluded to the fact 'that living in these closed communities was like living in a fish bowl. Lots of intrigue, everyone knew your business and gossip was rampant.' I suspect no different from any small isolated civilian community. Sometimes personnel, for various reasons, could no longer cope with the job and the isolation and they were transferred out to maintain the team spirit of the radar site. This did not happen soon enough for a sergeant at CFS Pagwa who turned up for the commanding officer's parade wearing shorts and a tee shirt; he left on the next train.

What was the status of the Canadian Radar Network at the time of the Amalgam Mute exercise on 10 May 1973? It had been eleven years since the Cuban Missile Crisis. The ongoing Strategic Arms Limitations Talks were helping to diffuse Cold War tension. As a result, the DEW Line was reducing, the Mid-Canada Line had closed in 1965 and the Pinetree Line was reducing the number of radar sites. CFS Ramore was one of the Pinetree sites that closed the next year, in 1974.

The three 'Lines' had served Canada well. They had protected us as we slept, worked and played. Unseen by most, unknown by many, the men and women of the 'Lines' ensured our safety 24 hours per day, every day. In conjunction with the Texas Towers, permanent offshore radar sites, the radar ships and airborne radar aircraft, the entire of North America was surrounded by a wall of early warning radar. Therefore, to use the NORAD motto – DETER, definitely, DETECT, certainly, DEFEND, no question!

CHAPTER FIVE

Mcdonnell CF-101 Voodoo

There was no mistaking the sound of a Voodoo taking off, the roar of the engines was shattered by the boom of the afterburners igniting as it hurtled down the runway. This aircraft sounded like it meant business and when it got 'upstairs' it would prove it. The Voodoo brought the RCAF into the supersonic fighter interceptor era. A highly efficient operational unit that consisted of a pilot, AI Navigator, and an aircraft with a fire control system that commanded the nuclear-tipped rockets and heat-seeking missiles. All these items said, 'Intruder beware.'

How did it happen that the RCAF and the CAF ended up flying an American-manufactured fighter interceptor? Surely Canada could produce another fighter to follow the very successful Avro CF-100? Why were the later marks of CF-100s cancelled? The military had requirements for a supersonic fighter interceptor, but the politicians would decide how, where and when to spend the budgeted dollars. Unfortunately, in the early 1960s that would not be in Canada; the dollars flowed south to the USA.

Interceptors came in two types: point defence and area defence. In the era of limited radar range it was necessary for the interceptors to takeoff and climb as rapidly as possible to protect specific targets. As radar improved and the Cold War continued, it became apparent that the requirement had changed to an area defence fighter interceptor. This interceptor had better radar, missile carrying ability and greater operational range than the point-defence aircraft. North America was a very large territory to defend.

In 1953, it was realised that a straight-wing subsonic interceptor would become obsolete in the fairly near future due to the speed of the developing Soviet bombers. It would be 'touch and go' to intercept the faster Soviet Bear and Bison bombers. A design contract was awarded to Avro that year, but by October it was halted and maximum effort was put into fixing the problems with the CF-100. Finally, in March 1954, a requirement for two prototypes and one static model of the new CF-105 aircraft was signed and, despite some misgivings as to performance, a contract for forty aircraft was signed. The Orenda engine manufacturing company, in the meantime, had been developing the PS-13 Iroquois engine and proposed it for the CF-105, now named the Arrow.

The next development contract that was signed, in 1956, called for five CF-105 Mark Is with the Pratt & Whitney J-75 engine and three CF-105 Mark IIs with the Iroquois engine to be completed by the end of 1958 and the thirty-two remaining Mark IIs by 1961. The first Arrow was rolled out on 4 October 1957 and was test-flown by Janusz Zurakowski, of previous CF-100 test pilot and Farnborough Airshow fame, on 25 March 1958. It had been six years since the original government Air 7-3 specification had been published with the intention of using the Rolls-Royce RB-106 engine. The aircraft was now airborne, but without any fire control system or weapons.

Costs were escalating at an alarming rate, about 300 per cent of the original estimate, and due to the RCAF preference for the RCA Sparrow missile and Astra fire and flight control system, the expenses were going to continue increasing. The debate raged on: manned interceptor or missiles, which was the best? A missile is good for one target, hit or miss, while the manned interceptor is good for multiple targets and can be sent up again on multiple missions. Another aspect to consider is that the interceptor can perform identification functions to prevent shooting down friendly or civilian aircraft, while the missile cannot. Air Marshall Hugh Campbell, Chief of Air Staff, and Air Marshall C. Roy Slemon, Deputy Commander NORAD, were both of the opinion that a manned interceptor was the requirement for the foreseeable future. The other chiefs of the Army and Navy felt that the programme was consuming too many dollars and that the less expensive missile defence was the cheaper and better way to go.

Then the proverbial straw that broke the camel's back occurred: Avro asked for another $40 million. The Conservative cabinet voted immediately to cancel the contract, pay the fine and destroy the aircraft. Nobody was interested in the completed aircraft or the Orenda engine, which was quite remarkable despite their superior performance, and, possibly because of the chance of espionage, the aircraft and its plans were totally destroyed. Could Prime Minister Diefenbaker have prevented the cancellation? He did not and we will never know. He made the announcement on Black Friday, 20 February 1959, that the programme was cancelled. Was he correct in his decision? Numerous books have been written on the subject and after reading some of them you will have to decide because the experts, after fifty years of fierce debate, cannot.

In the end, a 'no decision' to the debate of missile versus manned interceptor won and a combination of missiles and manned interceptors was instituted. The McDonnell CF-101 Voodoo was offered at such advantageous terms by their US allies that Canada could not refuse the offer. It was combined with a purchase of Bomarc missiles as a defence package. This was certainly a win–win situation for the USA. The US aircraft production industry was spared from the Arrow competition and had secured for itself a contract for aircraft and missiles, hence the flow of the Canadian dollars south to the USA. An additional condition of the package was that Canada would assume responsibility for the Pinetree Line radar stations. What type of aircraft was the RCAF getting and would it meet defence requirements? How did it evolve and would it have the Sparrow missile that the RCAF originally planned for the Arrow?

The ink of the last signatures on the Second World War VJ Day Japanese surrender was barely dry when the US military's attention turned to the new perceived threat: the Soviet Union. There was a need for a penetration fighter to escort the bomber force on its missions; this force became Strategic Air Command in 1946. The McDonnell Aircraft Company of St Louis, Missouri, USA, won the competition with the proposed XP-88 aircraft, called the Voodoo. The name was not out of place as the company had previously called their straight-winged aircraft such names as the Banshee, Demon and Phantom.

Robert F. Dorr in his book, *McDonnell F-101 Voodoo*, mentions that

> on the 20 June 1946 McDonnell Aircraft Company got the go-ahead to build two XP-88 aircraft designated United States Army Air Force serial numbers 46-525/526. In September 1947 a major change occurred; the USAF was formed and split from the Army Air Force. The USAF aircraft requirements of long range and high performance were at odds with each other. The former required lots of fuel storage space and the latter called for thin wings and fuselage. The swept wing design of the Voodoo was attributed to an engineer called Edward M. (Bud) Flesh who had studied German research which indicated that a 35 degree sweep back would work very well for the Voodoo.

There are three ways of extending range: carrying fuel internally, carrying fuel externally using drop tanks, or having an in-flight refuelling capability.

In August 1948, the now designated XF-88, F for fighter rather than the P for prototype, rolled out to be flown by McDonnell Aircraft Company chief test pilot Robert M. Edholm. It was vastly underpowered and work began to increase engine thrust and add an afterburner. The afterburner was restricted in size because the engines were mounted underneath the fuselage. The afterburner had to be short to allow the aircraft to rotate during takeoff and land with a high body angle, that is, nose up high attitude. The afterburner developed was the first turbojet engine to use a multiple-element or iris nozzle, which became the industry standard.

By June 1949, the XF-88A had flown supersonically and, although many proposals for production were put forward, by December the two test aircraft were put in storage.

However, all was not lost. North Korea's political and military antics were becoming more alarming and influencing military purchases. Air Materiel Command wanted to have a fly-off competition to decide on a fighter aircraft – a disappointment for the McDonnell Aircraft Company, who anticipated they would automatically get the contract. A fly-off was held at Edwards AFB, California, from 29 June to 7 July 1950. The other two aircraft in the competition were the North American YF-93A and the Lockheed XF-90. The McDonnell Aircraft Company was very confident that the aircraft's ease of maintenance and flight performance would ensure they were awarded the contract.

The three fighters were put through their paces by a select group of pilots. Among them was a Major Charles E. Yeager, who was the first pilot to fly faster than the speed of sound on 14 October 1947. The Voodoo won the competition hands down. It was to no avail. The funds were diverted to North American F-86D Sabres, Northrop F-89D Scorpion and Lockheed F-94A Starfire interceptors already being produced and combat-ready to cope with the Soviet bomber threat. The Voodoo contract as a fighter was dead. F-86A Sabres were rushed over to Korea in November to fight the Mig-15. Dorr mentioned that, 'The first Voodoo was converted to a propeller test-bed, a prototype aircraft, to examine the aerodynamics of a propeller at high speeds. It did its last flight in January 1958. The two Voodoos remained at Langley AFB, Virginia for some years and then were scrapped.'

McDonnell employees were devastated by the loss of the Air Force fighter production order. Production did continue with the Banshee for the Navy, so at least McDonnell Aircraft Company remained solvent. Strategic Air Command still had ideas for the fighter escort and with that in mind McDonnell Aircraft Company started an in-house proposal for an aircraft powered by Pratt & Whitney J-57-P-13s. The new fighter, based on the XF-88, was designated F-101A and was rolled out on 20 August 1954. With a view to our Canadian story, it must be remembered that this was the single-seat fighter escort version, not the dual seat interceptor. It was second in the 'century series' of aircraft, the North American F-100 Super Sabre being the first, and the F-101A was the heaviest single-seat fighter ever built.

Robert C. Little took it airborne on 29 September 1954. During its first flight it was flown supersonic at Mach 1.07, a truly remarkable achievement which also showed Little's confidence in the aircraft. However, the aircraft, both as the single-seat and later the dual-seat model, was not without some problems. One of the more serious was the engine compressor stalling, sometimes with an accompanying bang – not a confidence builder. The boundary layer air control in the engine inlet duct was modified in order to resolve the issues with the engine compressor. The landing gear remained a problem for the life of the aircraft; the side brace actuator of the main landing gear had a dual function and it was susceptible to failure, especially on the original 'A' models. The actuator's purpose was to retract and extend the main landing gear as well as to act as a side brace. The nose gear also had problems due to the fact that it retracted forward, against the air loads. If the pilot did not select the landing gear up quickly enough after takeoff, the air pressure would overcome the hydraulic actuator and the nose gear would fail to retract – this was known as a 'hang up'. The Voodoo was known to accelerate extremely fast when taking off, especially during the cold northern Canadian winters, and it was possible to 'hang up' the nose gear very easily.

The author remembers that in wintertime it was not unusual, among the 'hot dog' pilots, to see the main gear still on the runway with the nose gear retracting during the rapid acceleration of the takeoff. This meant that the pilot had selected 'gear up' with the main wheels still on the runway and the nose in the air. A very dangerous manoeuvre, but indicative of the fighter interceptor pilot pushing the boundaries. 'I wasn't going to be the guy that bought the beer that day because I had 'hung' the nose gear,' commented a 416 Squadron Voodoo pilot who wished to remain nameless!

Another unique problem was the tendency for the aircraft to pitch-up uncontrollably at high angles of attack. This pitch-up tendency was caused by air from the wings, at extreme angles of attack, disrupting the airflow over the horizontal stabiliser on the tail causing it to lose lift and to pitch the nose upwards. The eventual solution, after lengthy flight testing, was to install a redundant limiter system, an active inhibitor, which sounded an alarm and stopped the control column from moving further back to prevent the pilot pitching up the aircraft. These problems suggested that perhaps the Voodoo was not suited to the 'yank and bank' flying of fighter combat and would be better suited to a reconnaissance and intercept role.

George McAffer emphasised that, 'the Voodoo was not hard to fly but to fly it well was not that easy. The difference was in the feel. The Alpha gauge had two needles. The first needle was the safety factor and the second needle was where you were at. You could fly the needles close together by feel; the nose became light as they (the needles) came together.'

The author remembers one particular graphic illustration of the pitch-up phenomenon with 409 Squadron at CFB Comox, British Columbia. The squadron had chosen a team to send to the inter-squadron competition to determine who would represent Canada in the William Tell Meet in

Florida. The target squadron was providing electronic warfare training to further hone the skills of the team and evaluate the serviceability of the team fighter interceptors.

The target aircraft, flown by the author at 33,000 feet, was being routinely and electronically shot down on each successive pass. The author decided to put a red herring into the scenario on the last fighter pass late in the afternoon. Known only to the target force monitor (the fighter was unaware of the change), the target aircraft climbed to 43,000 feet. This was 10,000 feet higher than all the previous passes of the afternoon. This is where complacency and pride may have come into the equation: complacency in the attacking Voodoo fighter to not notice the sudden increase in altitude and pride to push the flight boundaries to hang on to the target lock-on and not get a Missed Intercept. The author watched the approaching fighter contrail as it rapidly climbed to make up the altitude difference and saw the change in vapour trail pattern as the afterburners were selected to maintain momentum of the climb. Everything looked good for the launch of the simulated rocket. Then, probably due to decreasing airspeed and control inputs to maintain radar lock-on, the fighter appeared to change direction suddenly and the nose pointed straight up – it had pitched up. Very quickly, it was falling away with the landing drag chute streaming behind it, a standard pitch-up recovery technique, and passed beneath the target wing and out of sight.

Was it a Mission Accomplished or Missed Intercept? The intercept is consigned to memory and history, but the fighter interceptor crew will never forget the experience. A wild ride for a few short minutes followed by some paperwork back at the squadron operations. No doubt a chat with the Flight Safety Officer would follow. It was also a few anxious moments for the author as a witness to a potentially disastrous situation. We, after all, were on the same side as we trained to maintain top proficiency to Deter, Detect and Defend.

A similar aerodynamic situation to the pitch-up phenomenon of the Voodoo was called roll coupling, which could also have disastrous results. This coupling was inherent in the design of high-performance swept-wing aircraft such as the Voodoo. A high roll rate of up to '360 degrees per second', according to Voodoo pilot Captain H. R. (Rick) Hovey, can produce 'highly undesirable yawing or pitching moments leading to overstressing of the aircraft' or the aforementioned pitch-up. It also occurs in a slow roll rate, such as in a snap-up attack recovery, where the unloading and subsequent roll, positioning the aircraft inverted to pull the nose below the horizon, produces yaw. The snap-up attack is where the fighter is level at a high speed and uses its momentum to 'snap-up', climb steeply, to aim at a target at a much greater altitude. The pitch-up and roll

-coupling phenomena remained the Voodoo's nemesis and its crews were very aware of the aircraft's bite.

A further problem for the Voodoo was the connection between the horizontal stabiliser and the trim system – either the pilot manually trimming or the autopilot trimming the aircraft. A weakness in the system, due to metal fatigue, was a constant concern. The stresses of flying the world's heaviest fighter took its toll on the engineering mechanisms of the 1950s. In spite of these problems, the Voodoo's real worth was as an excellent handling supersonic aircraft that finally, in July 1957, found a role as a nuclear strike aircraft with the 27th Fighter Bomber Wing, which subsequently was designated as a Tactical Fighter Wing.

Dorr stated that, 'On 12 December 1957, at Edwards AFB, California, the Voodoo set the world speed record at 1,943.43 km/h (1,208 mph).' The Voodoo was remarkably adaptable to many roles and saw duty as an atomic bomb research aircraft in the South Pacific and was deployed to England for eight years to serve in its nuclear strike role with assigned targets deep within the Soviet Union. This version of the Voodoo had 20-mm cannons mounted in the nose as armament. The photo reconnaissance version served in Korea, Thailand, South Vietnam, France, and Germany. It also flew more than eighty missions over Cuba during the Cuban Missile Crisis to verify Soviet missile site construction. In the late 1950s and early 1960s, some of the most experienced USAF pilots were found to be flying the Voodoo in the single-seat versions in either nuclear strike or photo reconnaissance roles.

This is a brief background to the fighter interceptor which would bridge the gap between the Avro CF-100 and the McDonnell Douglas CF-188. What happened to turn the single-seat F-101 A and C models into the B model, which was the backbone of the Canadian NORAD contribution? The range and speed of the first test flights in 1954, along with the growing Soviet bomber threat, contributed to the decision in 1955 to simultaneously build the heavier fighter interceptor version. The thinking was to intercept and destroy the Soviet bombers as far away as possible from North American cities. This would require an aircraft with range, speed and the ability to destroy the enemy; the Voodoo had found its niche. On 27 March 1957, the first B model became airborne, and the two-seat version was about to prove its worth.

It looked different from the single-seat model. An unmistakable difference was the two-place plexiglass canopy, which drew attention to the stretched fuselage that accommodated the extra crew member, and the new Hughes MG-11 weapon fire control system. It was also heavier and thus required modification to the landing gear and larger tyres that necessitated bulges in the landing gear doors. It had the capability of carrying two

Falcon heat-seeking missiles and two nuclear-tipped Genie rockets on a rotateable armament door. The four nose cannons were removed.

Canada was in a military bind: the Arrow cancelled, the CF-100 obsolete, and the defence network vulnerable as the Soviets continued to build its bomber and missile force. The solution, as previously mentioned, was the fighter interceptor and missile combination. The year 1961 saw major defensive acquisitions for the RCAF; under Operation Queens Row they purchased sixty-six F-101 Voodoos, fifty-six F-101Bs and ten dual-control F-101Bs from the 1959 production year. The RCAF serial numbers ran from 17391 to 17483 and agreed with the last three numbers of the USAF serial number. Canada designated single-control aircraft the CF-101B and the dual-control trainer aircraft the CF-101F. Simultaneously, Canada purchased the surface-to-air Bomarc missile, which will be discussed later in the chapter.

The Voodoos were an American-produced aircraft and, except for initial acceptance and major overhaul and repair work at Bristol Aerospace Ltd in Winnipeg, they did very little for the Canadian aircraft production industry. The first two aircraft were delivered by RCAF Flight Lieutenants Dobbin and Cromie and a symbolic USAF crew amid great fanfare at RCAF Station Uplands (Ottawa), Ontario, on 24 July 1961. The standard aircraft came with a retractable in-flight refuelling probe, which was never used operationally in Canada. It was displayed irreverently on more than one occasion; it resembled a large phallus protruding from the upper nose of the aircraft.

The first Voodoo ground school was held at Otis AFB, Massachusetts, on 31 July 1961 to prepare the Canadian instructors, nine pilots and eight Navigators, under Wing Commander R. D. Schultz, for the Operational Training Unit. Subsequently, the flying portion of the course was held at Hamilton AFB in California. The instructors then proceeded to RCAF Station Namao, Edmonton, Alberta, to reactivate 425 Squadron. In October 1961, crew training began for the operational squadrons. By July 1962, all the crews were trained and Canada had five operational Voodoo squadrons. The last CF-100 squadron in Canada stood down in January 1962 and handed the mantle of defence to the Voodoo – the supersonic era had arrived.

Air Defence Command shrunk in number with the arrival of the Voodoo; there had been nine CF-100 squadrons and now there were five Voodoo squadrons. These squadrons were 409, located at RCAF Station Comox, British Columbia; 410, located at RCAF Uplands (Ottawa), Ontario; 414, located at RCAF Station North Bay, Ontario; 416, located, initially, at RCAF Station Bagotville, Quebec, before moving to RCAF Station Chatham, New Brunswick; and 425, located at RCAF Station Bagotville,

Quebec. In 1964, 410 and 414 Squadrons were disbanded, leaving three operational fighter squadrons.

Nine years after the delivery of the first Voodoos to Canada, the USA was embroiled in the Vietnam War. In 1971, the American forces needed the Canadian Voodoos with their refuelling probes to enable them to penetrate into northern Vietnam. A trade was arranged for sixty-six older, but low-flying time, aircraft that had been in storage at Davis Montham AFB, Arizona. The last Voodoo ever built in March 1961, RCAF serial number 17483, was returned to the USA as part of the batch. A total of 807 aircraft were built.

The replacement Voodoos were delivered to CAF as part of Operation Peace Wings which lasted from 2 July 1970 until 10 January 1972. Bristol Aerospace Ltd in Winnipeg undertook the modification process to engines, ejection seats and communication equipment. Then the aircraft were returned to the USA for installation of the Hughes MG-13 fire control system and MB-5 autopilot. The new batch of Voodoos did not have a refuelling probe and could be readily identified by a heat source dome – an infra red sensor on the nose just forward of the canopy. This dome supplied information to the Falcon's heat-seeking missiles. The CAF serial numbers ran from 101001 to 101067, and had no relationship to the USAF serial numbers. They were referred to as the 'double I P' birds – Improved Intercept Performance.

Robert (Bob) D. Moore ran the test flight hangar for Bristol. He had extensive experience with MacDonald Brothers, Standard Aero Engine, and finally Bristol. The Korean War saw him retrieve aircraft out of storage and return them to operational status. He was also involved in maintaining the North American B-25 Mitchell for operational radar intercept training. Moore transitioned to the jet age by being involved in the modification of the Avro CF-100 Mark 3 to a dual-place trainer.

It was no surprise, then, that Bristol assigned Bob Moore to the test flight division for the McDonnell CF-101 Voodoo. He took classroom training from USAF instructors in Ottawa and then went to Hill AFB, Utah, to complete the practical training of engine run-ups, trimming procedures and structural repairs. He recounted that 'management did not realise the size of it [the CF-101 Voodoo]. When the first aircraft arrived they could not believe it, they walked around it with mouths open, totally overwhelmed.'

A new system of management was developed, using IBM punch cards to keep track of the overhaul procedures. The approach was so new that one of the managers asked, 'How do you know that the aircraft is ready to fly?'

'All the cards are back,' replied Bob.

'Alright, carry on!'

CF-101 Voodoo Infrared Sensor. (Courtesy of Author)

Management were very reluctant to install an expensive engine run-up area, not understanding the need. Moore had run-up experience at Hill AFB and decided the best way to get one installed was to demonstrate the procedure and let the managers come to the logical conclusion. He borrowed two Caterpillar D-14 tractors from the Ministry of Transport. He attached the engine run-up harness to the landing gear and anchored the harness, by using wire cables, to the two tractors. Moore assembled about 100 management and airport personnel in a horseshoe shape around the aircraft. Then, with Eddie Poirier in the cockpit, they started the engines. Advancing the thrust lever they brought one engine up to full power, engaged the afterburner and brought it back to idle. They did the same procedure with the second engine. By now, the assembled spectators had firmly placed their hands over their ears. Then, finally, they brought both engines up to full military power and engaged the afterburners.

Bob remembered that the 'the cable was whipping like a bloody banjo string, the dust was flying and it was tearing up the turf. Just a real uproar,' he laughed, and said, 'the crowd had had enough. They scattered in all directions. It scared the hell out of everyone.' Then, to finish off the demonstration, the two Pratt & Whitney J-57 engines 'pooped out' raw fuel on to the tarmac when they were shut down, a design feature. Management were convinced and the concrete engine run-up area was subsequently built in the north-west corner of the Winnipeg airport, where it still can be seen in 2011.

In the 1970s, Bob Moore was a founding member of the Western Canada Aviation Museum at Winnipeg Airport. At the time of writing, he is the Chief of Restoration for the museum. He does admit to having a soft spot for the Avro CF-100 and McDonnell CF-101 in the collection.

Canada ended up flying three versions of the Voodoo: the B, the F and one EF-101 model. Voodoo production had ended on 24 March 1961 and the first batch of Canadian Voodoos was among the last aircraft off the line. The one EF-101 aircraft was leased from the USAF in 1983 and used as a high-speed Electronic Countermeasures aggressor target by 414 Electronic Warfare Squadron. It was painted sinister black with low visibility national markings and was known as the 'Electric Voodoo'. It displayed the CAF serial number 101067. It originally had the USAF serial number 58-300.

In the RCAF livery, each squadron had their colours painted on the rudder: 409 Squadron – blue and yellow; 410 Squadron – red and white; 414 Squadron – black and red; 416 Squadron – black and yellow; 425 Squadron – black and silver. The tail flag was subsequently changed from the red ensign to the maple leaf. The CAF livery eventually changed the bilingual Canadian Armed Forces to Canada on the side of the fuselage.

CF-101 Voodoo Afterburners. (Courtesy of Canadian Forces Joint Imagery Centre, Department of National Defence)

101067 arriving in Canada, USAF paint scheme. (Courtesy of DND, Directorate of History and Heritage)

For the 60th anniversary of the Air Force, each squadron painted one squadron Voodoo aircraft uniquely: 425 had Lark One, 409 had Hawk One and 416 had Lynx One, with the appropriate stylised animal.

The Voodoo was a great attraction at air shows. The sheer size of the fighter and the sound of the twin afterburners were a sight and sound that few could ignore. Always a crowd pleaser, it was always in demand, whether as a single aircraft display or, more often than not, as part of a formation.

The most dramatic display ever flown by the Voodoo was during Canada's centennial celebrations in 1967. A Voodoo flown by F/L Jake Miller and AI Navigator F/L Rod McGimpsey, and a Starfighter flown by F/L Rene Serrao, performed an inverted formation pass. It was a spectacular sight at the Abbotsford Airshow on 13 August 1967, never to be forgotten and shortly after dropped from the routine because it proved to be 'a bit too close for comfort and long life' according to Serrao in Daniel Dempsey's book, *A Tradition of Excellence*.

In 1973, it was 425 Alouette Squadron's turn to have the display team at the Canadian National Exhibition Airshow in Toronto, Ontario. The team was called The Larks, an English translation of the squadron name. A five-plane Voodoo formation team was formed under the leadership of Major Gene Lukan. Gene, coincidentally, is the Voodoo pilot featured in our exercise on 10 May 1973 in Chapter Nine.

The William Tell Meet of air-to-air rocketry competition was a separate meet to the annual USAF Fighter Gunnery and Weapons Meet held at Las Vegas AFB in June 1954. William Tell took place at Yuma, Arizona, and

Voodoo and Starfighter, Abbotsford Airshow, 1967. (Courtesy of Gerald Vernon)

Voodoo and Starfighter inverted formation. (Courtesy of Gerald Vernon)

Major Eugene Lukan leading 425 Squadron Larks, 1973 Display Team. (Courtesy of Canadian Forces Joint Imagery Centre, Department of National Defence)

Air Defense Command and Air Tactical Command were the two USAF Commands involved. The separate meet was renamed 'William Tell' during the last meet held at Yuma in 1956. This meet had nine teams representing seven major USAF air commands.

In 1958, the William Tell Meet moved to Tyndall AFB, Florida, which became the home to the USAF Worldwide Air-to-Air Weapons Meet. The Q-2A radio controlled drone target and PARAMI electronic scoring system was introduced. Twelve teams competed that year, including an Air National Guard team and, for the first time, the aircraft were divided into categories. The three types of aircraft involved were the USAF F-102 Delta Dagger, F-106 Delta Dart and the F-101 Voodoo.

In 1965, seven years later, Canada was invited to attend the William Tell Weapons Meet with their CF-101 Voodoos. This meet was the largest in history, with sixteen teams and four categories. The Canadian team, comprised of 425 Squadron aircrew, did not win any awards that year, but came away with an appreciation of what would be required the next time! The next time would be in 1970, as the Vietnam War led to the cancellation of the competition for five years.

It is interesting to note that during the 1970s, Voodoo squadrons either won the coveted Top Gun award or the Top Unit award. The Voodoo had finally attained its proper status as the number one fighter interceptor.

The 1972 Meet introduced the subsonic BQM-34A Firebee drone and was the first year of an overall, instead of individual aircraft type, 'Top Gun' award. This particular meet was a special one for Canada and it is extensively covered in Chapter Six.

The Voodoo, 101063, that won the Top Gun competition in 1972, piloted by Captain Lowell Butters, later Major, and Captain Doug Danko, is sitting forlornly outside behind a fence at the Shearwater Aviation Museum, Halifax, Nova Scotia. It is actually owned by the Canadian Museum of Flight, Langley, British Columbia. The aircraft was earmarked for battle damage maintenance training but instead was sold through Crown Assets to the Museum. That is lucky for Canadians. The museum had hoped to move the aircraft to Langley and preserve it as a piece of Canadian Aviation history, the first Canadian Top Gun aircraft.

The debate continued whether the single-crew, fully-automated F-106 was more effective than the multi-crew F-101. Maybe, if the Hughes MA-1 integrated fire control system was working well, the automated F-106 had the edge. But if it was not, the pilot would have needed to further increase his multi-tasking and may have become overloaded, which would have led to Missed Intercepts. Perhaps the proof lies in the fact that at the William Tell Meets from 1970 to 1980, the 'Top Gun' award was won by the multi-crew American F-101 and Canadian CF-101 five times and the single-crew American F-102 once – no mention of the F-106. Canada had a formidable fighter interceptor in the hands of a well-trained pilot and AI Navigator.

What was the CF-101 Voodoo like to fly? It certainly had the speed, but to maintain a high speed it consumed fuel at a prodigious rate, especially at lower altitudes. Given the geography of Canada and the location of the fighter bases, would it be able to do its job effectively? It certainly was an impressive aircraft to look at. It was a very large, two-place, swept-wing jet aircraft sitting atop two predominant afterburner nozzles. It did not have the 'mean' appearance of its brother, the McDonnell Phantom, with its anhedral, downward-facing tailplane, but instead exuded a commanding purposefulness. It could be compared to the racing cars of the 1930s: big, fast and noisy.

The Lockheed CF-104 Starfighter had the reputation, by virtue of its cigar-shaped fuselage, stubby-thin wings and needle-nose appearance, of being the 'missile with a man in it'. However, as stated by author Robert McIntyre in his book, *CF-101 Voodoo*, 'On one cold day, (-18°c), a CF-101 reached 35,000 km from brake release in 92 seconds, 11.2 km from base. Even the CF-104 cannot do that!' The amount of fuel consumed for that full afterburner climb would restrict the range too much, so climb profiles were established. These were a compromise between performance and operational range considerations.

A VOODOO FLIGHT

The pre-flight preparations began with the pilot signing the maintenance record to accept the aircraft. The last inspection date and accumulated time record were annotated by qualified ground personnel. The status of the aircraft was fully documented and included any systems repair, serviceability statement, and quantities of fuel, oil, and hydraulic fluid onboard. It was recorded whether there are external fuel tanks as well as the type and quantity of weapons loaded. The crew then leisurely proceeded to the aircraft and installed their personal parachute in their ejection seat and placed their oxygen mask and helmet, irreverently called a 'bone dome', in an accessible place.

The first priority was to make the cockpit safe. In order to do so, the crew must check that the ejection seat pins are installed, the landing gear handle is down (prior to system hydraulic pressure) and that the armament switches are in the safe position. A walk around is then completed to check that all applicable safety pins are installed and that there is no visible aircraft damage or fluid leaks. The crew now entered the cockpit and strapped into their parachutes, and secured themselves to the ejection seats using the five point harness. The ejection seat escape envelope was very limited: a minimum of 100 feet altitude, 70 knots airspeed and no

CF-101 Voodoo on ramp. (Courtesy of Canadian Forces Joint Imagery Centre, Department of National Defence)

sink rate was required for a successful ejection. The survival gear container was hooked to the parachute. Oxygen masks – normal and emergency supply – were hooked up. The masks were required as the cockpit altitude could reach 20,000 feet, which requires supplemental oxygen. The helmet chord is plugged in to allow the oxygen mask microphone and headset for communication. A complicated series of belts, straps and hoses, which must be done in the correct sequence to ensure correct functioning in an emergency of the ejection seat and personal parachute, were the next series of tasks to be undertaken. The alert or exercise crews would have done all these checks previously to allow them to run out to their aircraft, jump in and get airborne within five minutes.

Both crew members then scanned their cockpits and prepared the aircraft for starting the engines. External electrical power and air – pneumatic pressure – is connected to the aircraft in preparation for the engine start. All switches were positioned, pointers set, circuit breakers checked, systems tested and armament confirmed secure. The aircraft is now ready for engine start. An unusual feature of the Voodoo is that it has no parking brake. It had to be chocked and wedge-shaped wheel restraints placed on the ground to prevent the wheel rolling prior to engine start. The explanation given was that 'the wheels absorb so much energy during the landing and the subsequent braking that they become extremely hot. To set a parking brake would weld the brake discs to the wheel.'

To give you some indication of the power of the Pratt & Whitney J-57 engine, the Aircraft Operating Instructions have the following warning: 'Suction at the intake duct is sufficient to kill or severely injure personnel drawn into or pulled suddenly against the duct.' Engines were started by rotating them with the external air and introducing fuel. Normally started individually, they could be started together if 'tactical requirements dictate it'. Two problems to be watched for during the start sequence were the hung start – low RPM – or a hot start – high exhaust gas temperature.

In coordination with the ground crew, the landing gear ground locks and pins were removed, the flaps were extended, the speed brakes closed respectively, the Redundant Limiter System was tested and the ejection seat pins were removed and stowed. The pilot had to remember to have their feet on the brakes prior to removal of the chocks, as there was no parking brake! The nose-wheel steering was engaged and the pilot taxied the aircraft to the runway for departure. The Aircraft Operating Instructions cautioned to 'not exceed 25 knots [46 km/h] while taxiing to prevent excessive tire wear and brake heat'. It also stated to avoid speeds where the aircraft develops 'excessive airframe shimmy'.

The aircrew completed twenty-six items on the pre-takeoff check during the taxi out to the runway. Each check was completed by a Verbal

Challenge and Response Checklist. It started with 'Fuel Switches' and ended with 'Flight Controls – Free and Proper Movement'. The takeoff clearance was obtained and the aircraft was taxied to the runway centreline for departure. The Pre-Takeoff Checklist was completed with the check 'Pitot Heat – On'. The pitot is a tube that uses air pressure to indicate airspeed. Heat is supplied electrically to prevent it from icing up when flying through cloud or in moist conditions.

A normal takeoff required the use of afterburners if the temperature was warmer than 18°C. Military thrust – no afterburner – was used for colder temperatures. Acceleration is rapid during either type of takeoff! The takeoff sequence began with the application of brakes and the throttles brought up to 80 per cent RPM, the maximum with the brakes on. The engine instruments and warning lights were checked. The brakes were released and the throttles pushed forward to the full military power position. The engine pressure ratio gauges were checked to confirm power setting and, if correct, the throttles were moved outboard to the afterburner position.

The nose-wheel steering was used to maintain directional control until 70 knots, when the rudder began to become effective. The rudder played an important role at slow speeds as the afterburners may not 'light off' simultaneously, which caused a yaw or swing. The thrust from the engine

CF-101 Voodoo takeoff roll. (Courtesy of Canadian Forces Joint Imagery Centre, Department of National Defence)

increases instantaneously from 10,200 lbs to 16,000 lbs of thrust, a 64 per cent increase. It was like getting a kick in the pants! The aircraft rapidly accelerates and at 155 knots the nose is raised to a five degree attitude, and at 175 knots it will lift off the runway. The aircraft has a fuel drain located beneath the rudder that vented excess fuel. During an afterburner takeoff, any excess fuel was vented and ignited and produced a torching effect; a dramatic visual sight, especially at night.

The landing gear had to be selected up immediately due to the rapid acceleration. As mentioned previously, it was very easy to 'hang' the nose gear against the air loads. Following the gear selection, the flaps were immediately selected up at 200 knots. The landing gear and flaps had to be fully retracted by 250 knots, otherwise extensive damage could occur. At 250 knots the pilot terminated use of the afterburner. At 5,000 feet the Redundant Limiter System was turned on, flaps were confirmed up and the correct fuel-feed sequence was confirmed. There were two climb profiles used by the Voodoo, depending if the requirement was for time to altitude or range.

The military thrust range climb was to accelerate to 350 knots and then raise the nose to ten degrees above the horizon to give a climb speed of 370 knots. When this speed intercepted Mach 0.80, at approximately 20,000 feet, the pilot maintained Mach 0.80 until level off. The maximum thrust, minimum time to altitude, afterburner climb is to accelerate to 350 knots and then raise the nose to 25 degrees above the horizon. Then maintain 400 knots by adjusting the pitch to a maximum of 30 degrees. When this speed intercepts Mach 0.85, at approximately 22,000 feet, maintain Mach 0.85 until level-off.

Level-off had to be anticipated. The military thrust climb required a smooth push over 1,000 feet below the desired altitude and the maximum thrust climb required a whopping 3,000 feet below to not overshoot the level-off altitude. Prior to any intercept or anticipated high-G manoeuvres, a Manual Control Limiting and Automatic Command Limiting check had to be performed to check that the aircraft operating limits were displayed correctly. This is done using the Redundant Limiting System and Pitch Boundary Indicator. A successful check constitutes a light to moderate buffet at 'limiting', while the Pitch Boundary Indicator indicated the limiting boundary +/- ¼ units on the gauge. During manoeuvring, such as during an intercept, it was important to monitor correct fuel feed sequence and oxygen supply. Both items, if not attended to, could have had disastrous results, from engine flame out to crew incapacitation, due to insufficient fuel and oxygen respectively.

That was a very orderly and unrushed departure. Can you imagine being fast asleep in the Quick Reaction Hangar and being woken by the scramble horn at 3:30 in the morning, running across the hangar to your aircraft, strapping in, starting the engines and taxiing out to be airborne in five minutes? It is during a winter snowstorm and as you hurtle down the runway and into the air, you have no idea where you are going. Checking in with the NORAD Fighter Controller, they give you a direction to fly and an altitude. Many things are going through your mind as you speed towards the unknown target. First of all is the intercept. Is this the real thing? What are we up against? Will we have to fire our weapons? Is there more than one target? Where are we going to land? What is happening to the weather and do we have enough fuel to complete the intercept? Meanwhile, your heart rate is finally settling down as you 'catch up' with the aircraft and the familiarity of your surroundings has a calming effect. Ten minutes ago, you were in bed and now you are flying supersonically at 35,000 feet towards an unknown situation – exciting, daunting, or what? It turns out to be an airliner off course, which is subsequently identified by the Identification Section down 'the Hole' in North Bay before you get to the target. It is time to return home and resume your Alert status.

To prepare the aircraft for descent, it was necessary to turn on defrost to prevent the windshield from misting up. A fuel check confirmed correct feeding and amount to calculate approach speed. Pre-Descent and Descent Checklists were completed by challenge and response. The descent profile is 300 knots, 80 per cent throttle and speed brakes out. Levelling off, the speed brakes were closed and the speed was set at 250 knots. The landing gear was selected down 10 miles (16 km) back from the airport, flaps selected down, speed brakes opened to give better engine control, and the speed reduced to calculated approach speed. This was 175 knots with 3,000 lbs of fuel, adjusted if necessary for gusty conditions. The AI Navigator had a peek-a-boo view of the runway around the pilot's ejection seat and shoulders during final approach.

Airspeed decayed rapidly with the nose-high attitude of the Voodoo so power was kept on until the flare, levelling off descent, began over the runway surface. The throttles were eased back slowly as the aircraft flared. A firm touchdown occurred about 10 knots less than approach speed. The drag chute was deployed as soon as the aircraft was on the runway and the throttles were at idle. The aircraft nose was raised for maximum aerodynamic breaking. A maximum of 10 degrees was used to avoiding scraping the engine tail pipes on the runway. At 120 knots the nose wheel was lowered to the runway and wheel brakes were used as required.

The drag chute was dropped during the taxi in, preferably off the taxiway for following aircraft. Normal procedure was to shut down the left engine first, which allowed checking of the right engine hydraulic system. It was permissible to taxi in with one engine shut down. The rotary armament door was driven hydraulically, so it was necessary to rotate the door prior to shutting down the second engine.

The author was privileged to fly on a supersonic target mission with Captain Mike Spooner of 409 Squadron, CFB Comox, British Columbia. The date was 27 June 1974 and it was in a CF-101F, a dual-control model, number 101007. The mission was in the military area north of Port Hardy, Vancouver Island, which allowed us to create the sonic boom in the wilderness, although I am sure some animals were not impressed by our noisy progress. I remember how quiet it got when you went supersonic and how the barometric gauges corrected their error as we passed through the transonic speed range to supersonic flight. The subsequent recovery above coastal Vancouver Island waters was spectacular. Unfortunately, 101007 crashed ten years later at CFB Comox on 22 June 1984. Both crew members ejected and, considering that they were flying over the sea, landed on Texada Island – their lucky day!

The Voodoo served Canada well for over twenty years. The exemplary CAF maintenance organisation and the 'above and beyond the call of duty' attitude of the line maintenance personnel kept the ageing aircraft serviceable to meet their NORAD commitment; not an easy task considering the vagaries of the Canadian climate. However, there was one

(Pre-IIP) CF-101 Voodoo aerodynamic braking landing. (Courtesy of Canadian Forces Joint Imagery Centre, Department of National Defence)

major problem that arose, with very serious consequences, that was not unique to Canada; it affected the Pratt & Whitney J-57 engine.

Lt L. (Larry) A. Lundquist, later Major, was on his first posting in the CAF and assigned to CFB Chatham, the home of 416 Lynx Squadron which flew the CF-101 Voodoo. Initially, he was the Mechanical Support Officer, responsible for safety systems, which included ejection seats, oxygen equipment, personal safety equipment and the landing drag chutes. In 1971, he became the Aircraft Repair Officer for the Voodoo and was responsible for second line maintenance.

Maintenance on the Voodoo was designated in three lines. The first line was the day-to-day operations and snag recovery. Snag recovery was the repairing of failed systems or broken parts. The second line was a yearly maintenance cycle that took five days for a minor check and twelve days for a major check. The aircraft flew about 300 hours per year and were checked for cracks, corrosion and all systems working correctly. The third line was performed at the contractor level, Bristol in the 1970s, and occurred every five to six years.

Larry did manage to get two supersonic test flights as an observer. On one of the flights, the pilot was Captain David Wilson in aircraft number 17467. Larry had been planning for months to get on the test flight and had hoped that it would be a dual model to get to actually fly the aircraf; unfortunately, 467 was not. The day came and that morning he went flying in the rear AI Navigator's seat. However, the flight coincided with a visit to the base of the Minister of National Defence, the Rt. Hon. Donald Macdonald, who had scheduled a walk through the hangars. Larry recounted 'that I stumbled through the hangar door as the Minister was walking by. I still had the oxygen mask marks on my face and my mind was still at 35,000 feet. He asked me a question and I did not have a clue how to respond. Luckily an old wizened Commissioned from the Ranks officer saw my predicament and answered the question.'

Larry mentioned that he was involved in three major maintenance projects with the Voodoo. They were Operation Peace Wings, the third-stage blade crisis while at CFB Chatham and the Pacer Rake project while he was at National Defence Headquarters in Ottawa, Ontario. The Operation Peace Wings aircraft exchange, 1970–72, was, according to Larry, 'Actually quite complicated. Each country kept its own engines – they were very big, expensive and storeable. It took four hours to take out and replace an engine.' Canadian engines had to be kept at the Ling-Temco-Vought plant at Greenville, South Carolina, USA, for the exchange process.

Towards the end of the aircraft exchange a further complication arose. The Pratt & Whitney J-57 engine had a third-stage compressor blade problem. The compressor blade was failing and destroying the engine when it disintegrated. The engine had been developed many years before and been installed in many aircraft, such as the Boeing B-52 Stratofortress and the early model Lockheed U-2, and by now had experienced a longer service life than initially envisaged. It is believed that two CAF aircraft losses occurred due to uncontained disintegration of the third-stage compressor. In the subsequent accident investigation of engine records, it was discovered that 80 per cent of Canadian engines had a high risk of the same problem.

The entire Voodoo fleet was immediately grounded in March 1971. This was a serious operational issue and affected the Canadian NORAD status. An exception was made to allow those aircraft on Alert status to fly only on an actual intercept mission of an unknown target. All training and practise ceased. Larry confirmed that 'this was a huge job to process all the engines. It took a year. A special speed line was set up to separate the cold, compressor section. Special tools and equipment were needed to remove the compressor which was then sent to Pratt & Whitney for overhaul.' In time the Voodoo fleet recovered and got back to full strength.

The afterburner, reheat as they call it in Great Britain, was different from other aircraft of the period. Larry remembered it as 'awesome! It was a hard light afterburner that had a distinctive explosion. Never totally together, there was always a random two "KABOOMS". Every pane of glass in the hangar and barracks rattled. The [afterburner] nozzle had two positions: fully closed or fully open. There was in fact a small amount of modulation available at the open position'. Larry then went on to explain the technique of igniting the afterburner fuel.

'Everything had to be timed perfectly. A special fuel cylinder would squirt extra fuel into one of the regular burner cans. This would cause over-fuelling and the flame would burn right through the engine (past the turbine blades). Meantime, a fuel pump was pouring fuel into the burner can area, making a giant fuel rich mixture. When the flame hit this mixture it would explode, KABOOM!' Spectacular by day, the resulting cone of flame and roar from both engines was totally awesome at night. This was one aircraft that looked and sounded like it meant business.

In 1972, it was recognised that the Pratt & Whitney J-57 engine was now becoming obsolete and so would require some modification to extend its life. Larry remarked 'that there were lots of [P&W J-57] engines in service and that there were big issues to be addressed or there could be more third stage blade crises'. By this time Larry had been transferred to National Defence Headquarters in Ottawa, Ontario, and was responsible for determining maintenance programmes for the Pratt & Whitney J-57, the Voodoo, the Pratt & Whitney J-75, and the Starfighter engines.

The Pacer Rake Project established twenty-two modifications, some mandatory, some on an 'on condition basis', to be performed on various parts of the engine by the contractor Pratt & Whitney, the third line maintenance level. It resulted in a multi-million dollar contract that was completed on about 160 engines. This ensured the long-term reliability and safety of the engine. It has been inferred that the J-75, in the more critical single-engine aircraft, had received more attention for reliability prior to the Pacer Rake Project than the J-57 in a multi engine aircraft.

The Voodoo aircraft throughout its service life was a weapons platform, whether the weapon was cannon, rocket or missile. The Canadian aircraft, the first batch Queen's Row and the second batch Peace Wings, were equipped with the Falcon heat-seeking missile and the Genie rocket. The two Genie rockets were carried internally and the two Falcon missiles were carried externally on the weapons bay rotary armament door. The Genie rocket was politically and socially controversial in Canada during the early 1960s because it had a nuclear warhead capability.

Initially, the Voodoo squadrons and supporting RCAF bases had difficulty passing the Initial Capability and Nuclear Safety Inspection due to the unfamiliarity of the new weapon and what exacting storage, handling area and procedures it required. From 1962 the Voodoo had only the Falcon missile as its primary, and only, armament. In spring 1965 all three fighter bases, RCAF Stations Chatham, Comox and Bagotville, passed their inspections. The Genie W25 warheads were delivered in May 1965 and the squadrons became operational in the summer of the same year.

The two air-to-air weapons, the Genie rocket and Falcon missile, had the ability to destroy the attacking enemy bomber aircraft. Their methods, however, were different. The Genie rocket used a target-proximity nuclear explosion and the Falcon heat-seeking missile used the exhaust heat of the target aircraft to guide the missile to an explosive collision. Together they formed a redundant weapon package. They were both radar-guided using the Hughes fire control system; in the unlikely event of the Voodoo fighter interceptor radar failure, the Falcon could use the independent infrared search and track system. This system is sometimes referred to as the infrared sighting and tracking system.

In the event that the target was above the service ceiling, of the CF-101 Voodoo, 54,000 feet, a method of delivering the Genie rocket was devised. It was called the 'Snap-Up Tactic' and overcame the deficiency of the Voodoo to reach the target's altitude. It was achieved by accelerating at a level altitude and then pointing the nose of the Voodoo upwards using inertia at a very sharp angle while the computer calculated the launch point of the rocket. Once released, the Genie rocket made up the altitude difference while the Voodoo recovered using the 'Escape Manoeuvre'. The recovery consisted of rolling the aircraft inverted and maintaining a zero-G curve until the nose fell below the horizon and airspeed increased a tricky procedure due to the ever-present pitch-up and roll-coupling tendency, and at night, flying in cloud, it presented a real challenge.

Shortly after the Second World War, the United States Army Air Force put out a bid to design a new type of aircraft armament system comprising of two main components. The first was an airborne radar Fire Control System and the second was a guided air-to-air missile system. Both bids were awarded to the Aerospace Group of the Hughes Aircraft Corporation. The proposed Fire Control System was an airborne radar operating in conjunction with an analog computer and was designated the Hughes MA-1. The missile was designated the Guided Aircraft Rocket-1.

The Falcon initially operated as a semi-active radar-homing missile using reflected radar signals from the host aircraft. The GAR-2 version subsequently changed to Airborne Intercept Missile-4, called the Falcon and was the first infrared homing version. It used the infrared radiation emitted by the hot engine exhaust gases of the enemy aircraft. This was sometimes referred to as the 'fire and forget' type of missile. The attacking fighter could fire the Falcon missile and immediately break away to safety, leaving the missile to track the enemy aircraft and destroy it with no further control required.

The CAF used the Falcon AIM 4-D version in the 1970s. The Falcon used a Thiokol solid fuel rocket motor and had a hemispherical heat-seeker nose radome. The radome was cooled by liquid nitrogen to make it more sensitive to a heat source. It had an infrared target lock-on life of just two minutes. It could only be cooled once, a one-shot deal, and took approximately seven seconds to achieve target lock-on and go through the internal firing sequence. The Falcon had a fairly short range, remember this is 1970, of approximately 10 km (6 miles). However, it covered the distance at a speed of Mach 3, three times the speed of sound. The Hughes Falcon was 1.97 metres in length and weighed 50 kg. It had a small explosive charge and relied upon the collision for detonation. The collision was most likely to occur up the tailpipe of the target engine exhaust and the resulting internal explosion would destroy the aircraft.

Canada got the Improved Intercept Performance Voodoos in the early 1970s and Lowell, the Top Gun pilot, offered the following explanation of the difference in getting a 'lock-on' and firing the Falcon missile system in the two aircraft: the first batch of pre-IIP Voodoos and the second batch of IIP Voodoos. The pre-IIP Voodoo is distinguished by the fact that it has no IRST dome on top of the fuselage in front of the cockpit windshield. The pre-IIP Voodoo had two options for the attack, he said:

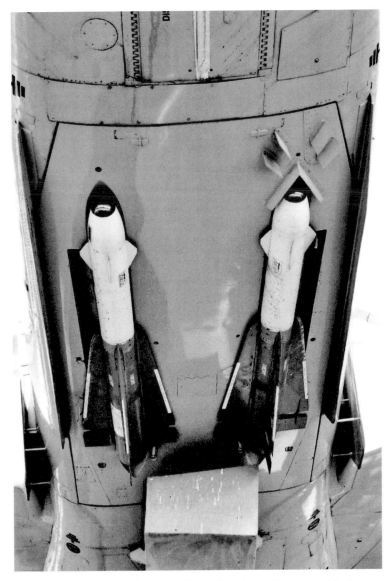

Falcon missiles on launch racks, CF-101 Voodoo. (Courtesy of Author)

Manually fly at the target using the 'bore-sight" in the front windscreen [a primitive heads-up display] to within the AIM-4D IR seeker head field of view (plus/minus 25 degrees) and let the missile seeker heads acquire the target Infra Red source (not recommended because if you did not have radar ranging info, you might be outside of the missile envelope); or obtain a radar lock on to the target in the stern – now the missile Infra Red seeker heads are slaved to the radar antenna thus looking directly at the target (recommended because the Fire Control System would fire the missile right in the heart of the firing envelope with all the 'lead-collision' angles solved and with the missile seeker heads looking right at the target).

The Post-IIP had the added option of obtaining an Infra Red lock on (rather than radar lock on) to the target and again, the missile seeker heads would be slaved to the Infra Red seeker head thus looking directly at the target. The Fire Control System and autopilot had the capability of doing a fully automatic radar lock on with the aircraft chasing the target radar return on the scope. This was, could be, a very rough ride and involved getting your head bumped around the cockpit as the aircraft aggressively pursued the elusive target dot. It was commonly referred to as the "Voodoo Dance".

The Voodoo was not the only aircraft to employ the Falcon missile. Over 12,000 AIM 4-Ds saw service with the Northrop F-89 Scorpion, the Convair F-102 Delta Dagger and F-106 Delta Dart, and the McDonnell F-101. It saw limited service in the Vietnam War on the McDonnell F-4 Phantom, but it was not suited to the yank and bank of close in aerial combat. The missile was used on the Swiss Air Force Dassault Mirage III and the Swedish Air Force Saab 35 Draken. Depending on the version, the Falcon tracked its target by infra-red or semi-active radar guidance systems. The Falcon was withdrawn from service in the USAF in the late 1980s and Canada when the last Voodoo retired at the end of 1984.

The other half of the Canadian Voodoo arsenal was the Douglas AIR-2A Genie unguided air-to-air rocket that was capable of carrying a 1.5 kt W25 nuclear warhead. Note the use of the word capable. The Canadian government of the day was adamant that Canada did not own, would never own, and did not have in *its* possession, any nuclear warheads for the Genie rocket on Canadian soil. Strictly speaking that statement was correct. The USA owned the warheads and kept them under their control in secure 'ammunition dumps' at each of the Canadian fighter bases. The warheads would be released to the Canadians under a dual-key arrangement when, and if, the DEFCON level reached the highest level of alert, meaning imminent war. The result was that Canada had a nuclear defence capability without the political fallout, no pun intended, of actually owning nuclear warheads. This was a truly unique situation between allies.

Canada had the capability of producing its own nuclear weapons, but chose not to. A nuclear research facility had been established at Chalk River, Ontario, by the National Research Council. By the mid-1950s, Canada had accumulated enough plutonium to make nuclear weapons but instead supplied it to the USA for its weapon programme. It supplied a necessary nuclear weapon component to its NORAD ally and, at the same time, continued to develop its technology for peaceful technology. Today, Chalk River supplies medical isotopes for the world.

Douglas Aircraft began a programme in the 1950s to develop a simple, reliable and unguided rocket with a small nuclear warhead. The idea was that the relatively large lethal blast area, calculated to be 304 metres, would destroy the bomber and any other aircraft in its immediate vicinity. It could be thought of as a proximity weapon.

The aircraft's Fire Control System would calculate the targeting, arming and firing of the weapon. The detonation was delayed by approximately ten seconds to allow the firing aircraft to perform an escape manoeuvre from the blast. This rolling and pulling manoeuvre had to be performed immediately and smoothly – remember roll coupling? The Douglas Genie's

Genie Rocket. (Courtesy of Canadian Forces Joint Imagery Centre, Department of National Defence)

flying performance was similar to the Falcon, with a speed of Mach 3 and a range of 10 km. It was 2.94 metres in length and weighed 373 kg. The Genie, too, had a Thiokol solid fuel engine. Test firings of the rocket were completed in 1956 with the weapon entering service in 1957. During development it had various names, such as Ding-Dong and Bird Dog, but was finally designated the Douglas MB-1 Genie.

The only live test of the Genie warhead occurred over Yucca Flats Test Site, Nevada, on 19 July 1957, and was called Plumbbob John Nuclear Test. The Genie was fired from an USAF Northrop F-89 Scorpion at an altitude of 15,000 feet. In 1962, the Genie was re-designated the AIR-2A, with an inert version – no nuclear warhead – called the ATR-2A which was used for training purposes. The Genie saw service on the Northrop F-89 Scorpion, the Convair F-106 Delta Dart, the McDonnell F-101 and the CF-101 Voodoo. Over 3,000 weapons were produced and they remained in inventory until the late 1980s. Canada's access to the weapon ceased with the standing down of the last operational Voodoo squadron on 31 December 1984.

There was an extensive handling protocol for the Genie rocket, both in the physical handling and release of the weapon to Canadian hands. The release of the weapon was controlled by the double-key and 'no alone zone' method. An American and Canadian officer would perform the required actions together after appropriate authentication to allow them to proceed. These routines were practised regularly and then tested during exercises such as the Amalgam Mute in Chapter Nine.

In discussion with WO Roch Roy, an air weapons technician in CFB Bagotville, Quebec, he remembered 'as a young Private, having completed his TQ5 qualification exam, being part of the Voodoo weapons load crew. The load crew consisted of a crew chief, a "B" man and a "C" man. In those days I was the junior "C" man and assisted with pushing the MF-9 Genie trailer into position at the aircraft. During my weekly schedule I also occasionally did rotation for a day in the QRA'. When asked about the practice loads he said, 'We were qualified to load both the Genie and Falcon rockets. We practised with the ATR-2N, a dummy Genie rocket, to maintain proficiency and qualifications. I did plenty of live loads on the flight line.'

The author observed these live loads from a distance as the area was roped off and secured by military police. Sometimes it involved many squadron aircraft and the pilots and AI Navigators were observed sitting in the cockpit with both hands clearly in view to prevent any inadvertent switch selections. A nuclear incident was termed a Broken Arrow occurrence. The Genie did have many safeguards built-in; one was that the detonation sequence to arm the warhead would not start until the Thiokol engine had burnt out and ceased operating.

There was a secure Quick Reaction Area compound close to the end of the prevailing wind runway at each of the four fighter bases, as previously mentioned in Chapter Two. The Quick Reaction Area consisted of two pairs of hangars separated by living quarters occupied by aircrew and ground crew for the aircraft on Alert. Two of the aircraft were on 'five-minute Alert', meaning that after the 'scramble call' from NORAD the aircraft had to be airborne in five minutes. Not an unreasonable proposition during the day, while the crews were reading the newspaper, but certainly a more different challenge awakened from a deep sleep at three in the morning! These aircraft were armed with the Falcon missile.

There were maintenance personnel assigned to duty at the 409 Squadron, CFB Comox, Quick Reaction Area hangars twenty-four hours a day. These would include: engine, airframe, communications, radar, instrument, electrical, armament systems, munitions and weapons technicians. The munitions and weapons technicians were called gun plumbers. Some of these technicians would also be designated for the start crew.

At the squadron itself, the daily maintenance duties were in two sections. The servicing section on the flight line looked after parking, towing, refuelling and starting the aircraft. The snags section looked after non-scheduled rectification of system faults and 'unserviceabilities'. It also had the NADAR debriefing room for the crews to review their performance: the joy of a Mission Accomplished and the agony of the Missed Intercept.

The five-minute-Alert aircraft were used for flying duties and actually held on Alert in the air. The NORAD requirement was to have them turned around ready for flight in a limited time; twenty to thirty minutes after landing had been mentioned. This procedure would also require that, if the five-minute aircraft had snags, another aircraft had to be readied to take its place. The airborne aircraft could, if needed, be held airborne until minimum fuel status was reached before landing. This would give the maximum amount of time to get the replacement aircraft ready and still meet the NORAD commitments, a version of NORAD chess.

The Genie weapons were kept in the custody of the USAF 425 Munitions Maintenance Squadron at each of the interceptor bases. The rockets and their W_{25} nuclear warhead, were inspected and rotated regularly. The Genie rockets were kept in a special armament storage area adjacent to the Quick Reaction Area for immediate use in the event of war, when all authentication and clearances had been satisfied. The warhead maintenance procedures did incur special USAF transport aircraft making secretly scheduled delivery flights to the bases in the middle of the night.

What part did the Genie rocket play in this readiness? Only those with the appropriate clearance know for sure and they are not telling. Despite being nearly forty years since the Amalgam Mute exercise it is difficult, maybe impossible, to get the 'Top Secret' operational files unclassified. The author had several requests denied and subsequent appeals with Library and Archives Canada to access these files prior to publication were unsuccessful. Likewise, access to some files at the Directorate of Heritage and History has also been denied.

The question that to date has no verifiable answer is whether the other two aircraft holding one-hour Alert in the secure Quick Reaction Area were armed with the nuclear-tipped Genie rocket? It should be noted that sometimes the backup 'one-hour birds' held alert on the non-secure hangar line, where they would only be armed with the Falcon missile. All of the interviewees for this book, which included a base commander, squadron commanders, squadron aircrew, weapons technicians and line maintenance personnel would not verify, or deny, that the aircraft were armed with nuclear weapons in respect for the Top Secret restriction on information.

The weapons did exist on Canadian soil. They were kept in a USAF ammunition compound next to the Quick Reaction Area. They would only be used in the event of war. What about imminent war? Would the Genie have been uploaded to the aircraft in preparation for hostilities? What happened during exercises such as our Amalgam Mute in 1973? We do know that there were live-load and inert/dummy-load practices. The protocol for both practises would be the same.

The only verbal, un-validated information was a chance remark by a Voodoo aircrew who admitted that 'he had touched a live Genie in the QRA hangar' while being escorted by an American and Canadian officer. However, the rocket was on a loading trailer and not on the aircraft. So the answer remains locked up in dusty Top Secret files. The only information unanimously offered by the interviewees was the fact that a live Genie rocket had never flown on a CAF Voodoo in Canadian airspace.

It is the personal opinion of the author that the backup aircraft, not the five-minute Alert aircraft, would be armed with live Genie weapons while in the secure Quick Reaction Area. There was no intention to fly these aircraft except in the event of actual hostilities. These two aircraft would have to be disarmed of their nuclear weapons as they were rotated through the five-minute Alert or general squadron flying duties. They would carry the Falcon missiles as five-minute Alert aircraft and then the McDonnell Simulated Rocket and Weapon System Evaluator Missile weapons simulators when used as squadron training aircraft.

The Weapon System Evaluator Missile was airborne test equipment, which used an oscillogram tape to record the analog and digital signals used to prepare, launch and guide the secondary weapon: the AIM-4D

Falcon missile. Post-flight, the light sensitive tape was removed from the aircraft, developed and analysed for proper missile preparation and delivery.

The McDonnell Simulated Rocket tested the fire control system for the primary weapon: the AIR 2A Genie rocket. It was a 41-kg, 2-metre-long cylinder that mounted to the aircraft's special weapon ejector rack. The McDonnell Simulated Rocket recorded the signal preparation, time of flight and firing signals for the rocket. Once it was confirmed that the Falcon and Genie aircraft weapons fire control systems were functioning correctly, an aircraft could assume NORAD Alert duties.

NADAR tape was another training and verification aid. It recorded both the pilot's radar scope display and flight data during the intercept and allowed the post-flight examination of the crew and fire control system performance. The tape was removed from the aircraft and played back on special video equipment. The proof of the Mission Accomplished was there for all to see, or not!

During the 1960s and 1970s, the only time a CAF Voodoo would fire its weapons was during the William Tell competition in Florida. However, during the 1980s this was changed and for certification purposes every aircraft had to go through a practical firing exercise of the Genie rocket. The weapons would be fired at target drones or remote-controlled aircraft. The Genie had a small self-destruct explosive charge as it was a proximity weapon.

In the 1970s, every aircraft in the CAF inventory was assigned a record-keeping card. The card for Voodoo 101003 indicates it was a CF-101F dual model with P&W J57-P-55 engines. It was accepted on Quartermaster Transfer Order 253 by Bristol Aerospace Ltd, Winnipeg, Manitoba, on 30 June 1970. It was sent to LTV Ltd, Greenville, South Carolina, USA, for Fire Control System testing, MB5 autopilot modifications and painting. On 3 August 1971, it was assigned by Quartermaster Transfer Order 239 to Air Defence Command, 410 All Weather Operational Training Squadron, Bagotville. The aircraft was assigned from 410 Squadron at CFB Bagotville to 425 Squadron, also based at CFB Bagotville, crew for the duration of the exercise on 10 May 1973.

The last Voodoo to fly in the world was on 19 April 1987. Aircraft number 101006, a dual-training model assigned to 414 Electronic Warfare Squadron, was flown to CFB Chatham, New Brunswick, to be displayed at CFB Cornwallis, Nova Scotia. For twenty-six years the Voodoo's afterburners shattered the Canadian skies and, notwithstanding its contribution to the defence of Canada, it will be best remembered for its noisy airshow fly- passes. How then does the Voodoo compare with the McDonnell Douglas CF-188 Hornet that is used as the present day CAF interceptor and, itself, will be replaced by another fighter in the next five years?

The Canadian Hornets are now thirty years old and have been upgraded throughout their service life. The Hornet is a single-pilot, multi-role attack aircraft that can be used as an interceptor. It has multi-type weapons ability, improved radar and navigation aids, inflight refuelling capability, which improves operational range, and a safer ejection performance envelope for the pilot. There is no AI Navigator, so a 'Hands on Throttle and Stick' and 'Heads Up Display' allows the pilot to operate the systems alone. Once again, like the USAF F-106, if the automatic features are working then all is well, but a Missed Intercept will occur if it is not. How well is it at avoiding jamming? We do not know, the information is classified.

The foregoing was the history of the defence aircraft of the post-Arrow cancellation era. What of the other segment of the defence system: the Bomarc? The defence package included the delivery of Bomarc missiles to supplement the Voodoo aircraft. Was this a case of the government hedging their bets wisely or was it a complete waste of resources? In peacetime, the following statements were applicable: the Voodoo aircraft permitted an identification function of an off-course friendly aircraft, the Bomarc missile could not; the Voodoo aircraft could be recalled from attacking the target if it was subsequently identified as friendly, the Bomarc missile could not; the Voodoo aircraft had multiple warheads, the Bomarc had one; the Voodoo aircraft could be rearmed and used again, the Bomarc missile could not.

In the event of war, using 1972 as an example, on any given day there were probably an equal number, or more, of Bomarc missiles to serviceable Voodoo aircraft. The Bomarc missiles were all located in Ontario and Quebec, there was no Canadian missile coverage on the west coast. The Bomarc range from their fixed bases was limited; the Voodoo could be deployed closer to the action and their range extended further by external fuel tanks that can be jettisoned when empty. The Bomarc missile had the advantage of not endangering aircrew life during their flight – at least not Canadian aircrew!

Storage, training, maintenance cost and the facilities needed were some of the many factors to be considered. The fact that the Bomarc missile was not very effective without its nuclear warhead was a very big political issue, which eventually brought about the defeat of the Diefenbaker Conservative government of the early 1960s. The Liberals, under Prime Minister Lester Pearson, initially agreed to have the missiles nuclear warhead-armed. The bottom line was that the Bomarc missiles left Canada in 1972, having been declared costly and ineffective, and have never been replaced. The Voodoo aircraft flew on until 1984, until they too were replaced by the McDonnell Douglas CF-18 – another aircraft.

The Bomarc was the first long-range, anti-aircraft missile in the world. It was created by the Boeing (BO) aircraft company and the Michigan Aeronautical Research Center (MARC). Hence it was named Bomarc. The first Bomarc flew in 1955 and, by the time Canada took delivery in 1962, a new improved version was available: the Coffin Intercept Missile CIM-10B. The Coffin refers to the protected horizontal storage unit which was at a combat-ready state and converted instantly to a vertical missile launch pad. Approximately 700 A and B model Bomarcs were built.

The CIM-10B version of the Bomarc (often called the Super Bomarc) had a first-stage Thiokol XM-51 50,000 lb thrust, solid-fuel rocket motor and two Marquardt RJ43-MA-7 ramjets with 2,000 lb of thrust. Its range had been increased to 644 km with a cruising altitude of 100,000 feet. The difference in weight distribution caused the wings to be moved forward, and the missile was shortened by over 2 feet compared to the original model.

The Canadian Bomarcs were converted to a nuclear warhead in December 1963. It had a W40 warhead, which had a calculated 7–10 kiloton yield. The explosion would be expected to be lethal to a bomber within 1,000 metres of the explosion. The effect of radiation on other aircraft in the vicinity would increase as the altitude increased. The warheads were rotated for routine maintenance every ninety days. The US-owned nuclear weapons remained in control of US personnel at all times and were stored in special ammunition storage facilities. Of course, the 'Two Man Rule' would apply to any phase of the Bomarc operation, such as exchanging warheads. This meant that there was always a minimum of two qualified military people involved with handling the Bomarc, and in Canada one of the people had to be from the USA. These individuals would also have been subjected to the Human Reliability Programme prior to handling any nuclear weapon, such as the Genie rocket or Bomarc missile.

The missile had a speed of 3,434 km/h, weighed 7,272 kg and was 13.7 metres long and had a wing span of 5.5 metres. The Bomarc was integrated into the SAGE network, which provided the necessary support to detect, track and intercept the hostile target. The Bomarc would launch and be guided by the SAGE computer to the general vicinity of the target. Then, the Bomarc would be instructed to 'lock on' to the target and carry out its own interception. The warhead would detonate at the closest proximity to the target.

In order to fire the Canadian Bomarc, a two-key interlock switch system had to be activated. The keys were held by Canadian and US personnel and would be deployed from the 22nd NORAD Region Headquarters deep in 'the Hole' at North Bay, Ontario, Canada. In addition to the switch system, the missiles required coded tapes that provided the flight and detonation information for launch. Where in Canada would these missiles be located? Once again, the two 'expected roads into town' would be covered, which would meet the requirement to protect major cities in eastern Canada and the north-eastern USA.

The two sites selected were North Bay, Ontario, to protect the polar route, and La Macaza, Quebec, to protect the Iceland/Greenland route. The 446 Surface-to-Air Missile Squadron was located at North Bay and 447 Surface-to-Air Missile Squadron was located at La Macaza. The two Squadrons were expected to provide a secondary ring of defence against the bombers that got passed the fighter interceptors. These were in addition to the eight USAF Bomarc units predominantly situated in the north-eastern USA.

Simultaneously, as the transition from the CF-100 Canuck to the CF-101 Voodoo took place, the construction began on two Bomarc sites. In North Bay, 446 Surface-to-Air Missile Squadron, motto 'Vigilance Swiftness Strength', became operational in August 1962 and then sat idle, waiting for the politicians to decide how they were going to arm the missiles. After a change of government and an Initial Capability Inspection in November 1963, the site was ready to accept nuclear warheads. On 31 December 1963, authorised by the President of the USA, the first shipment arrived, with full fanfare, at North Bay. The well-documented arrival of the warheads was probably a political photo opportunity for the Liberal government in order to bolster support for their decision to have nuclear weapons, because this, in fact, was the very reason they were in power.

Meanwhile, 447 Surface-to-Air Missile Squadron, motto 'Always Ready', in La Macaza, had its Initial Capability Inspection in November 1962. It too sat idle for a year awaiting the warheads. Finally, with all nuclear warheads in place, the Bomarc missile sites assumed full operational status in 1963. This was not without public comment and La Macaza, in particular, had its share of protestors who were against having nuclear weapons on Canadian soil. The summer of 1964 was very active for the peace protestors at the La Macaza site, a two hour drive from Montreal.

The Bomarcs were arranged in four rows of seven missiles each, giving a total of twenty-eight missiles at each base. It can be assumed there were some spare missiles to cover the ones being rotated for maintenance. The missile had four main components to be maintained, each with its own qualified personnel: the propulsion rocket and ramjets, the fuel, the warhead and the electronic system. The guidance, radar and fire control systems were sub-components of the electronic section. The Special Ammunition Storage and nuclear warhead shelters were in a patrolled

Canadian Bomarc missile firing. (Courtesy of Canadian Forces Joint Imagery Centre, Department of National Defence)

security area within the Station secure area. This area was also referred to as a 'No Lone Zone', with at least two persons working together and as previously mentioned one person had to be an American.

The danger of handling nuclear weapons was always present. Any occurrence of an irregular nature was code named Dull Sword for an incident and Broken Arrow for a potentially more serious accident. Broken Arrow was used to describe an accident that had the possibility of producing a nuclear explosion, a fire in the vicinity of the warhead and the unimaginable, but entirely possible, theft of the warhead. There were designated teams on each of the sites who were fully trained to handle all nuclear weapon emergencies.

What was it like to work on a Canadian missile base responsible for the operational status of a nuclear weapon? Who were these people? One of them was Captain Maurice J. Hanberg, a Missile Launch Officer at CFS La Macaza until the closure of the site in 1972. He was one of six aircrew Missile Launch Officers who worked in the command centre. All of them had been subjected to an intensive screening process called the Human Reliability Program. Maurice described his job as more of a 'Safety Officer' as launch capability was in the hand of the Combat Operations Center Duty Officers down 'The Hole' in North Bay. His job 'with at least two techs on duty was to make sure that the weapon was serviceable for launching if needed by North Bay [NORAD HQ]'. He was also qualified as the Broken Arrow team commander.

Hanberg was given a 'three week indoctrination course'. 'I had come from Air Training Command, on Air Defence Command, the meaning of the DEFCON levels, preparation in the event of war and the nuts and bolts of Bomarc. [This included information on] the time to launch, the launch angle about eighty degrees and the split roof on the shelter. The missile launched with a solid fuel rocket and then the ramjets took over. There were about 250 maintenance people. The USAF looked after the pointy end and the Canadians the power plant and communications.'

At the start of the twelve-hour shift Maurice said that 'everything had to be proved. That the lights on the [his] panel indicated that there were proper connections, showed serviceable and that all the warning lights were out. This was prior to going through a coded procedure to establish contact with North Bay. If signal problems occurred, a Demand and Reply Checklist procedure would be followed.'

Maurice related that he 'worked in the Interceptor Missile Strategic Operations Center. It was a secure windowless building with a constantly changing coded door lock. There was a small kitchen and a washroom immediately outside the locked door.' The personnel drilled and drilled so that they 'all knew their job really well, all fitted together'. The squadron was constantly checked by Operational Readiness Inspections and exercises such as the Amalgam Mute of our account.

When asked about the nuclear warhead, Maurice remarked that 'even on course nobody would tell you if they were real or not. I was told that for paperwork and procedures we will treat it as if it is. People did not discuss their job and when I asked a question I was told "not any of your business where you work" or asked "do you have a need to know?" So until the day I left I did not know.' So it seems that Top Secret even meant Top Secret among the CFS La Macaza personnel who were all cleared Top Secret.

'The missiles were exchanged for maintenance every ninety days and the warheads were exchanged annually. During the exchange the Station was locked down and no one could move. The other time that I saw such heightened security was during the FLQ crisis in October 1969. We all were confined to base for forty-eight to seventy-two hours. We had three levels of security: the outer security, the inner security patrolled by Air Force Police, and the Interceptor Missile Strategic Operations Center coded door itself,' related Maurice.

The Minister of National Defence, Donald MacDonald, announced in August 1971 that the Bomarcs would be returned to the USA and that both squadrons would be disbanded within the year. The change in policy was in response to the shifting Soviet threat from manned bombers to unmanned intercontinental ballistic missiles. Captain Hanberg worked the very last shift at La Macaza in March of 1972 and, as he said, 'I turned out the lights and went flying!' The warheads were quickly separated from the rocket, crated and flown by the USAF back to the USA. Canada's entry into homeland missile defence had ended and, to date, has never been repeated.

Should we have installed the Bomarcs? The accountants can give us a cost analysis for the nine years of operational service, but is that the answer? Remembering the NORAD motto – Deter, Detect, Destroy – the Bomarc was part of the deter factor and because of that we never had to destroy. There are very few examples of the Bomarc missile in Canadian museums. The reason was that it was very difficult to ensure decontamination of the rocket and ramjet fuel. A prime, preserved example is at the Canadian Aviation and Space Museum in Ottawa, Ontario.

After August 1971 it was up to the Voodoo alone to protect Canadian skies against the diminishing bomber threat. Or was it diminishing? The bombers still existed in large numbers and continued to fly probing missions on the Atlantic seaboard. The Voodoos were the last line of defence and the Improved Intercept Performance aircraft, the new second batch to Canada, shouldered this added responsibility. More than twenty years of service and not one rocket or missile fired in anger. The Voodoo must surely have contributed to the deter factor. Both weapons systems played their part in the 'warming up' of the Cold War.

Voodoo Flying Suit Badges

Pilot

AI Navigator

Maintenance Personnel

CHAPTER SIX

Fighter Squadrons

Canada emerged a stronger military nation after rallying to the successful defence of Mother England during the Second World War. Many Canadian squadrons owe their creation to the war as they were formed by the RCAF in England with Canadian personnel during the conflict. At its height, in 1944, the RCAF had seventy-eight squadrons in service, thirty-five overseas and forty-three at home. Six months after the cessation of hostilities, the Cabinet approved a new format for the peacetime RCAF. It consisted of four components: Regular Force, Auxiliary, Reserve and Royal Canadian Air Cadets.

The Regular Force had five established squadrons. There were two squadrons for aerial photography, two for transport and one for communication. The matter of air defence fell to the Auxiliary squadrons. Fifteen squadrons were authorised and they assumed the defence role until 1954. As the relationship between the Western democracies and the Communist Bloc countries continued to deteriorate, the RCAF decided to once again build up its squadron strength. In 1955, it reached an operational level of twenty-nine regular squadrons and twelve auxiliary squadrons. The RCAF then gradually decreased to eighteen regular squadrons, four training squadrons and six auxiliary squadrons. This was the squadron strength on 1 February 1968 when the three services, Army, Navy and Air Force, joined together to form a unified force: the Canadian Armed Forces.

Despite various name changes over the years, the Air Force command structure prior to unification was basically three commands. They were Air Transport, Maritime and Air Defence Command. In the early 1950s, the air defence of major cities was assigned to day-fighter Auxiliary squadrons flying the North American piston-engine Mustang or the jet-engine De Havilland Vampire. In 1954, this roll was assigned to regular squadrons flying the Avro Canuck. The defence of Europe was assigned in 1954 to an

CF-5, T-33, CF-100, CF-101 mixed aircraft formation. (Courtesy of DND, Directorate of History and Heritage)

Air Division flying the Canadair Sabre, later replaced by the Avro Canuck and finally, the Lockheed Starfighter.

NORAD had a major influence on the shape and growth of Air Defence Command from the late 1950s onwards. It took the immediate post-war mobile auxiliary radar units and developed them into the SAGE network. The number of regular defence squadrons continually decreased from nine Avro Canuck squadrons in 1955 to three McDonnell Voodoo squadrons in 1964. The two Bomarc missile squadrons were phased out in 1972. At the time of our exercise mission, 10 May 1973, there were three active fighter interceptor squadrons: 409, 416 and 425. There was also a training squadron, 410, that provided all Voodoo crew training and whose instructors were all combat-ready.

1. President Carter of the USA signing SALT 2 Agreement with General Secretary Brezhnev of the USSR on 18 June 1979.

2. CAF fighter interceptor crews 'scrambling' to get airborne in five minutes. (Courtesy of Canadian Forces Joint Imagery Centre, Department of National Defence)

3. Air Weapons Controllers' Blue Room in Underground Complex, North Bay, Ontario. (Courtesy of Canadian Forces Joint Imagery Centre, Department of National Defence)

4. CF-18 and Russian TU-95 Bear bomber. (Courtesy of Canadian Forces Joint Imagery Centre, Department of National Defence)

5. AN/APR-9 Radar receiver used by Electronic Warfare Officer in CF-100. (Courtesy of Wayne Scott)

6. Lt-Col. Dennis Kelleher, Air Weapons Controller, with scope that he operated in 1973. (Courtesy of Author)

7. Schematic of AN/FPS-27 Search Radar. (Courtesy of Radomes, Inc.)

8. Typical radar site. Two search radars and one height finder radar. (Courtesy of Canadian Forces Joint Imagery Centre, Department of National Defence)

9. CAF CF-101 Voodoo firing Genie rocket. (Courtesy of Canadian Forces Joint Imagery Centre, Department of National Defence)

10. BOMARC missile site, North Bay, Ontario. (Courtesy of Canadian Forces Joint Imagery Centre, Department of National Defence)

11. Quick Reaction Hangar. (Courtesy of Wayne Ralph)

12. Genie rocket (larger) and Falcon missile on Voodoo armament door. (Courtesy of Author)

13. CAF CF-101 Voodoo taking off in afterburner. (Courtesy of Canadian Forces Joint Imagery Centre, Department of National Defence)

14. CAF CF-101 Voodoo. (Courtesy of Canadian Forces Joint Imagery Centre, Department of National Defence)

15. CAF CF-101 Voodoo pilot's cockpit. (Courtesy of Western Canada Aviation Museum)

16. CAF CF-101 Voodoo Airborne Intercept Navigator's cockpit. (Courtesy of Western Canada Aviation Museum)

17. William Tell 1972 Top Gun winners, Captains Lowell Butters (left) and Douglas Danko. (Courtesy of Manny Soberal)

18. Major Lowell Butters, 2009, next to a Falcon missile. (Courtesy of Author)

19. 425 Alouettes Squadron CFB Bagotville, Quebec. (Courtesy of DND, Directorate of History and Heritage)

20. 409 Nighthawk Squadron Voodoos over coastal mountains. (Courtesy of Canadian Forces Joint Imagery Centre, Department of National Defence)

21. 414, 425, 416, 409 Squadron (front to rear) CF-101 Voodoos in formation. (Courtesy of Canada's Air Force, Department of National Defence)

22. CAF Avro CF-100 Canuck 414 Electronic Warfare Squadron. (Courtesy of Canada's Air Force, Department of National Defence)

23. CAF CF-100 flight line, 414 Squadron, CFB North Bay, Ontario. (Courtesy of Author)

24. CAF CF-100 pilot's cockpit. (Courtesy of Author)

25. Author flying CAF CF-100. Chaff pods and jammer antennas are clearly visible. (Courtesy of Author)

26. CAF CF-101 Electronic Warfare Voodoo, supersonic target. (Courtesy of Wayne Ralph)

27. Captain Ron Neeve, 2010, Airborne Intercept Navigator (first Soviet Bear intercept). (Courtesy of Author)

28. Colonel Eugene Lukan, 2010, beside McDonnell CF-101 Voodoo. (Courtesy of Wayne Ralph)

29. Lt-Col. R. (Tiny) McDonald, deceased 2007. (Courtesy of Lisa McDonald)

30. Lukan/McDonald's CF-101 aircraft, 101003, at 1976 CFB Moose Jaw Airshow. (Courtesy of John Kimberley)

31. Captains W. (Bill) Bland (L) and D. (Doug) Fitzpatrick, 2010, reunited after thirty-seven years, in the cockpit of a CF-100 at the Canadian Museum of Flight. (Courtesy of Wayne Ralph)

32. Fitzpatrick/Bland's CF-100 aircraft, 100779, at 1975 CFB Moose Jaw Airshow. (John Kimberley)

425 Squadron CF-101 Voodoo and TU-95 Bear. (Courtesy of DND, Directorate of History and Heritage)

Wing Commander Sydney Burrows, AFC, CD, supplied information on the peacetime flying fatalities of the Avro CF-100 and McDonnell CF-101. A hundred aircrew on the CF-100 and fourteen on the CF-101 gave their lives during service in the RCAF and CAF. This service included the NATO commitment in Europe and the NORAD commitment in Canada.

409 NIGHTHAWK SQUADRON

The Squadron was formed in Digby, Lincolnshire, England, on 7 June 1941. Its badge is a crossbow in front of a dark cloak, to indicate that it specialised as a night fighter squadron. The motto is: *Media nox meridies noster* – Midnight is our Noon. Its nickname is Nighthawk. It was adopted by the City of Victoria, British Columbia.

It was the RCAF's seventh, and second night fighter, squadron formed overseas. The formation flew Bristol Beaufighter and De Havilland Mosquito aircraft in the night defence of Britain and the Allied forces in north-west Europe during the Second World War. It was the first night fighter squadron to cross over the channel after the Normandy landings and operate from bases in Belgium and Germany. It was later disbanded at Twente, Netherlands, on 1 June 1945.

409 Squadron CF-101 Voodoo, CFB Comox. (Courtesy of Canadian Forces Joint Imagery Centre, Department of National Defence)

Reformed on 1 November 1954, 409 became an all-weather fighter squadron based at Comox, British Columbia, flying the Avro Canuck. The squadron converted to the McDonnell Voodoo in March 1962. The squadron call sign was Hotel Golf. At the time of our 1973 account, it was part of the 25th NORAD Region.

Lt-Col. G. W. (George) McAffer was commanding officer of the squadron in the late 1970s. He was a very experienced NORAD officer. George's previous postings had included the Combat Alert Center at CFB Val d'Or, squadron Voodoo pilot at 409 Squadron, commanding officer of the Fox Main DEW Line site, NORAD Headquarters in Colorado Springs and the Tactical Evaluation Team at 22nd NORAD region in North Bay, Ontario.

The Voodoo experienced an engine problem with the fuel pig tails in the afterburner section and when McAffer arrived to take command of the squadron, he discovered that all the aircraft had been grounded. There were no Voodoo aircraft flying for the handing over of command ceremony. George related that, 'if it had not been for the Search and Rescue guys flying it would have been very quiet'. It was discovered that the engine problem was in the bend of the fuel pipe and he related, 'couched in a form of advice from the Base Commanding Officer, it was expected that I would fly the first aircraft. I had been away from the aircraft for a few years but it did not bother me.' McAffer flew the successful test flight and his 409 Squadron Voodoos were returned to NORAD combat status. Great leadership displayed by the new Commanding Officer.

410 COUGAR SQUADRON

The squadron was formed in Ayr, Scotland, on 30 June 1941. Its badge is the face of a cougar in front of a decrescent moon. The cougar is a native Canadian animal noted for its speed and power of attack. The waning moon is to signify night operations. The motto is: *Noctivaga* – Wandering by Night. Its nickname is Cougar. It was adopted by the City of Saint John, New Brunswick.

The formation was the RCAF's ninth, and third night fighter, squadron formed overseas, like 409 Squadron. It flew Bristol Beaufighter and De Havilland Mosquito aircraft during night operations in the defence of Britain and the European theatre. The squadron was disbanded at Gilze-Rijen, Netherlands, on 9 June 1945. Among the squadron's aces, those pilots with five kills or more, was F/L R. (Joe) D. Schultz. He is generally credited with setting up the CAF Flight Safety organisation, becoming Director of Flight safety in 1966. The author was very fortunate to attend his Flight Safety Officer's course in CFB Trenton, Ontario, Canada.

Reformed in December 1948 at St Hubert, Quebec, 410 was the first Regular Force fighter squadron in the post-war era. It flew Vampires in a day interceptor role. It transitioned to the Canadair Sabre and, in 1951, moved to North Luffenham, England, to be Canada's first day-fighter squadron to be part of the North Atlantic Treaty Organisation (NATO). In subsequent moves to Baden-Soellingen, Germany, and Marville, France, it completed its NATO commitment and was disbanded in October 1956.

The squadron was reformed in Canada in November 1956 and was assigned the Avro CF-100 Canuck at Uplands, Ottawa, Ontario. In 1962, it converted to the McDonnell Voodoo as part of NORAD until it was disbanded in March 1964. In April 1968 it reformed as 410 All-Weather Operational Training Unit (OTU) in CFB Bagotville, Quebec, responsible for all training of aircrew on the McDonnell Voodoo. In 1973, it trained thirty-seven pilots and twenty-nine AI Navigators to combat ready status.

In 1973, the commanding officer of the squadron was Lt-Col. R. (Ron) L. Bell, later Brigadier General, who became the first Navigator to command a supersonic fighter squadron in the Canadian Air Force. Bell had extensive NORAD experience as a CF-100 and CF-101 AI Navigator, as well as an Air Weapons Controller. He mentioned that, 'I flew on 10 May 1973. My log book shows a night low level airborne intercept mission for 1.1 hours in aircraft [101] 020.' The Amalgam Mute exercise must have been an important one to have the 'Boss' flying in the middle of the night. In addition to his military accomplishments, Bell was famous for his unlimited card tricks to keep the troops amused.

416 LYNX SQUADRON

The squadron was formed in Peterhead, Aberdeen, Scotland, on 22 November 1941. Its badge is a lynx leaping in front of a maple leaf. The lynx is indigenous to Canada and is noted for its fierceness. The motto is: *Ad saltum paratus* – Ready for the Leap. Its nickname is Lynx. It was adopted by the City of Oshawa, Ontario.

The squadron was the RCAF's fifteenth, and sixth fighter, squadron formed overseas. It flew the Supermarine Spitfire on defensive and offensive operations in Britain and in support of the Allied forces in north-west Europe. It was disbanded at Utersen, Germany, on 21 March 1946.

The formation was reformed at Uplands, Ottawa, Ontario, in January 1951 with the North American Mustang, later Canadair Sabre, before moving to Grostenquin, France, in September 1952. It was deactivated in January 1957 and returned to Canada to reactivate in February 1957 at St Hubert, Quebec, as an all-weather fighter squadron flying the Avro

Canuck. Deactivated in September 1961, it reactivated in January 1962 flying the McDonnell Voodoo. The squadron call sign was Golf November. It moved to Chatham, New Brunswick, in November 1962 and remained there until 1984. On 26 June 1968, it was the first Canadian squadron to intercept a USSR Tupolev TU-95 Bear bomber on a reconnaissance flight, described in Chapter Two.

During the 1970s, the CAF had exchange postings with the RAF and USAF. All aircrews received valuable experience outside their normal environment. The exchange postings included flying and non-flying positions. The American, British and Canadian military worked together in NATO, so it is not surprising that NORAD should have exchange postings. An exchange posting was looked upon as a 'plum job', no matter what it was, and an opportunity not to be turned down. On one ground exchange tour, a Canadian officer in England became unwittingly involved in the 1982 Falklands War. When things got 'too hot', the RAF decided that a Canadian should really not be participating at this level and he was asked to 'leave the room!'

RAF Flight Lieutenant David Trotter, an experienced AI Navigator, was selected to be the RAF exchange AI Navigator and started the course in March 1971. David took his Voodoo training at 410 Operational Training Unit, CFB Bagotville, and was initially paired – crewed up – with

416 Squadron CF-101 Voodoo formation. (Courtesy of DND, Directorate of History and Heritage)

the pilot who would be his future boss at 416 (AW) Fighter Squadron, the commanding officer, Lt-Col. Lew Twambley. Dave recounted that at times 'we had a few problems with the language' during the training.

Trotter's previous posting had been as an AI Navigator, or Observer in naval terms, on the Hawker Siddeley FAW.2 Sea Vixen aboard the Royal Navy aircraft carrier HMS *Eagle*. He completed his tour with 899 Squadron after 153 carrier deck landings. He mentioned that 'the major operational differences between the Vixen and Voodoo were the data link, the Infra Red for low levels, and that I was now supersonic and had the ability for the attack and re-attack. All my previous attacks had been from the stern in the Sea Vixen.'

'I have never forgotten my first impressions of Canada. I had spent most of my time flying over the sea and now all I could see was this vastness of trees, fire breaks, lakes and very few inhabitants, it was quite the change.' He also enjoyed 'flying without an immersion suit. In Canada we never flew [training missions] over the sea in winter. The Voodoo had a superbly roomy cockpit and now I had my own canopy.' He also was impressed with 'the normal operations on runways covered with snow and ice. The Voodoo landed at 165 knots!'

One mission that he remembered was when 'we, Major George Herbert and I, were scrambled out of ground training to CFB Goose Bay on 29 February 1972 and sat there until 4 March whilst a Soviet submarine floundered around off the Labrador coast. I was very pleased when some clean undies and toiletries were finally sent up from Chatham. The Soviets were sending aircraft [close to Canadian airspace] to provide possible assistance to the submarine.'

The crew remained at Goose Bay, Labrador, 'On Alert' to show the flag, and more, if any Soviet aircraft posed a threat. The multi-national crew, Canadian and British, demonstrated the close ties, post Second World War, between the RAF and the CAF. The fact that an RAF officer in a CAF aircraft was part of a NORAD crew, trained and ready to use weapons, and defending North America against Soviet aggression, truly reflects a close and trusting association between the CAF and RAF. Trotter, of course, had taken the required checks and tests and was cleared to the same level of security clearance as the Canadian crews.

Trotter completed 490 hours with 416 Squadron prior to returning to the RAF in September 1973 to join 111 Squadron flying the McDonnell F-4 Phantom in Scotland. He recalled that: 'the Voodoo was a straight line interceptor and I called it "the poor man's Phantom". An earlier generation of fighter than the F-4, the Voodoo just could not turn and perform like the Phantom.'

A little known fact was that the CAF investigated the possibility of replacing the Voodoo in the early 1970s with the Phantom. Ron Neeve was part of the team that went to the McDonnell Douglas factory in St Louis, Missouri. Upon arrival they were told 'sorry, we cannot spare the aircraft from the production line. They are needed in Vietnam. However here is a model of the Phantom in CAF colours!' See a photograph of Ron's model in the colour section.

Trotter also recounted that: 'I ejected from Phantom FGR2 XV416 just off the runway at RAF Coningsby on 3 March 1975. We had an engine failure and zone A fire warning on takeoff. The pilot was relatively inexperienced and possibly could have stuck with it. However both Martin Baker seats worked perfectly and thankfully nobody was seriously hurt. I always was concerned about the low altitude capability of the Voodoo seat.'

David Trotter visits Canada regularly but has never returned to CFB Chatham. The 416 Squadron Voodoos ceased operations in 1984 and the base subsequently closed in 1996. His son, Neil, was born while David was on squadron at CFB Chatham, New Brunswick, and, after returning to England, Neil subsequently emigrated to Canada. Now, David has a permanent connection to Canada after his two-and-a-half-year military posting protecting the land, with the next generation of Trotters. A perfect example of the twists and turns of the journey we call life!

425 ALOUETTE SQUADRON

The squadron was formed in Dishforth, Yorkshire, England, on 25 June 1942. Its badge is a hovering lark, which was intended to represent a bomber overhead its target about to release its bombs. The motto is: *Je te plumerai* – I shall pluck you. Its nickname is *Alouette*. It was adopted by the City of Quebec, Quebec, and the *La Presse* newspaper auxiliary, Montreal, Quebec.

It was the RCAF's twenty-second, and fifth bomber, squadron formed overseas. It flew Vickers Wellington and Handley Page Halifax bomber aircraft on strategic and tactical bombing missions. It was a unique formation within the RCAF in that the organisation order designated it 'French Canadian'. Bomber Command was encouraged to fill its ranks with French Canadian personnel. It saw action in North Africa as well as Europe. It was disbanded at Debert, Nova Scotia, on 5 September 1945.

It reformed in 1954 at St Hubert, Quebec, flying the Avro Canuck aircraft. It reactivated in October 1961 on the McDonnell CF-101 Voodoo at RCAF Station Namao, Edmonton, Alberta, and assumed an instructional

425 Squadron CF-101 Voodoos, CFB Bagotville. (Courtesy of Canadian Forces Joint Imagery Centre, Department of National Defence)

role for the other squadron's conversion training. The squadron call sign was Kilo November. It returned to Bagotville, Quebec, in July 1962 and a 425 Squadron crew was the fighter interceptor crew in the Amalgam Mute Exercise.

In 1973, the CAF fighter interceptor squadrons were located at three locations: 409 Squadron at CFB Comox, 416 Squadron at CFB Chatham and 425 Squadron at CFB Bagotville. 410 (OTU) Squadron also maintained combat ready crews at CFB Bagotville. Each squadron protected Canadian airspace under the auspices of NORAD. CFB Comox was in the 25th NORAD Region and CFBs Bagotville and Chatham were in the 22nd NORAD Region. Each base was positioned to give effective fighter coverage, but, perhaps, dare it be suggested, there was also a political factor in the placement. Each base had a long runway, 10,000 feet (3,048 metres), with arrestor gear (barrier) for the Voodoo tail hook in case of braking problems.

CFB Comox is situated on a headland in the Comox/Courtenay area of Vancouver Island, British Columbia. It is positioned west of the city of Vancouver and north-west of the provincial capital, Victoria. It was originally constructed by the RAF in 1942 to guard against Japanese invasion or bomber activity. In 1943, the RCAF assumed control of RCAF Station Comox and used it for training transport aircraft crews. Mothballed from 1946 to 1952, it was reactivated as a permanent base due to the escalating Cold War tensions. In 1954, a CADIN/Pinetree Line radar site was established and at that time housed two squadrons: 407 Maritime Patrol Squadron and 409 (AW) Fighter Squadron.

To meet the expected Soviet bomber threat route down the west coast of North America, 409 Squadron was located strategically on Vancouver Island at Comox. Initially, 409 Squadron was equipped with the Avro CF-100, which was subsequently replaced by the CF-101 Voodoo. In 1973, 409 Squadron was a very active unit. It is now the home base of a Maritime Command patrol squadron and a search and rescue unit. Apart from occasional CF-18 deployments from CFB Cold Lake, the sound of afterburners has disappeared from Comox.

CFB Chatham was situated at the mouth of the Miramachi River in eastern New Brunswick. It was north-east of the provincial capital city of Fredericton. Selected for its better maritime area flying weather, it hosted the British Commonwealth Air Training Plan and trained pilots, Navigators and radio operators from 1941 until 1945. RCAF Station Chatham trained a phenomenal 131,553 British Commonwealth aircrew, a worthy contribution to the war effort.

Operational units such as Bomber-Reconnaissance Submarine Hunting Detachments flew missions in the 'Battle of the St Lawrence' against German Kriegsmarine U-Boat operations during 1942. Seven years later, in 1949, 421 Fighter Squadron, flying the Canadair F-86 Sabre, arrived

CFB Chatham, QRH in foreground. (Courtesy of DND, Directorate of History and Heritage)

and brought Chatham into the jet age. A CADIN/Pinetree Line radar site, St Margarets, was built close by.

In 1959 the base hosted the Golden Hawks, predecessors to the Snowbirds, the Sabre aerobatic team. The team was established to celebrate two anniversaries: the 35th anniversary of the RCAF and the 50th anniversary of powered flight in Canada. Its first leader was Squadron Leader, later Lt-Col., F. (Fern) G. Villeneuve. In 1972, Fern Villeneuve was the author's commanding officer at 414 Electronic Warfare Squadron, CFB Uplands (Ottawa), Ontario. In 1962, the first CF-101 Voodoos arrived with 416 Squadron and the Miramachi River echoed to the sound of the twin afterburners.

CFB Chatham was in a position to meet the Soviet bomber threat approaching through the Greenland/Iceland gap route towards the industrial north-east of the USA or coastal surveillance flights. Its geographical location also allowed rapid deployment to CFB Goose Bay, Labrador, or CFB Gander, Newfoundland. NORAD developed a plan as well, code plan 'College Shaft', to deploy Convair F-106 Delta Darts of the 27th Fighter Interceptor Squadron, Loring AFB, Maine, to Goose Bay to meet the increasing number of USSR surveillance flights. 416 Squadron was deactivated in 1984 and the base remained open, with army units stationed there until it was closed in 1996.

CFB Bagotville is situated near the town of Bagotville on the Baie des Ha Ha of the Saguenay River. It is north of the provincial capital city of Quebec City. It was constructed in 1942 under the British Commonwealth Air Training Plan and trained 940 pilots for the war effort. A resident defence unit was established during the Second World War, specifically to protect the hydro-electric facilities needed for the nearby aluminium smelter. Closed in 1945, the escalating Cold War tensions caused the base to be reactivated in 1951. The base was used to train fighter crews for the Canadian NATO commitment in Europe, initially with Canadair F-86 Sabres, and then with Avro CF-100s. (Canadian squadrons were based on the NATO frontline facing the USSR in England initially, and also West Germany and France.)

In 1961, the base role changed, and it became home to the CF-101 Voodoos of Air Defence Command. CFB Bagotville guarded the north-east approaches to Canada and the USA. In 1973, it also supported CFB Val d'Or further to the west, which guarded the expected Soviet bomber route down to Hudson Bay and James Bay. CFB Bagotville remains an active fighter base and is home to a McDonnell Douglas Hornet squadron, which continues the fine tradition of airborne intercepts.

TOP GUN

The rivalry between the squadrons was good natured, but intense. All the crews in the 1970s had been trained by 410 Squadron in CFB Bagotville before being posted to an operational squadron. The Air Defence Command squadron component of the CAF was relatively small, so chances were that the aircrew had worked or trained with one another in the past. This created a close-knit group of fighter interceptor aircrews that were proud of their proficiency and their heritage. The 416 and 425 Squadrons were responsible for the east coast of the 22nd NORAD Region, so they interacted frequently. The lone Canadian squadron on the west coast, 409, was responsible to the 25th NORAD Region.

Canada's triumphant Top Gun win started with events held in 1965. From 1958 to 1965 the USAF and Air National Guard had met regularly at Tyndall Air Force Base near Panama City, Florida. A suitable name was required for the air-to-air rocketry portion of the USAF annual Fighter Gunnery and Weapons Meet, a demonstration of courage and prowess. In 1958, it was decided to use the name of a Swiss legend that everyone was familiar with: the story of William Tell. William was an expert marksman with the crossbow who lived in Switzerland in the early fourteenth century. One day, he failed to properly recognise the local Austrian official, Gessler.

His punishment was to shoot the apple balanced on the top of his son's head with his crossbow and arrow. He would be put to death if he refused. He succeeded in splitting the apple and became a legendary folk hero. The USAF felt that the symbolism of the story reflected the kind of steely-eyed aircrew they wanted for their fighter interceptor aircrew. The William Tell Meet was created.

Following the Second World War, the RCAF fighter crews, flying day fighters or the all-weather fighter interceptors, would have regular 'meets' in Canada at the Weapons Proving Unit in Cold Lake, Alberta, or Chatham, New Brunswick. The overseas squadrons used Rabat in North Africa, and later Decimommanau in Sardinia. In 1961/62, the Canadian Air Defence Squadrons had been re-equipped with the McDonnell Douglas CF-101 Voodoo, which carried the Genie and Falcon weapons. The RCAF would not have the opportunity to test these weapons and the aircraft Fire Control Systems until three years later in 1965. Would they work as advertised? Would they even come off the ejector racks? This was during the time of the Cuban Crisis, October 1962, and the Canadians had no idea if their weapons would work!

The problem was solved on 5 February 1965 when General H. B. Thatcher, commander of the USAF Air Defense Command, extended an invitation to Air Vice Marshall Murray Lister, the air officer commanding the RCAF Air Defence Command, to send a team to the 1965 William Tell competition. There is no doubt that this invitation grew out of the close working relationship of the two nations in NORAD. An officer, Flight Lieutenant T. (Tom) W. Murray, was assigned to the position of William Tell Project Officer. A William Tell restriction was that all members of the team had to be from the same squadron.

There was insufficient time to organise a 'shoot off' at one location so a team was sent to evaluate each squadron's performance. One day was spent assessing the weapons loading team and two days evaluating the flying team. A standard set of mission profiles were used, simulating what the teams could expect at the William Tell meet. By mid-June the winner had been declared. After an extremely close race, 425 Squadron in Bagotville, Quebec, had come out on top. There were only one hundred days left to prepare the aircraft, the aircrew and ground crew for the competition.

In spite of an intense effort to prepare the team, led by Wing Commander M. (Mike) J. Dooher, the competition was plagued by bad weather, faulty weapons and target drones. They did not win. However, the team could take comfort in the words of USAF Major General Beeson, Commander 73rd Air Division, when he was quoted in the *High Flight* magazine as having said,

In a competition such as William Tell the breaks could fall either way and anyone could turn up a loser or a winner. But for his money, although all the teams were good, only two were really outstanding. The 326th FIS, from Richards Gebauer AFB, flying 102s and the RCAF 425 AW(F) Squadron. The 326th because they flew all their sorties successfully the first time and completed the Meet flying the minimum 16 sorties and the Canadians as they suffered every bad break imaginable, flew 53 sorties to complete the required 16, and on the final day of the Meet still came within an inch of winning. Such a performance was unique and the manner in which the Canadians conducted themselves was an example for all to follow.

The William Tell Meet had awards that acknowledged different aspects of the competition, including: the Top Unit (aircrew), the Weapons Loading Team and the Ground Controller Intercept Team. However, the most coveted was the Top Gun Award, given to the fighter interceptor crew having the best score for the Meet. They, for that day, were the elite of the elite among their peers. They were the 'Top Dog' and had an achievement award to prove it. It is no coincidence that the movie industry saw the potential of making a movie of the fighter aircrew at work. The result was the 1986 blockbuster movie entitled, appropriately enough, *Top Gun*.

Here is a quote from the movie.

Viper: In case some of you are wondering who the best is, they are up here on this plaque. (turns to Maverick)
Viper: Do you think your name will be on that plaque?
Maverick: Yes, Sir.
Viper: That's pretty arrogant, considering the company you're in.
Maverick: Yes, Sir.
Viper: I like that in a pilot.

Due to the demands of the Vietnam War, the competition was not held for another five years, until 1970. Canadians attended the meet again in 1970. In 1972, Canada's third attendance at the William Tell Meet, the Top Gun Award went to two Canadians. Captain T. L. (Lowell) Butters and Captain D. (Douglas) M. Danko of 425 AW (F) Squadron based at CFB Bagotville. The success was especially significant in that it was a Top Gun Award of all aircrew that participated in the competition. Prior to 1972, a Top Gun Award was awarded to each individual aircraft type aircrew, such as the Top Gun for the Convair F-102 Delta Dagger, the Convair F-106 Delta Dart, etc.

Lowell Butters recounted the details of their experience and the events leading up to the Top Gun Award in an interview in 2008. Lowell commented that it was 'a bitter sweet recollection for me'. Memories of the prestigious award were sweet, but also bitter because Douglas Danko, who was his friend, fellow crew-mate and brother-in-law, was later killed in a 421 Squadron flying accident in Europe in 1977. Being a fighter pilot is a very dangerous occupation; there is little room for error, both for the aircrew and the ground crew that overhaul and maintain the aircraft.

Butters had some family connection to the Air Force. He had uncles that had been in the First World War Royal Flying Corps and an uncle in Bomber Command in the Second World War. A BC (British Columbia) boy, he had lived in West Vancouver, Kamloops and Victoria. On his twentieth birthday he was on the beach in Puerto Rico working as a water sports instructor. He mentioned that at the time, 'I realised that I could not be a beach bum all my life.' He observed an airliner flying overhead and he decided that he would return to Canada and apply to be a pilot in the RCAF. It was during officer cadet training in Victoria that he was motivated to try and become a Voodoo pilot after seeing a 409 Squadron Voodoo formation perform at the local Pat Bay airshow.

Initially, he suffered from air sickness, a common complaint, but was able to defeat that and continue training. He mentioned that, 'I transitioned quite well (from the Chipmunk) to the Tutor and frankly did very well in the Tutor and T33 training.' He particularly enjoyed the precision of the instrument and formation flying. The stage had been set by his performance on jet aircraft and he was posted after Wings graduation to T33s with 410 Operational Training Unit in Bagotville, Quebec. He subsequently was posted to the 410 Voodoo Operational Training Unit and upon completion of training was assigned to his first operational squadron – 425 AW (F) 'Alouettes' Squadron, also at Bagotville, Quebec.

The next three years were spent honing his skills as a Voodoo pilot and learning as much as he could about the aircraft and weapons performance. Tactical evaluations, exercises, mutual interceptor combat and holding 'Alert' all contributed to the accumulation of knowledge and skill. I suspect that Lowell's 'I loved it' answer to my many questions was a big part of his development and understanding of his role as a fighter interceptor pilot.

He has very fond memories of the changeover of the Alert crew in CFB Val d'Or. The schedule was set up to return two Voodoos from Val d'Or to Bagotville and to simultaneously send four new Alert Voodoos from Bagotville to Val d'Or. The idea was that the two Voodoos from Val d'Or would do anything, yes anything, to get past the four incoming Voodoos.

The battle was on. The two target Voodoos could be anywhere from terrain following the hills and lakes to supersonic at 45,000 feet. 'I loved it.'

Butters had obviously gained a respect among his peers and squadron commanding officer because during the spring of 1972, he was selected to be on the 425 Squadron Team vying for the right to represent Canada. The 425 Team would be in a competition, called CALLSHOT, with other teams from 409 and 416 Squadrons to determine which of them would go to the William Tell Meet. Intercept missions were set up and assigned marks; the team with the most marks at the end of the competition would head to Florida – quite an incentive!

He recalled that there were four mission profiles flown during CALLSHOT. The first two were a high-altitude supersonic target and a low-altitude, high-speed target, which could 'be very difficult due to ground return'. This was before the days of 'look down shoot down' radar systems which eliminated the clutter from the radar picture and allowed the weapon to lock on to the target. The last two missions were an Electronic Counter Measure target and a high-altitude stern attack.

The team from 425 Squadron, with Butters and Danko as number three crew, won the right to go to the William Tell Meet. The team consisted of four aircraft and crew, and four Ground Control Intercept controllers and Air Defence Technicians. Butters and Danko were team three with Captain Ron Willard as their initial air weapons controller and a supporting ground crew. Unfortunately, Willard had to return to Canada for compassionate reasons and was replaced by Captain Bill McKeigan. There was also a fifth aircraft and crew as reserve, just in case. The team was led by Major Bryce McDonald.

| #1 | Maj Bryce McDonald |
| | Capt Rick Phoenix |

| #2 | Capt Wayne Choptain |
| | Capt Al Oostenbrug |

| #3 | Capt Lowell Butters |
| | Capt Doug Danko |

| #4 | Capt Roger Ayotte |
| | Capt Pete Pellow |

| Spare | Capt Garth Dockery |
| | Capt Bob Leblanc |

The author had the pleasure of attending the CAF basic officer training course in 1968 with Al Oostenbrug and, while researching this book, was saddened to learn that he had been killed in a Voodoo landing accident at Ottawa on 19 February 1980.

Butters and Danko, both in their twenties, flew south to Florida in their million-dollar Voodoo interceptor with their names stencilled on the side of the cockpit. It must have been akin to the Knights of the Round Table, the highest Order of Chivalry at the Court of King Arthur, whose members were supposedly the cream of British chivalry and who followed a strict code of honour and service, setting off with King Arthur for another adventure. It is interesting to compare the military code of conduct of the 1970s CAF version, 425 Squadron, 'Knights of the Air', to some of the basic rules of this select group of knights of the twelfth century:

> To fight for the safety of one's country
> To give one's life for one's country
> To seek nothing before honour
> Never to break faith for any reason

Tyndall AFB, named after the American First World War fighter pilot Francis B. Tyndall, is situated on the Gulf of Mexico in the Florida Panhandle. It is a very large base that encompasses 38 square kilometres (15 square miles). The base was associated with the USAF Air Defense Command from 1 July 1957 to 1 October 1979. The USAF Air Defense Weapons Center and associated 4756th Drone Squadron (later Air Depot Squadron) were resident units. The drone squadron provided supersonic and subsonic target drones for the William Tell Meet.

Landing at Tyndall AFB, Lowell commented on 'the sheer size of the tarmac and the number of aircraft parked there'. He was aware that there were twelve teams present for the William Tell Meet, each with five aircraft: three F-102 teams, three F-106 teams, five F-101 teams and the lone CF-101 team. Lowell and Doug, along with their teammates, were representing Canada, representing the CAF, representing 425 Squadron and representing themselves.

The teams were welcomed, briefed, fed and housed. The USAF was a generous and well-organised host. This was the third year that the invitation had been extended to the Canadians. They had come close in the past but were unable to capture the team trophy or the coveted Top Gun award. Would this be the year that Canada would add its name to the illustrious list of winners?

The four crews were each required to fly a set of four profiles, three live-fire and one dry-fire, and would be marked on the results. The primary

Tyndall AFB, Florida, USA.

weapons system – the Genie rocket – would be marked by the Multiple Airborne Trajectory System. The system computed the position of the fighter interceptor aircraft, the rocket time and space calculation to the detonation point and the position of the target. Marks were assigned as per the accuracy of the result. The secondary weapons system – the Falcon missile – was assigned marks on whether it hit the target or not.

The heart of the Meet was a large scoreboard where you could observe your progress and that of the other teams. The days became an exciting and fast-paced series of briefings, mission and aircraft preparation, and flying the profiles. Coordination between the Weapons Loading Team, the maintenance team and the Ground Control Intercept controllers kept the crew busy. Everyone worked towards the same goal: to get an armed, serviceable aircraft in the air to the right place to shoot down the target.

Captain Lowell Butters (L) and Captain Douglas Danko. (Courtesy of Manny Soberal)

Butters observed 'that 6 of the 8 team members were pipeliners', meaning that this was their first squadron tour after graduation.

By the time Butters and Danko climbed into their aircraft, number 101063, they had trained for four months and now was the time to show their peers and teammates that they deserved to be on that team. Their first profile was the low-level, between 500 and 1,000 feet above the sea, Teledyne Ryan TDU-25B towed target. They had one Falcon missile, one chance to hit the target. Their controller had set them up nicely and, in spite of the ground clutter, Doug was able to give Lowell a good radar picture, which assisted them and the seeker head in the Falcon missile to find the heat source of the target.

They had one shot at this intercept. Lowell took the ARM SEL knob and turned it to the MISSILES IR position. At the same time, he was flying the dot in the F scope to ensure that the aircraft and the infrared sensor were both pointing at the target. Lifting the red guard, he placed the MASTER ARM switch on. Now the FCS system was calculating the envelope to fire the missile – it was very narrow at these low altitudes. Holding the trigger to the Trigger 2 position, he waited for the missile to fire. The Falcon left the Voodoo's weapons door rail and streaked at Mach 3 to the target. Lowell was very close by now and he saw the missile hit the target. No doubt about the mark for this profile. This was the very first time that the crew had ever fired a live missile and they had hit the target.

The second profile was the supersonic Firebee BQM 34F Drone. This was more work for the AWC, as he had to calculate the geometry correctly for the intercept, which was happening at extremely fast speeds. Lowell and Doug were flying at 35,000 feet and the target was at 50,000 feet. This was a frontal attack using the Genie rocket and a 15,000 feet snap-up. This profile was one with which they were very familiar. Lowell reached behind the control column to unlock the ejector racks. The Genie rockets were stored internally until just before firing, when the ejector door rotated and the rocket hung out below the fuselage.

He turned the ARM SEL knob to the SPL WPN FCS position, raised the guard on the MASTER ARM switch and turned it on. Doug once again had a good radar picture; the maintenance guys had the tube driven radar and FCS working well in spite of the Florida humidity. Lowell was concentrating on steering the dot on the F scope and holding the trigger on. He moved the throttles into afterburner to maintain the speed as they performed the 15,000 feet snap-up climb manoeuvre. The crew heard the rumble beneath their feet as the ejector door rotated, a very good sign. Then Lowell got the next good sign, the large X on his screen signifying that the weapon had fired. Small charges blew the rocket off the racks, followed by the rocket motor lighting off. Once again the rocket streaked

off, leaving a trail of smoke which was easy to follow. It was all up to the
Multiple Airborne Trajectory System to assign a score. Two down, two to
go.

The next profile, the dry night-time Martin EB-57 ECM run, proved to be
'the most difficult from a technical point of view', said Lowell. The EB-57
was a formidable target due to its jamming capacity, both electronic and
mechanical. It had multiple India band jammers for the fighter radar and
multiple Delta, Echo, and Fox band jammers for the ground-based radar
sites. Not to mention the mechanical chaff jamming. This was going to take
all their skill, some luck and perhaps some yank, bank and crank to get the
MA. Lowell and Doug would have to work as a team extraordinaire to
put an X on the board for this profile.

Bill McKeigan, their Ground Control Intercept controller, had put them
in a good position to pick up the target at around 46 km for a frontal attack.
That was the last time they got a steady target acquisition. The closing
speeds now meant that Team #3 had to get their aircraft manoeuvred into
position in less than two minutes. The heavy jamming and suspected high
humidity was causing Doug's radar to break lock frequently. He tried all
his tricks to stay away from the jamming, but the crew on the other end
were determined that no Canadian was going to shoot them down.

Lowell recounted, vividly reliving every moment of the attack as his
voice became quite animated: 'We were probably about a mile from firing
– that was going to be tough, actually to get the lock on – get dot in –
centred, because if you did not get the trigger down, it would abort. I had
to trick the system. The dot was still out there. We locked on again, I had
to take trigger 2, the door started to open. I pulled and pulled and pulled
until I centred the dot. The (firing) X came on and the radar broke lock.
We broke off. A bit of luck – incredible skill in the back seat and I did
pretty good in the front seat too.' They had done it again – 3 for 3 – a
perfect score.

The last profile was a front-stern re-attack. This involved a successful
attack approaching the target head-on, and then immediately reversing
direction and attacking the target from behind. Bill set them up again and
they successfully carried out the two attacks. Lowell and Doug knew that
they had done well. However, bad luck appeared and the scoring system
failed to work. There was no official record of the attack. They had to
repeat the attack sequence the next morning. They did, and Murphy's
Law reared its ugly head – the scoring system had failed again. They knew
they were in contention and just had to keep doing what they had done
in the past. Once again, they repeated the profile in the afternoon. This
time there was a score: they were tied for first place with two other USAF
Voodoo crews.

The Meet was extended for a day to arrange a shoot-out. Each aircraft would be given one AIM-4D Falcon missile to fire at a fully-manoeuvrable, remotely-controlled Firebee BQM-34A Drone. The three fighters would be held on Combat Alert Patrol and one at a time would be cleared to attack the drone when it entered a defined area. It could only be shot down within this area, time was paramount. Bill would be ready with initial directions as soon as the Drone passed over the line.

A 'Happy Hooligans' crew from the Fargo, North Dakota Squadron, went first and never got a shot away. Next was the Voodoo crew from the Bangor, Maine Squadron, and missed the target. Then it was Lowell's and Doug's turn. The target was flying in an evasive pattern, right to left at 20 degrees off their nose. Lowell had to be careful as he manoeuvred his aircraft that there was no 'G' loading on his aircraft when he fired the Falcon weapon. He recalled that 'the missile went up and then down before taking the wing off the Drone. It blew it out of the sky. Kind of cool as it fell in the ocean.' He asked Bill how they had done compared to the other crews. He said, 'I think you are going to like it'.

After landing, they taxied onto the ramp and saw the crowd of approximately 2,000 people cheering the Canadian crew. They were the first CAF crew to win the coveted NORAD Top Gun Award. In addition, they were awarded the 'Apple Splitter' Award for shooting down the

Captain Lowell Butters (L) and Captain Douglas Danko with Top Gun and Apple Splitter Trophies. (Courtesy of Manny Soberal)

Firebee drone. Tradition demanded that they were soaked with a fire hose as soon as they put their feet on terra firma. On that day, 28 September 1972, Lowell Butters and Doug Danko were at the pinnacle of their Voodoo flying career. They had achieved Top Dog status amongst their peers. The Olympic Gold Medal of the NORAD fighter interceptor crews.

Shortly after returning from the William Tell Meet to CFB Bagotville, Quebec, Lowell and Doug were posted to 410 (OTU) Squadron as instructors, where they could pass on their knowledge to the next generation of 'pipeliners'. Lowell finished off his twelve-year-Voodoo career with 2,012 hours flying time in his favourite '101'. He 'loved the aeroplane and its roll in Air Defence', seeds that were sown watching the Voodoo formation at the 1967 Pat Bay airshow. Now that is a Canadian with the 'right stuff', from spectator to Top Gun in five years.

Top Left: 409 Nighthawk Squadron.
Top Right: 410 Cougar Squadron.
Bottom Left: 416 Lynx Squadron.
Bottom Right: 425 Alouette Squadron.

CHAPTER SEVEN

Avro CF-100 Canuck

The good-natured fight was on, but there was always the same winner! Pilot: 'I am going to turn up the heat a bit.' Electronic Warfare Officer: 'No way – I am sweating!' Pilot: 'Too bad, I am going to turn it up anyway, I am so cold that I cannot feel my feet.' Electronic Warfare Officer: 'Go ahead, it won't make any difference – I have pulled the circuit breaker!' So, once again the age-old heat problem occurred in the only Canadian indigenous fighter to ever be utilised in squadron service.

In reality, the crew had to compromise. Judicious use of the heat bypass switch allowed the pilot to remain warm enough to land the aircraft safely and cool enough that the EWO did not pass out from heat exhaustion! The Avro CF-100 Canuck, affectionately known as the Clunk or Lead Sled, was notorious for the lack of, or too much, heat, depending on where you sat in the cockpit. The pilot froze and the Electronic Warfare Officer sweated.

The particular aircraft in our story, aircraft number 100779, was assigned to 416 Squadron, Air Defence Command at St Hubert, Quebec, on 6 November 1958. It returned to the manufacturer, A. V. Roe Canada Ltd, on 23 June 1960 to be converted to an electronic warfare version, the Mk 5C. It returned to service on 26 October 1960 with the Electronic Warfare Unit, also at St Hubert, Quebec.

While researching this book for specific aircraft information, J. (Jerry) E. Vernon said, 'No problem I can get you that information. It is all on the aircraft record card.' Jerry is President of the Canadian Aviation Historical Society, Vancouver Chapter, and is widely respected for his aviation knowledge and enthusiasm. His favourite phrases are: 'You might want to try ..., have you looked at ..., there was a book written about ..., if you cannot find it give me a call.' The above information on 100779 was supplied by Jerry.

Thirteen years later, the same aircraft was one of the target aircraft in the Amalgam Mute exercise on 10 May 1973. The pilot, Lt Douglas

Fitzpatrick, still froze and the Electronic Warfare Officer, Captain Bill Bland, still sweated! Perhaps the answer to the heat mystery lies in the fact that the parent company in England supplied some of the original wartime staff to Victory Aircraft, now A. V. Roe Canada Ltd, and that the air-conditioning designers were not familiar with Canadian winters!

Canada had successfully built aircraft under licence during the Second World War, the Avro Lancaster bomber and Hawker Hurricane fighter being two examples. The fledgling industry had acquired a great deal of expertise of building other people's designs. Was the time right for a Canadian team to design and produce an aircraft? What kind of aircraft should it be? This chapter will examine the Canadian aviation industry during the later stages of the Second World War, the Canadian defence requirements after the war and the evolution of the Avro CF-100 to meet those and future requirements.

The National Steel Car Company established an aircraft manufacturing plant at Malton, Ontario, in 1938, which subsequently became Toronto International Airport. National Steel Car Company was part of a consortium called Canadian Associated Aircraft, where many companies pooled their expertise to build British military aircraft in Canada. Initially building Westland Lysanders and Avro Ansons, the company became a Crown corporation, Victory Aircraft, and finished the Second World War building the famous Avro Lancaster bomber.

Larry Milberry, in his book *The AVRO CF-100*, stated that

> Canada could see a post-war economic slump happening at the end of the war and was concerned of the plight of its aircraft industry. The white knight for Victory Aircraft turned out to be an Englishman, Sir Roy Dobson of A. V. Roe Manchester, who returned to Canada to form A. V. Roe Canada Ltd, commonly referred to as Avro Canada or just Avro. He was given favourable terms by the government to operate the new company. For example, he had the Malton wartime plant rent free until the company turned a profit. After the end of the Second World War the skilled workforce had dropped from 9,600 to 300 people.

Sir Roy kept the workforce employed on non-aircraft work until he could negotiate a contract for an aviation project. He realised that the future of the company lay in the design and manufacture of a Canadian aircraft. He actively recruited design personnel from such English companies as Hawker Siddeley, De Havilland and of course A. V. Roe. Two projects were being considered at that time: a commercial jet aircraft known as the C.102 Jetliner for Trans-Canada airlines and a jet fighter for the RCAF. The Jetliner became a casualty of the 1950 Korean War and was scrapped in favour of production of the new fighter aircraft. Avro Chief Engineer Jim Floyd maintained that the abandonment of the commercial Jetliner was an even greater tragedy for Canada than the cancellation of the Arrow interceptor.

Early 1946 was a turning point for the company. The National Research Council, and later a Crown corporation called Turbo Research Limited, had been doing work with jet engines in the latter stages of the war. The government did not wish to continue the engine development and Sir Roy saw the opportunity to avail himself of the previous development and make Turbo Research part of Avro. He did so in April 1946. Their experimental jet engine, the 4,057-pound thrust TR-4 Chinook, first ran on 17 March 1948. It was a fortuitous move as Turbo Research became the famous Canadian jet engine manufacturer of Orenda engines, which would power both the Canadair CL-13 Sabre and the Avro CF-100 Canuck.

Everything was in place for a military contract, but who, or what, would make it happen? Existing and developing designs were examined by the RCAF, including the British Gloster Meteor, the English Electric Canberra and the American Lockheed Starfire. None of these aircraft met the unique RCAF requirements that included long range, high altitude, fast climb, capacity to carry arms and ammunition to destroy an invader, and the ability to operate in very cold temperatures. Avro had been negotiating with the RCAF regarding proposal 'Air-7-1' while simultaneously considering the development of the Jetliner. The Air-7-1 stipulated a Canadian-designed, twin-engined-jet, all-weather interceptor to defend Canada's northern frontier.

Avro submitted three proposals in August 1946. A design was accepted in October by the government and the detailed design of the XC-100 commenced in May 1947. Avro had managed to secure not only the design of the airframe but also the contract for the engines. It is interesting to note that Avro stayed with the straight-wing concept, although Germany had built swept-wing jet fighters in the latter stages of the war. This was possibly due to the British heritage of the designers, or the fact that the straight wing was a tried and true design. Always striving for aerodynamic efficiency, the engines were moved forward and down, and subsequently rearwards, because the centre of lift was too far forward; this required the main spar to be notched to accommodate them. More importantly, the engine relocation caused the notches to create a flexible structure in a heavy stress area that would shortly cause a major problem in the fighter development.

The Chinook engine evolved into the TR-5 Orenda engine, which, at 6,500-pound thrust, was suitable for the CF-100. Orenda is an Iroquois word meaning in a general sense 'Magic Power' or 'Great Spirit'. The engine first ran on 10 February 1949. It was the first Canadian-designed production jet engine used in a Canadian-produced aircraft. A preproduction agreement was signed on 17 May 1949 for ten aircraft: the Mk.2 with Orenda 2 engines. However, only one aircraft was ever built, 18103. Meanwhile, work continued on the two Mk.1 prototypes which would use the British Rolls-Royce RA.2 Avon engines until the Orenda engine was available.

Ron Page recounted in his book, *Canuck: CF-100 All Weather Fighter,* that,

> The first prototype flew on 19 January 1950 with Bill Waterton at the controls. He had been leant to Avro by Gloster Aircraft in Britain as they required a very experienced test pilot. Waterton had experimental flying experience and hundreds of hours flying single and twin jet fighters with the Avon engine. A coup also for the Public Relations department in the matter of national pride; the first Canadian designed and built jet fighter aircraft was being test flown by a Canadian, he had been born in Camrose, Alberta in 1916.

The CF-100 took to the skies in just over three years from design acceptance to first flight. Avro had grown to 4,000 employees and the cost had grown to $140,000,000 before the Mark 1 prototype, aircraft number 18101, flew. High-speed taxi tests had been completed in the previous two days. It was a cool and clear January day when the CF-100 went airborne for the first time. The cool air gave the Avon engines lots of thrust. The aircraft performance was enhanced by a light fuel load. The full power of acceleration was tremendous. In less than 550 yards (503 metres) it lifted cleanly off the runway, according to Ron Page.

The undercarriage, the British term used by Avro in that era for landing gear, would not retract and was left down for the rest of the flight. The aircraft climbed to 5,000 feet for testing of the flying qualities, albeit with the undercarriage down. The air brakes and flaps were also cycled. The test flight lasted 40 minutes and was completed with an uneventful landing, only using 550 metres of the runway length, remarkable for a jet fighter. The subsequent flight, after the undercarriage safety lock system was fixed, occurred on 25 January and explored low-speed flight and stalling characteristics.

The third flight was where the design flaw showed up. The innocent notches, previously mentioned, created the problem. Following the test flight with high-speed passes and tight turns, it was discovered that the fairings – aerodynamic covers at the wing root, joined to the fuselage – were torn and twisted. This was an indication of flexibility in the spar and wing attachment area – where the wing meets the fuselage – and a lack of flexibility in the engine nacelle fairing. Avro had to find a permanent solution to the problem quickly. The whole CF-100 project was at risk: the ten preproduction Mark 2 aircraft, the $140 million spent already and a production contract. Who would be the saviour?

It turned out to be Waclaw Czerwinski, an aeronautical engineer who first worked in the stress office and subsequently as a project engineer. There had been attempts with spar end and doubler plates to solve the problem over the years, but the fix was now critical as the production line was underway. The solution had to be simple and applicable to components already built. He strengthened the spar at the notches or dips and inserted a pin joint where the wing joined the engine nacelle. His redesign solved the problem and by late 1952 was applied to all production aircraft. The airframe was now acceptable, but what was happening to the Orenda engine?

The Orenda engine continued to accumulate hours and had run for 1,000 hours by 23 September 1949. The development was not without its problems, which all had to be solved. During the period from 1948 to the end of 1949, for instance, the engine suffered from several seventh-stage compressor rotor failures. It flew for the first time on board an Avro Lancaster test bed aircraft on 13 July 1950. It was installed in a North American F-86A Sabre, USAF serial 47-616, which flew 'on its own' for the first time on 5 October 1950. By 5 February 1951, the engine had accumulated 5,000 hours running time. Thoroughly tested by 20 June 1951, the Orenda flew in the third CF-100 built, the Mark 2 serial number 18103.

Canada's first indigenous jet fighter was now complete. The Canadian airframe, the Canuck, and Canadian engine, the Orenda, had started down the path to eventual aircraft production for the RCAF. The American Mustang and the British De Havilland Vampire would relinquish their Canadian defence roles to the Canadian all-weather CF-100 fighter interceptor. A glorious and exciting time for the fledgling Canadian aviation industry as it demonstrated its ability to conceive, design and produce a military aircraft suitable for its own requirements.

The toll this development exacted on people's lives should not be underestimated. The Soviet explosion of their first atomic bomb in September 1949 and the Korean War in June 1950 greatly concerned the Canadian political and military leaders. There was tremendous pressure on the young company to get the aircraft approved and into production. Setbacks were dealt with swiftly. The tragic loss of test pilot Bruce Warren and observer Robert Ostrander in the second prototype, 18102, on 5 April 1951 was one of those setbacks. It was suspected that an oxygen problem had caused the crash. Warren was quickly replaced by Peter Cope, a test pilot from Armstrong Whitworth Aircraft in England.

Cope recalled, when first flying the CF-100, that, 'My first reaction was extreme disappointment. I heard so much about this airplane in England and what it could do, and when I flew it and found out how far short it fell of what I heard it had many shortcomings that would not be acceptable to the air force and it was a job sometimes to convince Avro that they had to fix these things.' It would be up to Cope and his colleagues to improve the later versions to the superior aircraft that it eventually became.

One of his colleagues was Jan Zurakowski, the best-known name of test pilots in Canada due to his work on the CF-100 and CF-105 Arrow. A war-time Polish Air Force ace, he was a graduate of the RAF Empire Test Pilot's School and flew as a test pilot with Gloster Aircraft in England. His demonstration, 'Zurabatics', of the Gloster Meteor F-8 at the Farnborough International Airshow in 1951 amazed the public and colleagues alike. Peter Cope describes him as 'the most brilliant test pilot we ever had in England'. Zurakowski was renowned for his built-in ability to diagnose airplane responses in terms of its performance ability, its handling ability and overall stability.

He arrived at Avro on 22 April 1952 and by 11 October 1952 he test-flew the Mark 4 on its first flight. His legacy with Avro had begun. Two months later, on 4 December 1952, he flew 18112, a Mark 4, supersonically. It was the first time a CF-100 had flown supersonically; Zurakowski always pushed the flight envelope in search of further knowledge in the advancement of aviation. He flew the Arrow's first flight on 25 March 1958 and retired as Avro's Chief Development Test pilot in October 1958.

The first Mark 3 CF-100, 18104, was handed over to the RCAF at Malton, Ontario, on 17 October 1951, after four days of demonstration and handling trials. It had now been five years since the first proposals had been prepared by Avro. The handover was more symbolic than practical; there still was not a single CF-100 flying in the defence of Canada. The programme needed this handover of pomp and ceremony to appease some bad press and doubters in the government. However, time was still the issue. With the spar problem resolved, the first aircraft was delivered to the RCAF for actual use on 22 July 1952. A Mark 3, 18108, was delivered to North Bay, Ontario, for No. 3 All Weather (Fighter) Operational Training Unit.

The three Mark 3 aircraft in North Bay were all preproduction aircraft and had poor quality control and detail design. Like other preproduction machines, they had 'bugs' which would require further development, including nose gear retraction problems due to air load rigging sensitivity, unreliable solenoid fuel transfer valves, hydraulic pumps failing and erratic radios. The fuel management system was very complicated and required particular attention. The first aircraft had the Hughes AN/APG 33 radar, suitable for gun-laying or curve of pursuit tactics. By this time Avro was

Avro CF-100 production line, Malton, Ontario. (Courtesy of DND, Directorate of History and Heritage)

considering variations of the CF-100, including the use of rockets to supplement and/or replace the guns, high altitude, jet-assisted takeoff, and engine afterburner versions.

The various Marks, five built and two proposed, of CF-100 evolved as experience, innovations, developments in engines and armament, and requirements changed. The production line responded to these changes and modified the assembly as necessary. The various parts, about 30,000, came together at the Avro factory at Malton, Ontario. These parts included those made in-house and from the hundreds of sub-contractors. The fuselage, including engines, was assembled in one bay and then moved to the final assembly bay,~ where the wings and equipment were added. Page mentions 'that in 1954 40,000 Canadians were involved in the production of the CF-100', and he includes a description of the various Marks.

MARK 1

The Mark 1 was the prototype design and two were built using a Rolls-Royce Avon engine.

MARK 2

The Mark 2 was the preproduction design using the Orenda 2 engines. Only one aircraft of the original ten ordered was built to this specification. Four were converted to dual controls (2T), four were converted to dual controls, Mark 3 standards (3T) with the Orenda 2 (unverified) engine, and the last one to a Mark 4 trials installation standard. The Mark 2T, serial 18105, was assigned to the Air Force Central Experimental and Proving Establishment at Rockliffe, Ontario, for jet-assisted takeoff and rocket pod trials. One curious design feature was the offsetting of the control column to the left. The row of fuel instruments across the top of the instrument panel caused the blind flying instruments to be located lower in the panel. By offsetting the control column, the artificial horizon was clearly visible. This undesirable situation (the natural tendency to centre the control column caused the aircraft to roll to the right) was remedied in subsequent Marks by moving the fuel instruments.

MARK 3

The Mark 3 was the initial fighter version which would take over the squadron defence responsibilities. It was produced in various models: the Mark 3A and 3B with Orenda 8 engines, the Mark 3CT production gun fighter, the 3D production dual-control gunnery trainer, and the Mark 3T, the converted Mark 2, dual-control flight trainer. The wing to nacelle fairing on the Mark 3 was greatly enlarged to prevent high-speed buffeting at high altitudes.

MARK 4

The last of the preproduction group, serial 18112, was used as the Mark 4 prototype. There were two easily visible external changes from the Mark 3: the round bulbous nose housing the Hughes MG-2 fire control system and the larger AN/APG-40 airborne gun laying radar, and the one-piece clear canopy without any middle bracing. The Mark 4A and 4B were powered by the Orenda 9 and Orenda 11 engines respectively. It is interesting to note that by June 1954, the CF-100 Mark 4 was coming off the assembly line at the rate of one a day!

In 1955 Zurakowski demonstrated the Mark 4B at the Farnborough International Air Show. It was the first time that an aircraft produced outside England performed there. Similar to his demonstration of the Gloster Meteor

CF-100 Orenda 11 Engine. (Courtesy of Author)

years before, he once again put on a spectacular show. He started with a high-speed pass into a series of vertical rolls, then his trademark falling leaf, only to recover by a spin and a recovery over centre stage. It was an incredible display for a large fighter, all within the confines of the airfield.

MARK 5

The Mark 5 originated as an Avro proposal to modify the Mark 4 with updated weaponry, afterburning engines and a new, thinner wing. Cost was the deciding factor. The compromise, to extend the CF-100 life, was to lighten the fuselage, remove the gun pack and extend the wings and tailplane. The Mark 5 had the Orenda 11 engines. This added about 5,000 feet to the absolute ceiling of the Mark 4, enabling the Mark 5 to reach over 49,000 feet. AI Navigator Captain Ken Penny recounted that, 'when I was flying the Mark 5 at (CFB) Bagotville we could get the Mark 5 to 54,000 feet'. The problem was that the limiting Mach and stall speed were so close together at that altitude. In the event of a pressurisation problem, it was very difficult to descend. A limit was set of 45,000 feet. The first production aircraft flew on 12 October 1955.

Fifty-three Mark 5 aircraft were supplied to the Belgian Air Force under the Mutual Aid Plan. This was the only sale of the aircraft outside

Canada. The Americans were very protective of their aircraft industry and, as seen by their attitude towards the Arrow, were not interested in any foreign military aircraft purchases, no matter how good the product. Towards the end of production in 1958, five Mark 5s were converted to 5M configuration. These aircraft were modified to carry the Sparrow 2 missiles in support of the Arrow weapons development program.

The CF-100 carried out its defence duties until replaced by the controversial, US-produced CF-101 Voodoo aircraft in 1962. The Air Force found itself with surplus CF-100s. Further investigation revealed that the longevity of the airframe, 20,000 hours life to destruction, and the improved performance of the engines, made it feasible for the aircraft to assume other roles. This new role would be electronic warfare.

The CF-100 in our mission story, Chapter Nine, was a Mark 5C. The 5C and the 5D were converted from the Mark 5 by removing the wing tip extensions, increasing the fuel load, filling the fuselage weapons bay with electronic counter-measure equipment and adding chaff dispensers to the hard points under the wings. Captain Richard Sopczak was assigned to the Canadian Experimental Proving Establishment in 1962 to work on the installation of the AN/ALT-501 jammer in the CF-100 Mark 5D. The jammer was made in Toronto, Ontario, until the company closed in 1966. This fighter interceptor jammer, he said, 'could have up to 6,000 volts in it and use 1 amp of current. It generated large amounts of heat and required a liquid cooled radiator and airflow to remain cool. It was mounted in the old machine gun pod and could be lowered on four cables for maintenance.' Richard mentioned that the first prototype Mark 5D was destroyed in a hangar fire at St Hubert, Quebec.

Serial 18472, delivered to the RCAF on 28 June 1955, had flown the most of any CF-100. It had nearly 6,000 airframe hours when all CAF CF-100 flying ceased in December 1981. It was quite the career for the CF-100, a fighter aircraft, from the prototype first flight in January 1950 to its Mark 5C/D phase-out, which amounts to nearly thirty-two years flying the skies of Canada and Europe. The author checked his log book and noted that the last time he flew 100472, new CAF number designation, was on Thursday 2 May 1974 from CFB Winnipeg to CFB North Bay in 2.0 hours with Electronic Warfare Officer Captain Larry Parakin. We had just spent ten days at CFB Comox, British Columbia, flying exercises in the 25th NORAD Region. Noted in the log book margin was the fact, obviously concurred to by Larry (!), that we did a 'roll off the top' manoeuvre prior to landing to celebrate coming home after the long deployment. Zurakowski would have been proud.

Author and Captain Peter Maunsell over Alaska in 1973. (Courtesy of Author)

MARK 6

The Mark 6 was to be a Mark 5 with engine reheat – afterburners – to increase the thrust with the addition of Sparrow or Falcon missiles. The Falcon was subsequently used on the CF-101 Voodoo.

MARK 7

The Mark 7 was to be the same wingspan as the Mark 4, but with more area and thinner chord section. Both the Mark 6 and 7 were attempts by designers struggling to make the subsonic, straight-wing CF-100 last longer. The horse had already left the stable. The USSR had bombers that could easily outpace the CF-100 and what was needed was a supersonic fighter interceptor. The Avro Arrow was already on the drawing board but, as we saw in Chapter Five, it was not to be. Avro Canada's '15 years' of military aviation fame was coming to an end.

MARK 8

The Mark 8 proposal was for a long-range missile version using the Bendix Eagle missiles mounted on the wing tips. The basic Mark 4 wing and Orenda 11 engines would be used. Further modifications, such as thin wings and different engines, were being considered. The Mark 8, like the Mark 6 and 7, did not stand a chance against the political will of the day to buy American. The Avro Arrow had met the criteria for a supersonic fighter, but the government had already decided on abandoning it and reequipping with the CF-101 Voodoo and Bomarc missile.

TRAINING CREWS

On 22 July 1952, the delivery of a Mark 3 CF-100 was the start of No. 3 All Weather (Fighter) Operational Training Unit in North Bay, Ontario. During 1950, two experienced Canadian Second World War night fighter/ intruder crew were sent to England to observe the RAF and to the USA to observe the USAF train their all-weather fighter organisations. Then, a core group of similarly experienced pilots and Navigators went to the USA to train as fighter interceptor instructors. Finally, in mid-summer 1952, there were three CF-100s at the Operational Training Unit ready to train students.

The first chief instructor was Squadron Leader R. (Joe) D. Schultz, a very experienced jet pilot. Part of the training was to practice scrambles and he, reportedly, was one of the fastest to get airborne after the horn sounded. He was subsequently appointed director of the Canadian Armed Forces Flight Safety organisation in 1966. The author had the privilege of taking his excellent Flight Safety Officer's course in 1973.

Milberry extensively covers the CF-100 crew training and said,

It was not long, 1955, before the Operational Training Unit moved to Cold Lake, Alberta, where there were better facilities for the firing of live weapons. The training course generally ran thirteen weeks and was divided into three phases. Phase 1 introduced the pilots to airborne interception theory and techniques and the Navigators to the Hughes MG-2 fire control system. The first ten days was all academic study. Phase 2 trained the pilots on the CF-100 Mark 3 dual-control aircraft and the Navigators to high level navigation and Air Defence Command procedures. Crew cooperation was being taught at the same time. Phase three, the next six weeks, consisted of half a day studying and half a day flying the dual-control Mark 3s. At the same time, pilots and Navigators were getting to know each other and through social and professional interaction 'married' to form a crew for further training. The next week was spent in the simulator to hone their skills and familiarise themselves with the Mark 4 before the crew did their first live air intercept.

Captain Peter Maunsell mentioned that 'the North American B-25 Mitchell bomber was used by the RCAF to train the AI Navigators on the APG-40 radar before the advent of the simulator'. During the following three weeks the days were split between flying and simulator. The final three weeks were spent flying afternoon and nights.

All sessions were carefully monitored by the instructors and crews would be debriefed and instructed as required. An exercise would be repeated, if needed, to the full satisfaction of the instructor; there was no room for misunderstandings or errors. The aircrew worked very closely with the third member of the team, the Ground Control Intercept Controller. The controller controlled the target and the fighter to complete the exercise. 'Butting heads' was a common term used to describe the two aircraft approaching each other head-on for the attack.

The crews came in to the course as individuals and left as a highly efficient team to assume the defence of Canada. At its peak in the 1950s, RCAF Station Cold Lake was training up to seventy-five crews simultaneously. Some of the participants remarked that 'these were the glory days of the post-war RCAF' as it reequipped and formed Sabre and Canuck squadrons. The exciting era of the jet fighter had arrived. The sheer speed, noise, performance, tactics and agility of the new jet aircraft ensured that the crews became the new generation of the 'Knights of the Air'.

ARMAMENT

The CF-100 was initially armed with eight Colt Browning M3 50-inch (12.7-mm) calibre machine guns mounted in the belly of the aircraft. Each gun had 200 rounds of ammunition and was contained in a gun pack unit: a big magnesium casting to store, feed and fire the ammunition, which was designed to be detachable from the aircraft. Replenishment was fast and efficient because the gun pack could be removed and a fully loaded one replaced in its position. In contrast, the Second World War armourers had to replace each ammunition box and feed the belts into each gun separately. Initially, however, the standard of manufacturer tolerances did not allow interchange ability, which frustrated Avro and the RCAF.

The primary design had called for a retractable ventral forty-eight rocket belly pack to extend behind the gun pack. This belly pack contained the 2.75-inch Folding Fin Aircraft Rockets. Simultaneously, the wing tip rocket design was being developed. Aircraft serial 18112 completed the ground test of the belly rocket pack and in January 1954 it started flight testing. It was discovered immediately that with speeds in excess of 300 knots (345 mph 556 km/h), the aircraft nose pitched up and the airframe began to

CF-100 Colt Browning gun pack. (Courtesy of Author)

buffet. On 23 August 1954, Zurakowski was flight testing 18112 when several explosions occurred and he lost control of the aircraft and ejected. His observer, John Hiebert, unfortunately died in the crash. The cause of the crash was surmised to be the ignition of a fuel leak caused by the buffeting of the aircraft during extensive rocket-pack testing. Shortly thereafter, the rocket-pack project was abandoned in favour of the wingtip pod design.

A wingtip pod design of twenty-nine 2.75-inch Folding Fin Aircraft Rockets was decided upon after extensive studies showed that twenty-nine was the most effective salvo size. It should be noted that the whole pod, one on each wingtip, was fired in one salvo, fifty-eight rockets at once. The pod sequence was that the tail cone was explosively jettisoned, the centre rockets fired first to break the nose cone and then the empty pod was jettisoned from the wingtip. These primitive rockets sometimes were very unstable and gained the nickname 'Fickle Fin Rockets'. It was not unknown for the rockets to hit each other or to be embedded in the firing aircraft!

When mated with the Hughes APG-40 radar system, however, the rockets gave the CF-100 a formidable weapons presence for the 1950s. The machine-guns were used in a curved pursuit attack and the rockets were used in a Lead Collision Course attack. A Lead Collision Course is the calculated timed release of the rockets to arrive at the same location and same time as the target. To cut the cost down of training a three, and later seven, tube pod design was used. A fully armed shot, fifty-eight rockets, was reputed to have cost $6,000; you would not want to miss!

The Mark 3 had guns only and the Mark 4 had guns and wing tip rocket pods. The Mark 5 had the wing tip rocket pods on the extended wings and had removed the gun pack to reduce weight. By the time of Mark 5 production, heat-seeking missiles and nuclear warhead rockets carried by supersonic fighters were becoming the weapons of the day. With the cancellation of the Arrow, neither weapon has been carried by a Canadian-designed fighter aircraft since the CF-100.

SQUADRONS IN EUROPE

The CF-100s were coming off the production line at one a day in the early 1950s and were assigned to various squadrons and units at home, and eventually overseas to support Canada's NATO commitment in Europe. A total of 692 aircraft were built during the contract. In 1957, the Belgian Air Force had three squadrons, numbers 11, 349 and 350, flying the CF-100 Mark 5.

The CF-100 had served in many squadrons in many locations in the ten years from the handover in 1952 of aircraft 18108 to No. 3 Operational Training Unit at North Bay to the last flight as a fighter in December 1962; the first squadron to fly the CF-100 was 445 'Wolverine' Squadron in April 1953 based at North Bay, Ontario. It was the first CF-100 squadron to go to Europe as part of No. 1 Air Division and took over from 410 'Cougars' Squadron in Marville, France, in November 1956. Similarly, 423 'Eagle' Squadron was formed at St Hubert, Quebec, in June 1953 and went to Grostenquin, France, to serve in No. 1 Air Division. 440 'Red Bat' Squadron was formed at Bagotville, Quebec, in October 1953 and joined No. 3 Wing, No. 1 Air Division at Zweibrucken, Germany, in May 1957. 419 'Moose' Squadron formed in North Bay in March 1954 and was deployed in August 1957 to No. 4 Wing at Baden-Soellingen, Germany. In 1958, Europe was the CF-100's playground – four RCAF and three Belgian squadrons defending it from Communist aggression.

Who was looking after the home front? Nine squadrons were formed over the space of three years to provide vital defence support in Canada: 428 Ghost Squadron formed in June 1954 at Uplands (Ottawa), Ontario; 425 Alouette Squadron formed in October 1954 at St Hubert, Quebec, at the same time as 432 Black Cougar Squadron formed at Bagotville, Quebec; 409 The Nighthawks Squadron formed in November 1954 at Comox, British Columbia, at the same time as 433 Porcupine Squadron at Cold Lake, Alberta; 410 Cougar Squadron formed at Uplands, Ontario,

CF-100, NATO camouflage and black prototype paint. (Courtesy of Canadian Forces Joint Imagery Centre, Department of National Defence)

in November 1956, followed by 413 The Tuskers Squadron at Bagotville, Quebec, in May 1957; 416 Lynx Squadron formed at St Hubert, Quebec, in February 1957, followed by 414 The Black Knights Squadron in August 1957. There were nine squadrons of CF-100s on the home guard as Canada was negotiating the 1958 NORAD agreement.

Other units that flew the CF-100 were the Central Experimental and Proving Establishment/Aerospace Engineering & Test Establishment at Cold Lake, Alberta, and Uplands, Ontario, No. 3 All Weather (Fighter) Operational Trainig Unit at North Bay, Cold Lake and Bagotville, the Weapons Proving Unit at Cold Lake, Alberta, and the Airborne Sensing Unit at Uplands, Ontario. The Electronic Warfare Unit and 414 (Electronic Warfare) Squadron, which were described in the previous chapter, ended the life of the CF-100, flying as Mark 5C and 5D target aircraft.

FORMATION TEAMS

All the squadrons had formation teams for special occasions, either military or civilian, that would perform on request. Some were more visible and widely seen than others. All large formations contributed to maintaining the skill of the crews involved and demonstrated to the public that Canada could hold its own on the world stage of fighter crews. Formation flying was part of the daily life of all operational crews. It was a quicker and more efficient way to dispatch and recover aircraft in formations of two or four.

Red Ravens Formation Team, EWU, CFS St Hubert. (Courtesy of Leonard Jenks)

There were two permanent CF-100 aerial display teams during the years 1959 to 1962. The Bald Eagles of No. 3 OTU performed as the warm-up act for the Golden Hawks Sabre aerobatic team during the summers of 1959 and 1960. The author flew with two members of that team, Flying Officers, later Captains, Glenn Emerson and Nick Chester, in the 1970s with 414 (Electronic Warfare) Squadron. The Red Ravens team, from the Electronic Warfare Unit in St Hubert, Quebec, performed during 1961 and 1962. Flying Officer Len Jenks flew number three in the team. He was very helpful in getting contacts for this book. One of the aircraft used by that team, serial 100791, will feature in a serious 1973 flying incident mentioned later in this chapter.

INCIDENTS/ACCIDENTS

Aircraft, like any machinery, are inherently hazardous. The CF-100 had been jokingly referred to as '30,000 parts defying gravity for a short time with the knowledge that gravity will ultimately win'. Or as another phrase stated, 'what goes up, in the lower atmosphere, must come down'. It is more hazardous if you make that aircraft an all-weather machine that, at times, is operated to its human and mechanical limits. It is certainly a dichotomy to talk to a fighter interceptor crew about limits as they attempt to shoot down the target and return to base with the big X, the Mission Accomplished.

The teething problems of the CF-100, as it assumed its role in the RCAF, occurred in two main areas: machine and human. The new aircraft – the machine – had mechanical faults in various systems that were discovered through operating it and the adaptation of crews – the human – to an all-weather operational role. The rapid acceleration of the CF-100 in cloud and at night caused vertigo, an inner ear problem causing dizziness, which the crews had to be trained to deal with. 'Believe your instruments' became the motto of the fighter pilot. A crew had a discussion on a flight one night flying out of RCAF Station Comox as the Navigator felt that they were flying upside down!

Only 110, 16 per cent, of the 692 CF-100s built, were destroyed in air accidents or written off in ground incidents or fire over nearly thirty years of operational service. A fitting tribute to the robustness and integrity of the aircraft and crew as it operated 24/7 in the extreme cold of a Northern Ontario or Labrador winter, the fog and ice of a Vancouver Island day in January, the warm, moist air of a Sardinia weapons range in summer, and the extreme dry heat of Nellis AFB in Nevada. An enviable record for the aircraft as it defended Canada and Europe against Communist aggression and later, ironically, assumed the part of the Communist aggressor for the Voodoo interceptor for nearly twenty years.

The years, however, were not without its human tragedy. The CF-100 had an escape system for the crew if things went terribly wrong. Previous wartime experience indicated that it was quicker to replace the aircraft than a fully trained crew. In the early years of military flight, the crew were issued with individual parachutes to use in an emergency and return them safely to earth and, hopefully, to fly again. One of the problems encountered as aircraft became faster and more complicated was the ability to get out of the aircraft quickly. The result was the invention of a rocket-propelled seat that would remove the crew from the aircraft rapidly and then float them to the earth using a parachute.

The ejection seat used in the CF-100 was the British-made Martin-Baker Mark 2E model seat. The Martin-Baker ejection seat was responsible for saving 3,000 lives between the first ejection in July 1946 and July 1971, a valuable contribution to the preservation of resources – highly-trained crews – during the Cold War. I am sure the crews involved were very happy to get to fly another day! How does the crew use the ejection seat for normal operations as well as in an emergency?

The ejection seat combines two functions. Firstly, the normal crew sit with an integral parachute in the backrest and a survival gear pack acting as the seat pan. This was not the most comfortable of sitting arrangements and, combined with the fighter aircraft environment of 'yank, bank and crank', could result in back problems. Secondly, it also functioned as the ejection seat, which left the aircraft with the crewmember firmly strapped to it.

When the crew entered the cockpit they strapped into the parachute first and then strapped into the seat, remembering to thread the leg restraint straps through the leg stirrups. These straps prevent the legs from flailing about as the seat exits the confined space of a cockpit during an ejection. No mean feat with a bulky winter flying suit. The width of the cockpit at the canopy sill caused the shoulder badges to be gradually worn away with normal movement. Once firmly strapped into the seat, the oxygen mask, complete with communications cord, emergency bailout oxygen bottle and main aircraft oxygen system hose, was hooked up. The crewmember was now secured to the parachute and the ejection seat, leaving only the arms and legs free.

In an emergency the crewmember had to grasp the overhead firing handle and pull the handle and blind down over their face, which caused the canopy to jettison immediately. One second later, the seat rocket fired and propelled the seat up its rails and clear of the aircraft. The automatic jettisoning of the canopy only occurred with the Electronic Warfare

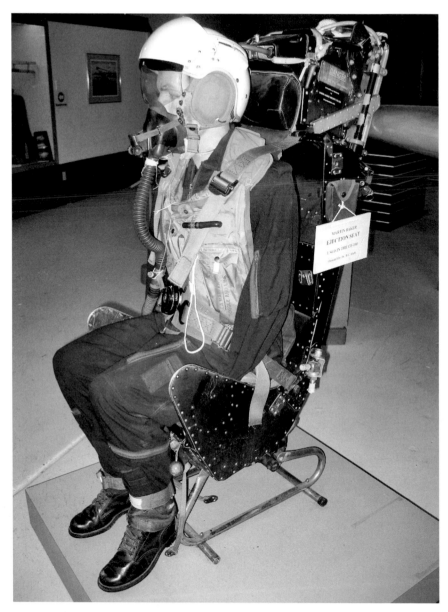

Martin-Baker 2E ejection seat. (Courtesy of Author)

Officer's seat; the pilot would have to manually jettison the canopy to eject first.

Once the seat left the aircraft, the automatic sequence continued with a 5-foot drogue chute deploying to stabilise and slow the seat. There was a barometric control set at 10,000 feet which prevented deployment of the automatic parachute until below 10,000 feet. Then the pull of the drogue chute was transferred from the seat to an apron, commonly called the butt-snapper by aircrew, which tightened and threw the crew out of the seat. Next the drogue chute pulled out the main parachute pack closure pins and apex of the parachute from the pack. The main 24-foot Irvin parachute fully deployed and the occupant had a slow, controlled descent to earth. The Issue 10 seats provided safe ejection from an aircraft at ground level, or low level with no sink rate, at speeds greater than 90 knots.

The next time you are in an aviation social scene take a look at the apparel of the people around you. Look specifically at the tie being worn and the lapel pins. The Martin-Baker company has a tie specifically designed for anyone whose life has been saved by the use of their ejection seat – The Ejection Tie Club. Similarly, the Irvin Air Chute Company has a Caterpillar Club pin for anyone who bailed out of a disabled aircraft who used an Irvin chute to save their life. The significance of the caterpillar is that the original parachutes were made out of silk threads, thus recognising the debt to the silkworm, and the caterpillar had to climb out of its cocoon and let itself down to earth by a silken thread or fly away. There is also a Goldfish Club pin, gold for the preciousness of life and fish to signify water, for those who used an Irvin chute to save their life and ended up in the water or crash-landed in the water and used a flotation device such as Mae West to save their life.

Approximately one hundred crewmembers lost their lives in the CF-100 during its flying career. During the author's time with 414 (EW) Squadron, there was one successful crew bail out and one crew fatality. Captain Vint Weldon and Captain, later Major, Rudy Willhauk successfully ejected from aircraft 100792 near La Macaza, Quebec. A trim tab malfunction had made the aircraft uncontrollable. Rudy had previously ejected from aircraft 18321 on 25 September 1958, flying with 445 Squadron out of Marville, France. Much to the annoyance and anger of the Base Surgeon at CFB Uplands, Ontario, the commanding officer, Lt-Col. Fern Villeneuve, debriefed the crew upon their return from the bush, submitted the paperwork, closed the squadron for the day, and all crew adjourned to the lower bar in the Officer's Mess to celebrate. After much celebration, the hurting Vint and Rudy were dropped off at the base hospital for medical testing!

The second accident and loss of aircraft 100788 unfortunately also resulted in the loss of two crew members. Captains Garry Hunt and Tom

Campbell were killed in the crash of their CF-100 short of the runway at CFB North Bay in the early morning of 17 October 1973 while returning from a NORAD exercise. Garry shared a house with his friend Doug Fitzpatrick in North Bay. Fitzpatrick is the CF-100 pilot in the Amalgam Mute exercise. It had been ten years since the last fatality of an electronic warfare crew member. A full military ceremony and burial was held for Garry Hunt at North Bay; Tom Campbell was buried elsewhere. I remember standing as the graveside honour guard and thinking that it was very exciting to fly fighter aircraft, but it could exact the ultimate sacrifice. Unbeknown to me at the time, I too would have too much excitement and face my own demise only eight days later.

TEST FLIGHT CARD

Major overhauls of the CF-100 were done at CFB Trenton, Ontario, during the 1970s. Routine maintenance, including engine changes, was done by 414 (Electronic Warfare) Squadron Maintenance at CFB North Bay. Each aircraft that had been repaired required an air test before returning to regular squadron service. It was the responsibility of the Squadron Flight Safety department to follow a prescribed series of tests done during a local flight. The test card would be flown and any snags would be reported to the Maintenance Department for further repair.

The following is a strange tale of seemingly unrelated circumstances, or were they? The author's secondary squadron duty was as part of the Flight Safety department and as such carried out maintenance Air Test Flights. On 27 September 1973, I was flown from CFB North Bay, Ontario, to CFB Bagotville to do an Air Test Flight on aircraft 100791, which had been repaired there. It must have been a serious problem, requiring the aircraft to have an Air Test Flight before returning to squadron service. The problem is lost to history, but as the Air Test Flight could not be performed at night it was decided to do it on the way back to CFB North Bay the next day.

Working through the standard '414 (EW) Sqn CF100 Air Test Card', the aircraft was flown back to CFB North Bay with, as it happens, Captain Rod MacPherson, who will feature later in the account, as the Electronic Warfare Officer and returned to squadron service. A few days later on 4 October, I was taking off in the same aircraft and noticed a slight binding in the elevator control during the takeoff run. I immediately rejected – abandoned – the takeoff and wrote the aircraft up unserviceable for control problems, grabbed another aircraft and departed for two days of target work at CFB Bagotville. Upon my return, I was informed that no fault could be found with the aircraft and that it was ready for an air test again. By now I was very concerned about aircraft 100791.

I discussed the problem at great length with the maintenance department. In the end, my friend Corporal Barrie Laycock offered to go with me as he had looked at the aircraft and also found nothing suspicious. An air test on 6 October found nothing and the aircraft was declared serviceable and returned to service. I still had an uneasy feeling about 100791; something 'was not right in the state of Denmark'. I took aircraft 100784 and headed west to an exercise in the 25th NORAD Region, flying as a target out of McChord AFB, Tacoma, Washington. Upon return I was assigned to fly 100791 to Chatham, New Brunswick, for some training with 416 Squadron. Some of the details are repeated, but here is the story as I recounted them for my personal memoir.

JAMMED CONTROLS

Both wine glasses sailed through the air and found their target – the back of the fireplace. They shattered upon impact, making a satisfactory crash. All was well until a voice of authority interrupted our revelry, 'Gentlemen, it is time to call it a night.' Captain Rod MacPherson and I looked around to see the imposing figure of the Orderly Officer, the Base Commander's representative, darkening the doorway. Perhaps he was right; it was time to call it a night.

Rod and I paid our large bar bill and stumbled out of the Officers' Mess at Canadian Forces Base Chatham, New Brunswick. As we made our way to the barracks, I said to Rod: 'That was two close shaves we had tonight! No use tempting fate. Have a good sleep. I'll see you in the morning!'

Rod and I had just survived one of the worst potential disaster scenarios that you could have in an aircraft – jammed controls. Next to a fire in flight and a mid-air collision, jammed controls are about as bad as it gets when you are trying to land a high-performance jet fighter that has a limited amount of fuel at the end of a flight as you try to sort out the problem.

It was 25 October 1973 and Rod and I were members of 414 Electronic Warfare Squadron, based in Canadian Forces Base North Bay, Ontario. We flew the Avro CF-100 Canuck aircraft in missions designed to test the NORAD system. I was the pilot and Rod was the electronic warfare officer – or EWO. My job was to fly; his was to keep us off the fighter and ground radar screens. We were equipped with electronic gear designed to trick radar detectors. It was all part of the role we played in mock battles. We were the enemy – simulating Soviet bombers attacking North America during the Cold War.

That night, which also happened to be my fourth wedding anniversary, we were flying from North Bay, Ontario, to Chatham, New Brunswick, to work with 416 All Weather Fighter Squadron the next day. We were to fly missions against the squadron's Voodoo fighters to test their ability to detect and eliminate incoming Soviet aircraft.

I had had some misgivings before takeoff. The particular Canuck we were flying at the time was serial 100791, or 791 for short. I had flown 791 before. I knew there was something not quite right about it.

As a Flight Safety Officer, it had been my responsibility to test-fly this aircraft a month earlier. On one subsequent flight, there had been a problem during takeoff as I tried to raise the aircraft nose to increase lift; I had felt a restriction in the flying controls, as if something was stuck somewhere. I abandoned the takeoff and returned to the hangar line. I could not duplicate the fault so, for safety's sake, I declared the aircraft unserviceable. There was a lot of pressure to make the aircraft serviceable because I could not duplicate the fault. I stuck to my guns and the aircraft went in for another inspection.

A few days later, I was again on a test flight with 791, this time with Corporal Barrie Laycock, a member of the squadron maintenance team, who had worked on the aircraft and had been unable to find any fault. The aircraft flew perfectly with no indication of any control problem. Even though I had some misgivings, I had no choice but to return it to active flying status.

When I learned I would be flying 791 on the 25 October mission, I felt a little shaky, but I quickly shook this off. I told myself the aircraft had flown without a hitch last time. Why should it be any different this time? Things started out well enough. Rod and I took off from North Bay without incident. As we approached CFB Chatham, Voodoo fighters intercepted us. As part of the exercise, Rod operated our electronic jammers in an attempt to block the fighters' radar and make their weapons systems unusable. The Voodoos managed to override our blocking techniques and, in spite of our best efforts with chaff and electronic jammers, we were electronically 'shot down'.

Having lost yet another round of electronic warfare, we decided it was time to land and head for the Officers' Mess for a beer. This aerial warfare was thirsty work. The plane had flown perfectly up to this point, and I had forgotten all my earlier misgivings.

We prepared to commence our descent to 20,000 feet, 'Angels 20' in pilot talk, from where we could start our approach to land. It took us three minutes to drop to that altitude, descending at 3,000 feet per minute. Conditions were good: clear skies and 1 °C. The lights of Chatham welcomed us as we came near. I started to ease back on the controls to level out; it was all very routine, or should have been.

Disengaging the autopilot, I grasped the control column and prepared for manual flight. The control column allows you to roll the aircraft using the ailerons, and so turn the aircraft, and also control the elevator. The elevator controls the pitch of the aircraft, allowing the plane to climb or descend. As I pulled it backward, I encountered resistance. A chill went up my spine. I tried again, just to be sure I was not dreaming. But it would not move more than a slight amount forward or backward, nowhere near enough control to make a safe landing. This had to be a one in a billion occurrence – I had never heard of this situation before or since in my forty-year flying career!

'Rod,' I said, trying to keep my voice calm as my heart raced, 'you are not going to believe this but the elevator is partially jammed.'

'Are you sure?' Rod asked incredulously. Rod was a very experienced Navigator, but he had never come across anything like this either. Still, he stayed calm and steady, a good guy to have along on a night like this. Unbeknown to me at the time, Rod had bailed out from a CF-100 five years before. On 20 August 1968, Rod and his pilot had bailed out of aircraft 18474 near St Hubert, Quebec. I cannot imagine what was going through his mind as he faced the same possibility again.

With a sense of growing dread, I wondered if any other controls were affected. I tried the ailerons and rudder. To my relief, they were free. Only the elevator was restricted. Even so, our lives were in peril, for there was nothing that I could do to stop our descent!

'You talk to Air Traffic Control and I will fly, Rod, until we get things sorted out.'

Rod got on the radio and declared an emergency. I noticed that we were heading east over Miramichi Bay. I had no wish for us to eject in the dark into ice-cold water; even if we survived the impact, we would only have minutes to spare before hypothermia overtook us. I asked Rod to get us a vector – an Air Traffic Control heading – to keep us above land in case we had to abandon the aircraft. We started a slow turn with the ailerons to the west and headed away from the water. One problem solved. All this time we continued to descend slowly at about 700 feet per minute. We were totally at the mercy of the jammed controls. I remember thinking that it looked very dark below and uninhabited, if we had to bail out.

I played with the throttles to give us the minimum rate of descent and a good, controllable, clean, no flaps extended, speed of around 200 knots (230 mph 370 km/h). Too much power and the aircraft accelerated downwards, too little power and the airspeed decreased and got very close to the point where it would stall and cease flying all together. With the aircraft slowly heading for the ground, we prepared for an emergency ejection. 'Let's go through the Ejection Checklist, Rod, but don't eject until you get my command. I am going to try and free the elevator first.'

I had some ground school training on the ejection procedure but, as I found out later, Rod had ejected before. It depended on a series of events happening in sequence, very little of which we could control once the ejection sequence was initiated. The likelihood of injury was high from the ejection, as well as the subsequent night landing. It was still a better position to be in than some of the early Soviet fighters, which did not have an ejection seat at all.

The checklist ensured that we were prepared for the ejection sequence. Rod and I discussed the procedure and rechecked that all our straps were tight to keep us in the ejection seat and the parachute, which was an integral part of the seat. The sequence was for Rod to eject first, providing automatic jettisoning of the canopy, followed by me. We were transmitting an emergency code on our transponder so that radar could monitor our position. This would assist search and rescue to find us in the New Brunswick bush.

Suddenly, my twenty-six years of age did not seem enough. I remembered how proud I was to get married on the military base in uniform. Emily and I had not been married long and we had many plans for our future, which included children and a house with a white picket fence! The notion crossed my mind that this life could end shortly, and that I would have no time to say goodbye. I thought: 'I have been married for four years today. Is it all going to end like this?'

We were now at 15,000 feet and ready to bail out. But we still had some time. With nothing to lose, I tried again to move the control column, but it only budged a few inches. We continued to descend in the darkness; there no visible welcoming lights now as we were getting farther to the west and away from civilisation.

Soon we were at 12,000 feet. My throat was dry now. An altitude of 10,000 feet was about as low as we wanted to go before it started to become more dangerous to escape by parachute. With only a few minutes of grace time, I once more tried to unlock the controls.

'Okay Rod, nothing to lose now, one last try', I said.

I jammed the control column forward with all my might, and then quickly pulled back with all the force that I could muster. I probably never used so much force in all my life. To my immense relief, the control column suddenly broke free. The aircraft immediately pitched up sharply towards the starlit sky.

'I have it, I have it, I have elevator control Rod!' I shouted as I eased the nose down to level flight.

'We are OK! We are OK!'

I returned the aircraft to level flight and tried to get my breathing to slow down! Holding our breath, we started a wide descending for a radar vectored approach to the easterly runway at CFB Chatham.

It was comforting to see the emergency vehicles with their red flashing lights alongside the runway. We landed and taxied to the parking area, set the parking brake and moved the throttles to the cut off position. The engines ceased their roar and suddenly all seemed eerily quiet after all the commotion of the last thirty minutes. Was it only half an hour? It seemed more like a lifetime. Still wearing my oxygen mask, all I could hear was the sound of my own breathing from the mask's microphone.

Out of the silence came Rod's voice. 'Are you alright Gord?'

'Yeah, fine. You?' I replied.

'OK.'

There was not much else to say at that moment. The next voice I heard was that of the maintenance corporal, who appeared on the cockpit ladder.

'Good evening sir, a bit of a problem tonight?'

'Just a bit,' I replied in the deepest voice I could muster, hoping to hide the fear that I was still feeling.

The reality of what we had been through was now hitting us. With unsteady legs we climbed out of the cockpit and down the ladder to the welcoming feel of the ground. Rod and I headed for the hangar blister, the maintenance office, to fill out the paperwork to declare the aircraft unserviceable. We notified 416 Squadron Operations that there would be no electronic warfare training the next day until after the repair of our aircraft.

It was heaven to be alive and walking in the cool air up the road to the Officers' Mess. We went straight to the bar and ordered doubles. Many doubles later, we were gently but firmly ordered out. 'Gentlemen, it is time to call it a night.' We adjourned to our barrack rooms to sleep off the results of our adventure, but that was not the end of the story. An urgent voice woke me out of deep slumber.

'Wake up, wake up! The flight line maintenance is on the phone for you!' I roused myself in the painful fog of an early morning hangover and staggered to the phone.

'Sir, the aircraft is ready to go, it just needs you to air test it,' said the line maintenance sergeant. I was surprised they had fixed the problem so quickly. I woke up Rod and we grabbed a hurried breakfast. We were just legal to go flying after our last drink, eight hours being the minimum required.

Everyone was keen to get our aircraft back in the air. There was pressure for us to meet our training commitments to NORAD. Crews and aircraft were waiting to carry out the Electronic Counter Measures missions, and our aircraft was a part of those missions. I was glad the aircraft was now serviceable and very curious to know what the problem had been to cause such havoc.

'Did you find the problem?' I asked the maintenance sergeant.

'No sir. We traced the elevator control cable and were unable to duplicate the problem, it is working perfectly.'

That was not exactly what I wanted to hear. I walked out to the aircraft with the maintenance personnel and asked them to show me how they had traced the control cable from the cockpit to the elevator in the tail of the aircraft. They demonstrated this, but admitted there was one area they could not look at. The part of the cable that passed behind the British-made Martin-Baker ejection seat. It would take a specially trained safety systems technician to remove it. Unfortunately, there was no such technician at the base.

Still, they assured me the controls were free. They had not been able to duplicate the problem. I had my doubts that the aircraft had been fixed. I had, after all, been through this before in North Bay. I was not about to risk going through what I just went through a second time. I might not be as lucky.

In the middle of my thought process, the phone rang. It was my Commanding Officer in North Bay. What he wanted to know 'was the hold up with the aircraft? The squadron needed it immediately for the training exercise.'

To this day I do not know why I made the decision I did. I had a lot of pressure on me at that moment to get the aircraft off the ground, but I stood my ground.

'Sir, I will not fly it until I can see behind the ejection seat to satisfy myself that all is well,' I told my Commanding Officer.

He did not receive the news well. He emphatically reiterated the fact that maintenance had checked the aircraft and found no fault. I repeated the fact that the area behind the seat had not been checked and that 'there was no way I was flying that plane'.

I hung up the phone and both Rod and I headed back to the barracks to catch up on our rest. While we slept, our Commanding Officer arranged to fly a specialised safety systems technician down from CFB North Bay to CFB Chatham. By lunchtime, the technician had removed the seat and I received another phone call.

'It is the flight line maintenance sir, I think you should come down and look at this.'

When we arrived the plane was stripped down, with panels strewn everywhere and the ejection seat sitting beside it on the ground. I was shown the Pac-Man shaped bellcrank, a circle with a wedge shape cut out, that the elevator control cable ran on and there it was for all to see, it had a another piece missing from it. The missing piece was one of the sides of the Pac-Man wedge. The missing piece had broken off when I forced it past the obstruction. The obstruction turned out to be a piece of fibreglass on a fuselage joint that had worked itself into the cable run and interfered with the bellcrank on the fourteen-year-old aircraft. This is what I had felt three weeks previously as I pulled back on the control column to raise the nose for takeoff.

I was lucky that it had not jammed on takeoff this time, a critical phase of flight close to the ground, as we probably would have bailed out immediately with the loss of the aircraft and possibly our lives from the low-altitude ejection. We were lucky that we had the time at altitude to try and solve the puzzle.

Rod and I had a more sober evening that night as we waited for the new part to be flown in. The next day we did a quick air test, but not without some trepidation. All seemed fine though, and we departed for home.

What did I learn from this experience? By working as a crew, Rod and I were able to solve the problem safely and avoid the loss of the aircraft and our lives. I learned to stand up for my convictions, no matter what the pressure and from whom, and to see any situation through to a satisfactory conclusion acceptable to me. Otherwise, I may not have been here today to tell this story.

On 18 July 1979, aircraft 100791 went to the scrap yard at CFB Mountain View, near Trenton, Ontario, after eighteen years of valuable service to the Canadian Armed Forces. I live in Surrey, British Columbia, and recently found out that part of 791 lives on close by. Its left wing is the left wing of the Avro CF-100 on display at the Canadian Museum of Flight in Langley, British Columbia, of which I am a member.

Thirty years after the last CF-100 flew, it is still possible to see aircraft in five countries of the world. Milberry mentioned that 'Belgium has kept an example to remember the fifty-three aircraft of their three squadrons. The Belgians had dismantled and destroyed all their aircraft and had to ask Canada for an example to put on show.' Germany has one on display at CFB Baden. It was flown there in December 1981 by Captains Bud Milne and Peter Maunsell, who is mentioned elsewhere. Britain has a Mark 4B, 18393, in the Imperial War Museum at Duxford to commemorate the CF-100's roll in NATO. The USA has an example of a Mark 5 at the Castle Air Museum in Atwater, California to commemorate its association with NORAD. The CF-100, 100779, in Chapter Nine is preserved at NORAD, Headquarters in Colorado. A well preserved example of a Mark 4 displayed can be seen at the National Museum of the United States Air Force at Wright-Patterson AFB, near Dayton, Ohio. It is a fitting tribute to the CF-100 that individuals, organisations and museums have made the effort to preserve Canada's only indigenous production jet fighter.

Canadians have, over the years, ensured that their aviation history is well preserved. Aviation Museums, CAF bases and municipalities across the country honour aircraft in permanent displays. A Mark 3, serial 18138, is on display at the Canadian Museum of Flight, Langley, British Columbia. A Mark 4A, 18194, was restored at CFB Borden, Ontario. A Mark 5, 100785, is painted in the black prototype colour scheme and has been lent by the Canadian Aviation & Space Museum in Ottawa, Ontario, to the Canadian Warplane Heritage Museum in Hamilton, Ontario. It was the last CF-100 to fly in the world as it was delivered to the Canadian Aviation & Space Museum at Rockliffe Airport (Ottawa), Ontario, on 10 February 1982.

A CF-100 cockpit is open to the public, at the time of publication, at the Canadian Warplane Heritage Museum, and is available for visitors to sit in under the supervision of a museum guide. It is a truly unique experience to sit in the fifty-year-old Cold War fighter and think of the work done by the aircraft and crew, as described in other chapters of this book. Aviation museums are surely worthy of our financial support as they preserve Canadian aviation history for this, the second century of powered flight in Canada. It is important to remember our aviation roots as Canada progresses in the exploration of space.

CF-100, 100500, pedestal at North Bay, Ontario. (Courtesy of Author)

THE CF-100 FLIGHT

What was it like to fly the CF-100 Mark 5C&D? The aircraft, no longer a fighter, was laden with tons of electronic and mechanical jamming equipment. The electronic equipment was located in the original belly rocket bay area and the rear fuselage. The jammer antennas were placed above and below the fuselage to give the most effective coverage. The mechanical chaff dispensers were attached to each wing, outboard of the landing gear. It no longer had the requirement to climb quickly and perform tight turns at high altitude. The aircraft had become a stable platform to carry electronic warfare equipment airborne for lengthy flights. It carried extra fuel in wing tip tanks, to enable the fighter interceptors to get in multiple attacking runs, and its thrust-to-weight ratio and aerodynamic performance, as a straight-wing subsonic aircraft, was similar to the Canadair T-33.

Pilots were already familiar with the T-33, having flown it as the advanced jet trainer during their ab-initio pilot training and subsequent 410 Squadron training prior to their assignment to the CF-100. This made the flying portion of the transition course, from T-33 to CF-100, fairly straightforward for the pilots.

Just as well, because in the 1970s there were no dual-control versions of the CF-100 left in service. The first flight was a solo flight! The conversion course, T-33 to CF-100, did include ten hours of training in a fixed-base simulator, so the pilot was familiar with the cockpit before getting into the aircraft for the first time. All normal and emergency operating procedures had been practised and performed to the satisfaction of the instructor. The pilot did have the moral support of the back-seat instructor, a pilot, until checked out on the aircraft and then it was up to the experienced EWO to keep an eye on him! It was a brave instructor pilot that got into an aircraft with no flying controls available for the instructor!

The weather was checked and the flight plan filed in the Squadron Operations room. The aircraft was signed out from maintenance after checking the L-14 log for snags. The personal issued helmet and oxygen mask was carried out to the aircraft. The difference between the CF-101 Voodoo and the CF-100 Canuck was that the parachute remained as a part of the CF-100 aircraft seat and it was necessary for the crew to wear calf straps to prevent their legs flailing about in the event of an injection. This was called a leg restraint system and was part of the Martin-Baker ejection seat.

The walk-around, external pre-flight inspection was performed, followed by an extensive checking, arming and strapping-in procedure to the ejection seat. It was very important to get the correct sequence of

The infamous CF-100791, see jammed controls, on ramp preparing for departure. (Courtesy of Canadian Forces Joint Imagery Centre, Department of National Defence)

straps, both strapping into the seat parachute and then to the ejection seat. Especially important on a cold and dark winter's night when the thought is to get the canopy closed and the engines started for heat. The engines used an electric starter generator, unlike the Voodoo air starter, for the start sequence. The Orenda engines had a slow ignition pulse rate and it was possible to turn the fuel on between pulses and cause, according to the Aircraft Operating Instructions, a loud rumbling noise and some flame. The flame out the tailpipe could be quite dramatic at night. It was rumoured, but of course never confirmed, that some of the young pilots did it on purpose for effect, especially when operating out of a USAF base.

The 1950s-era cockpit gave the impression that the crew were an afterthought. Milberry quoted, "'A cockpit small and cramped and dark" as F/O McArthur described it in his poem, 'The Clunk'." You could tell a CF-100 crew because the shoulders of their winter flying suits were worn from rubbing on the canopy sills; a tight fit compared to the spacious cockpit of the Voodoo. The resulting cockpit shape had the operating switch panels tucked away underneath the curve of the fuselage. The interior lights were adjusted, dim enough just to see the switches, but not bright enough to reflect off the canopy and diminish night vision. When the crew got accustomed to the cockpit switch position, their selection was often by feel and position rather than visually. Look down and inside during any acceleration at night and you would run the risk of disorientation.

Engine start took about thirty seconds to reach a stable and idle rpm. The Electronic Warfare Officer handled the alternator and inverter as all the circuit breakers were in the rear cockpit. A complete cockpit scan followed, with recycling of the speed brakes and setting of the flaps observed by the ground crew for correct operation. Taxi clearance from ground control and a wave-off from the ground marshaller completed the pre-taxi procedure. A loaded CF-100 with full fuel load, 14,719 pounds, electronic jammers and chaff now weighed just over 40,000 pounds. Judicious use of thrust in confined busy areas was required to get the aircraft moving and maintain speed in tight turns. At low rpm the engines had a decided lag and care had to be taken not to advance the throttles too far and suddenly have too much thrust.

The Taxi/Pre-Takeoff Checklist was a challenge and a response check was read by the Electronic Warfare Officer as the pilot steered the aircraft with the nose-wheel steering. The steering was activated by holding a button on the control column and using the feet gently on the brake pedals. One dark snowy night the author taxied into a snowdrift while looking in the cockpit, responding to the checklist. The Electronic Warfare Officer, Captain Ross Brewer, just recently forgave me after thirty-seven years, but it cost me after a few beers.

Lined up on the runway, the engines were spooled up to 85 per cent of their thrust. The ten-stage compressor and two-stage turbine gave approximately 7,275 pounds of thrust at 7,800 rpm. It is interesting to compare the weight-to-power ratio of the CF-100 Canuck and CF-101 Voodoo poised for takeoff. At maximum weight the CF-100 is 2.8 and the CF-101, if afterburner is used, is 1.6. Engine temperatures and pressures were checked before the brakes were released and the throttles advanced fully forward for maximum thrust.

The control column was eased back gently until the nose wheel lifted off the runway. At heavy weights, this occurred at a lift-off speed of 140 knots. The control column was then eased forward to avoid the aircraft getting an excessive nose-high attitude. At standard temperatures the aircraft would become airborne in 4,300 feet. Safely airborne, the wheels were braked and the landing gear retracted. In cold weather, opposite to the CF-101, the retraction was delayed to allow the nose-wheel oleo to extend so that upon retraction, the hook on the nose landing gear would engage the bail on the nose gear doors.

The landing gear was checked up and locked, followed by the flaps retracted at a safe altitude. The speed was initially increased to 200 knots before the climb. The throttles were then reduced to the maximum continuous setting of 93 per cent rpm and the speed allowed to increase to 300 knots. The airspeed restriction of 325 knots indicated air speed was imposed to avoid high 'G' loadings in case of turbulence, to prolong airframe life, and to protect the chaff dispensers which had been added to the Mark 5C & D. The climb speed was adjusted to maintain Mach .68 above 15,000 feet. It was very important to monitor the correct transfer of fuel sequel during the climb. The auxiliary tank and tip tanks had to be monitored at all times for correct feeding until empty.

The CF-100 took 11 minutes and 139 km to reach 35,000 feet. At altitude, the throttle was set for normal cruise of approximately 420 knots true air speed. The maximum speed at cruise was Mach .8, which was 480 knots. There was a rudimentary autopilot installed which had heading, pitch and altitude hold functions. The cockpit altitude at 35,000 feet was 19,000 feet, which required the crew to wear oxygen masks. In comparison, in an airliner at 35,000 feet the cabin is around 5,200 feet. The Pre-Letdown/Circuit Entry Challenge and Response Checklist was performed at altitude. Throttles were brought to idle 120 kilometres away from destination and the speed set at Mach .68 until transitioning to 300 knots at 15,000 feet. A rapid descent of a cold aircraft into warm, moist air could cause visibility fogging problems on the windshield. It was heated by electrical current and hot cockpit air.

Initial approach speed was 260 knots, reduced to 200 knots downwind to select the landing gear down and position the flaps to the twenty-five degree position. The speed was further reduced to 150 knots minimum for all manoeuvring with full flaps down until on final approach. The pre-landing check was completed by challenge and response to ensure the aircraft was in a safe configuration to land. Speed was adjusted to cross the airport boundary at 125 knots, the runway threshold at 120 knots and touchdown at approximately 110 knots. Normal foot braking, with the Dunlop Maxaret 1950s first generation 'non-skid' braking system, resulted in a 4,000 feet landing distance over the standard requirement 50-foot (15-metres) obstacle clearance.

Post-landing check was completed during the taxi. One of the items was to install the pin in the ejection seat alternate handle, between the crews' legs, to ensure it was safe for the ground crew to install the main pins. During engine shutdown the hydraulic pumps were checked for serviceability for the next flight. The remaining ejection seat pins were installed prior to leaving the aircraft. A stable aircraft to fly, but it was an old jet fighter whose engines took time to spool up – increase rpm speed – from idle and so demanded the respect of the pilot. Low altitudes at high sink rates in approach phase, as in any jet aircraft, were to be avoided.

DEFUNCT CLUNK CLUB

The thousands of CF-100 aircrew ensured that there would have to be a special party to send off the aircraft when it came to the end of its service life. The decision was made to cease CF-100 operational flying on 31 December 1981, so the last operating squadron of the aircraft, 414 (Electronic Warfare) Squadron at CFB North Bay, committed to have a fitting farewell. There were seven Clunks still flying in December 1981 and these aircraft are now on display: 100472 at Bagotville, Quebec, 100476 at Edmonton, Alberta, 100500 at North Bay, Ontario, 100504 at Atwater, California, 100784 at Baden Airpark, Germany (flown there by Captains Milne and Peter Maunsell) and 100785 presently (2011) at Hamilton, Ontario.

A Defunct Clunk Club was formed and by the time of the farewell party from 10 to 13 September 1981, the membership stood at 1,283. It seemed from the large crowds at the party that all members attended! The Defunct Clunk Club was chaired by Major Peter Growen, a distinguished CF-100 pilot, having flown over 3,000 hours in the aircraft, and among the sixteen committee members was Captain Peter Maunsell, mentioned in Chapter Two. Six Defunct Clunk Club newsletters were mailed to members throughout the preceding year recounting the history of the CF-100. Anecdotes and an updated membership list filled the newsletter pages.

Lt-Col. Otis C. Newport, Commanding Officer of 414 (Electronic Warfare) Squadron in 1981, wrote for the programme dedication page:

As we gather this weekend to pay tribute to the grand old CF-100, we should reflect on a moment why we are really here. The CF-100, in her final days, is a rallying point for us to renew the comradeship of years past – comradeship that was born with the birth of the aircraft itself.

The CF-100 was the common denominator that joined together the builders, air and ground crews, controllers and other members of the air defence team into a partnership that would last for over 30 years.

We learned the business of air defence together. Those lessons are still of value in developing new generations of equipment and in training new generations of people.

Because of this, the CF-100 will continue to play an important part in the defence of our country long after she flies for the last time. Thus, her last flight will not be a sad event. It will be celebration of years of achievement and of challenges met and mastered.

The final bash weekend had all the activities of a successful party. It included tours, dedications, displays, a dinner and dance, parades and the two highlights of the weekend were a monster beer call on the Friday and an airshow on the Saturday, which included the remaining CF-100s and the Snowbird formation team. The Clunk formation team had over 15,000 flying hours experience. The crews of the four-plane formation included Captains Bill Bland, featured in Chapter Nine, Peter Maunsell, mentioned in Chapter Two, and Nick Chester, mentioned earlier in this chapter. It certainly was a 'band of brothers'.

To quote Major Deanna Brasseur, one of Canada's, and the world's, first female CF-18 fighter pilots, 'I had the best time ever when I flew into the Bay in a Tutor for the Defunct Clunk Club Reunion! Never before, nor since, have I seen a CF Air Force Mess packed and over flowing into the street and parking lots!' Yes, it was quite the party.

Enjoy your well-deserved retirement, Clunk, we all will remember you with fond memories!

Canada Day formation, North Bay, Ontario. (Courtesy of Greg Montgomery)

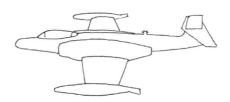

CHAPTER EIGHT

Target Squadrons

Just like the row of bottles on the fence for a casual target shooter, it was necessary for the fighter interceptor squadrons to have something to shoot at to hone their skills. At first the fighter crews used each other as mutual targets, but the need for practicing in a realistic radar jamming environment brought about a change. Target squadrons were the solution. Not only did the fighter crews get practice, but the whole air defence organisation was involved in the target squadron training missions and exercises.

The RCAF initially purchased two De Havilland 106 Comet 1s for transport and NORAD target aircraft; dedicated target squadrons would follow two years later. The RCAF became the first military organisation in the world to operate the Comets as a passenger transport service. The aircraft were assigned to 412 (Falcon) Squadron of Air Transport Command and both were operational by June 1953. Senior officials of the Canadian government were enjoying VIP jet travel long before the President of the USA. He did not get jet transport until nine years later in 1962!

The Comets, according to the Autumn 2006 edition of *Airforce* magazine, 'Would take off from Ottawa, streak north of the DEW Line and then zip south, mimicking Russian invaders as they were locked on radar. Ground control would then dispatch fighter jets to intercept the incoming passenger jets. Flight Lieutenant Dean Broadfoot (Comet pilot) enjoyed the game partly because the Comet could outrun a CF-100 jet interceptor.' The Comet era for the RCAF came to an end in October 1963, when it was replaced by the larger turboprop Canadair CC-106 Yukon.

In 1955, it was decided that the fighter crews needed electronic counter-measure training to maintain their effectiveness in an ever-changing electronic warfare environment. A small group of personnel from 104 Communications Unit, based at RCAF Station St Hubert, were selected to provide Electronic Counter Measures training for the CF-100 crews.

The first target with the capacity for radar jamming was the Douglas C-47 (Dakota) aircraft, which released large bundles of aluminium chaff from an open window to interfere with the fighter radar.

The following year, two Fairchild C-119 (Packet) aircraft were added to the target force. A specially equipped Avro CF-100 was also assigned to the unit, aircraft number 18225. The crews for the unit CF-100 aircraft were readily available from the two resident CF-100 squadrons at RCAF Station St Hubert: 416 and 425. The unit had grown in size, and on 1 April 1959 it was designated the Electronic Warfare Unit. The role of the Electronic Warfare Unit was to train the ground-based radar and airborne interceptor radar operators how to deal with Electronic Counter Measures.

By 1960, the Electronic Warfare Unit C-119 (Packet) aircraft trained the ground-based radar operators. The CF-100 and Canadair T-33 (Lockheed T-33s built under licence in Canada) aircraft were used as the airborne target force to train fighter crews. These aircraft, the T-33 and the CF-100, had a realistic target speed, as they were comparable to the speed of the early 1950s Tu-4 'Bull' of the Soviet bomber fleet, which cruised at 300 knots (345 mph 558 km/h) at 34,000 feet (10,250 metres). However, since 1956, the Tupolev TU-95 'Bear' had been in production and its cruising speed exceeded the speed capability of the CF-100. The CF-100 was reaching the end of its operational life as a fighter, and was replaced by the McDonnell CF-101 Voodoo in 1962. As a result, spare CF-100 aircraft were becoming available to be used as target aircraft. The unit had become a very active force within the NORAD system and provided ECM training during exercises for RCAF and USAF crews. It had a detachment at RCAF Station Comox, British Columbia, to train RCAF and USAF crews on the west coast.

The Unit CF-100s were basic Mark 5s with the wing extensions removed and the installation of wing tip tanks. The extra fuel gave an extended range, or more loitering time, which was necessary to allow plenty of time for Electronic Counter Measure training. The two variants were designated as Mark 5C and Mark 5D. The Mark 5C had the ability to electronically jam and interfere with fighter radar, while the Mark 5D had the ability to jam both ground and fight radar sets. Both Marks could use streamlined chaff dispensing pods mounted on the outboard bomb racks, underneath the wing, to jam the ground and airborne radar. The appropriate chaff, strips of aluminium foil cut to specific lengths to interfere with the specific frequency of the ground or radar set, was loaded in the chaff dispenser prior to departure.

The Mark 5C and 5D had the AN/APR-9 ECM receiver, the AN/ALR-18 I band receiver, the AN/ALT-6B I band transmitter and two MX-900A/A chaff dispensers. The Mark 5D had extra jammers, the AN/ALT-501 for ground radars, and could be recognised by the extra cooling vents visible in the previous gun pack location on the belly. In addition, the 5D had the MD188A/ARA3 UHF communications jammer and two MX-900A/A chaff dispensers.

The AN/APR-9 radio frequency receiver had a range of 1,000 to 10,750 MHz. The AN/ALR-18 and AN/ALT-6B operated in the India band from 8,000–12,000 MHz for the airborne fighter radar. The AN/ALT-501s operated in the Delta band, from 1,000–2,000 MHz, for ground-based search radar and the Echo band, 2,000–4,000 MHz, for the ground-based height finder radar. The chaff dispensers were normally loaded with the India band in one side and the Delta and Echo band in the other.

At first, the Unit T-33s did not have any Electronic Counter Measure capabilities, but in later years it carried an Electronic Counter Measures pod externally. The Unit CF-100s had a crew of two, the pilot and an Electronic Warfare Officer, which was a new designation for a Navigator involved in Electronic Counter Measures. The Electronic Warfare Officer looked after the active and passive jamming devices. The unit also had some Mark 3s. These aircraft were used as training aircraft for the unit crews.

The RCAF became the CAF during the 1 February 1968 unification of the Army, Navy and Air Force. All flying units became squadrons and the Electronic Warfare Unit was designated 414 (Electronic Warfare) Squadron on 15 September 1967. The squadron was first formed during the Second World War as an Army co-operation unit at Croydon, Surrey, England, on 13 August 1941. It was the RCAF's twelfth squadron formed overseas. The squadron was re-designated a Fighter Reconnaissance Squadron on 28 June 1943. It flew the North American Mustang Mk I and Supermarine Spitfire Mk IX. The squadron disbanded at Luneburg, Germany, on 7 August 1945.

It served briefly as a Photographic Squadron from 1947 to 1950, based at RCAF Station Rockliffe (Ottawa), Ontario, flying the Douglas Dakota Mk 3. In 1952, it reformed as a Canadair Sabre Mk 5 and 6 Squadron at Bagotville, Quebec, before going overseas to join No. 4 (Fighter) Wing at Baden-Soellingen, Germany. It returned to Canada and became an All Weather Fighter Squadron flying the Avro CF-100 Mk 5 and subsequently the McDonnell CF-101 Voodoo based at RCAF Station North Bay. It was disbanded on 30 June 1964.

The squadron badge is a medieval black armoured knight on a charger over a cloud. It became known as the Black Knight Squadron, signifying chivalry with no 'quarter given'. The cloud was symbolic of taking the fight to the air. The motto is: *Totis Viribus* – With all our Might. The squadron was adopted by the City of Sarnia, Ontario.

Captain Ken Penny's 414 Squadron mascot. (Courtesy of Ken Penny)

In September 1967, it was once again an active squadron as part of Air Defence Command at RCAF Station St Hubert, Quebec. In September 1968, the squadron moved to CFB Uplands (Ottawa), Ontario, and then in August 1972 to CFB North Bay, Ontario. In 1973, 414 Squadron had T-33s and three types of Electronic Counter Measure CF-100s. They were the Mark 5C, 5D and aircraft 100757, which had chaff pods only. Without the weight of the electronic jammers, 100757 was a real performer and could climb faster and higher than any other aircraft in the squadron.

CF-100 Line, 414 Squadron [note 100779 is the first aircraft in line]. (Courtesy of Larry Faulkner)

The CF-100 and T-33 were joined in the Electronic Counter Measure role by the Dassault Breguet CE-117 Falcon in 1977, in preparation for the retirement of the CF-100 as a target in the CAF. The CF-100 had by now continued on its Electronic Counter Measure role for twenty years in retirement from being an all-weather fighter. It ceased operational flying on 31 December 1981 and its final flights were to display sites and museums.

Similarly, the CF-101 Voodoo retired from active fighter operations in the mid-1980s, but two aircraft joined 414 (EW) Squadron. One aircraft, 101067, an EF-101, was equipped as an Electronic Counter Measures target with electronics similar to the USAF Martin EB-57. The other aircraft, 101006, a CF-101F, was used for crew training as well as a passive non-jamming supersonic target. At the end of its serviceable life, 101006 was the last Voodoo to fly anywhere in the world. On 19 April 1987, it flew to CFB Chatham, New Brunswick, to be prepared for display at CFB Cornwallis, Nova Scotia.

The Falcon aircraft was replaced, after twenty-two years of service, in 1989 by the Canadair CE-144 Challenger. It, together with the venerable Canadair-built T-33, now designated CT-133, provided Electronic Counter Measures training from CFB North Bay, Ontario, until 1992. The squadron was divided in 1992: one section went to CFB Comox, British Columbia, as 414 Composite Squadron and the other section to CFB Greenwood,

Nova Scotia, as 434 Composite Squadron. In 1993, the squadron changed its name to 414 Combat Support Squadron when it was equipped with the CT-133 Silver Star. The squadron was disbanded in 2002 when its duties were contracted out to a civilian company. The squadron spent forty-seven years providing targets for the fighter squadrons, a long time, but not quite as long as the fifty years of its last aircraft, the venerable 'T Bird'. The Canadian CT-133, built under licence from Lockheed with the Rolls-Royce Nene engine, first flew in 1952. It initially served as a jet-conversion trainer. It is interesting that Rolls-Royce named all their engines after rivers in the British Isles.

A formal ceremony at Gatineau Airport, near Ottawa, on 20 January 2009 marked the official reformation of 414 Electronic Warfare Support Squadron. The new independent flying unit will not have its own aircraft, but uses eight former Luftwaffe Dassault-Breguet Dornier Alpha Jets provided by Canadian civilian contractor Top Aces. 414 Electronic Warfare Support Squadron would provide electronic warfare support to the Canadian Forces for combat training purposes. It is interesting to note that in 2011 the CAF still uses trained Electronic Warfare Officers, albeit flying in civilian aircraft, to provide Electronic Counter Measures training for the McDonnell Douglas/Boeing CF-18 'Hornet' fighter.

What was so special about the training and where did the CAF get it? Canada's NORAD partner, the USA, had the training and technology resources and was willing to provide Electronic Warfare Officer training for Canada. The highly secretive nature of electronic warfare dictated that certain parts of the course were omitted for foreign nationals because they contained training for the latest USAF electronic technology. Course material, during certain classes, would appear as 'No foreign nationals access' and the Canadians had to leave the room. The course did provide both academic and practical training in the art of electronic warfare. Ground school training included classes on basic electricity, electronic circuits, radar systems, transmission and reception and fifty hours of practical training in an electronic warfare simulator.

The training was provided by the USAF's 3535th Navigator Training Wing, based at Mather AFB near Sacremento, California, USA. The Navigational Training School was located at Mather AFB from April 1958 until 1 April 1973. The Electronic Warfare course commenced in 1961 and was a part of the Navigational Training School. Captain Bill Bland, the Electronic Warfare Officer in our account, was on one of the last courses at Mather AFB. His course, 7202, included 556.0 ground school hours and 61.8 flying hours on special, electronic-warfare-equipped Convair ET-29 aircraft. Captain Bland was in Sacremento from 9 August 1971 until graduation on 16 February 1972.

Pilot training in the 1970s for 414 Squadron was done in-house. It consisted of the Avro CF-100 ground school and fixed-base, no-motion, simulator training in normal and emergency procedures. There were briefings on NORAD and target flying procedures. The training was provided by active squadron pilots designated for secondary duty as instructors. The author's flying log book indicated that the flying component of the course was 7.7 hours on the T-33 and 7.6 hours on the CF-100, completed between January 20 and 2 February 1972.

The author's instructor was Captain Jim Cratchley and the flight section of the conversion course included handling, and night and formation checkouts. The squadron aircraft were all single-pilot control Mark 5 aircraft. The dual-control Mark 3 had long since departed from the CAF. The author's first flight was on 31 January 1972 with Captain Cratchley acting as instructor in aircraft 100780. He must have been a very brave man! Sitting in the rear cockpit with no control column of his own, he watched the new pilot fly the CF-100 for the first time and the only help he could offer was verbal.

414 (Electronic Warfare) Squadron was the only dedicated target squadron in the CAF. The USAF had very few target squadrons and as a result, 414 Squadron was always in demand for its services. The general priority was to keep the three CAF fighter interceptor squadrons, 409, 416, and 425, at operational readiness and to provide ECM training for the 410 OTU students. These missions were called 'Towlines' as the target aircraft went back and forth being intercepted by many different aircraft to provide maximum training value. Irradiate, the radio call sign of NORAD target control, was always asking, 'Do you have fuel for a couple more passes?' The squadron supported exercises, such as the Amalgam Mute exercise in the next chapter, throughout the seven NORAD regions and also fulfilled a NATO naval commitment.

It was quite an amazing logistical, planning and scheduling effort to support this unique aircraft, the CF-100, flying all over North America in every season. At the time of our account there were only sixteen CF-100s flying in the world, all with 414 squadron. Spare engines, aircraft parts, ground support equipment and maintenance personnel would be loaded on transport aircraft and taken to the deployment base for larger exercises. Sometimes the target aircraft would go unserviceable en route and a rescue aircraft would be dispatched with parts and a maintenance technician in the back seat to repair it. The CF-100 was so unique that the favourite question at the US bases was: 'Never seen one of these before, whadya all call one of these birds?'

The area covered by 414 Squadron was immense, from Elmendorf AFB, Anchorage, Alaska, south to Naval Air Station North Island, San Diego,

California, east to NATO exercises at NAS Roosevelt Roads, Puerto Rico, and NAS Bermuda, north to Goose Bay, Labrador, and all points in between! Fortunate were the crews that got the exercise in Bermuda during January; not so fortunate were the crews in Goose Bay! In 1973, the author calculated that he flew about 276,000 km.

The target flying was varied in type and location, which made the job interesting. The NORAD exercises were normally less than three hours flying time and the Towlines were longer, as the squadrons were loath to let you go. 409 Squadron in CFB Comox tended to have the longest Towlines as, due their distance from North Bay, they did not get to see 414 Squadron that often and always pleaded for 'just one more run!' It was always a treat for the target crew to leave North Bay in the depths of a Northern Ontario winter, with snow and extremely cold temperatures, and spend a week flying out of Comox with its green grass and mild temperatures!

Lt-Col. Jim Pocklington, commanding officer of 414 Squadron in 1973, wanted to expand the flying experiences of the squadron. He led, in aircraft 100785 with EWO Captain Nick Chester, a formation of two CF-100s that visited Churchill, Manitoba, on 26 November 1973. Churchill is situated at fifty-eight degrees north latitude on the western shore of Hudson Bay and is famous for its polar bear sightings on its streets. A 414 (Electronic Warfare) Squadron CF-100 flight to this airport had never been done before. Operationally, the flight gave the radar sites a surprise

CF-100, winter deployment, CFB Goose Bay, Labrador. (Courtesy of Dan Farrell)

CF-100, summer deployment, CFB Goose Bay, Labrador. (Courtesy of Larry Faulkner)

interception and jamming practice as the formation returned south into radar coverage and proceeded to CFB Bagotville, Quebec.

On 1 June 1973 he led an eleven plane formation, eight CF-100s and three T-33s, from CFB North Bay, Ontario, to CFB Chatham, New Brunswick, for the annual Air Defence Command 'Survival' meet. The formation was arranged to spell out the squadron number in the sky, 414. The CF-100s made up the '4s' while the three T-33s in line astern made up the '1'.

In 1973, Lt-Col. Pocklington, like his predecessor Lt-Col. Villeneuve, arranged for 414 Squadron to support NATO naval exercises in the Caribbean and Atlantic. The naval guns had radar targeting capability and the Electronic Counter Measures training was very beneficial for the ships' crew. Lt Fitzpatrick recalled an interesting naval exercise flown in October 1972 from CFB Shearwater, Halifax, Nova Scotia. He recounted that he 'flew towards the ships with a Canadair CF-104 Starfighter in formation on each wing. The CF-100 jammed the ship's radars and then released the CF-104s which went supersonic and simulated a missile attack on the ships.'

Pocklington continued the tradition of a deployment to the Alaska NORAD Region in September 1973. The author deployed to Elmendorf AFB, Anchorage, Alaska, in the back of a Transport Command Lockheed CC-130 Hercules along with maintenance personnel, engines, tires and

Lt-Col. Jim Pocklington assuming command of 414 (EW) Squadron. (Courtesy of Jim Pocklington)

414 Squadron formation arriving at CFB Chatham. (Courtesy of Author)

every spare imaginable. The author, with Captain Peter Maunsell in CF-100 aircraft number 100780, flew one particular daytime mission as far west as Nome, Alaska. The fighter interceptors were McDonnell F-4 Phantoms of the Air National Guard. You could practically see the Soviet Union across the Bering Sea! Pocklington remembered that deployment and said that he 'had a great week in Alaska, (Elmendorf) where we employed 12 aircraft to jam their radars and interceptors – US commander commended our guys for the best exercise he had seen.'

Lt-Col. Pocklington was on the first 'pipeliner' CF-100 course at RCAF Station North Bay. It was course number three and used the CF-100 Mark 2. The T-33, an old model with an Allison engine, was used for jet transition. Subsequent postings on the CF-100 Mark 3 and 4, F-86 Sabre and CF-101 qualified Pocklington as a very experienced fighter pilot when he took over command of 414 (Electronic Warfare) Squadron. It is thought that Pocklington was the only other person, other than the test pilot Janusz Zurakowski, to ever to fly a CF-100 supersonic. It was in aircraft 18175 on 1 October 1953. The fuselage was found to be twisted after the flight according to a rumoured report.

There were many people responsible for keeping the CF-100 serviceable and able to meet its NORAD commitments, but 'the buck stops here' at line maintenance. These were the people who, by night and day, snow and rain, hot and cold, kept 'the birds' in the air. They are often the unsung heroes of squadron serviceability, 'all in a day's work, sir'. The author remembered it was always a good feeling to get out of the aircraft at an unfamiliar base and leave it in the hands of a recognised face to be looked after.

The CAF 414 (Electronic Warfare) Squadron sister squadrons in the USAF during the 1970s were the 158th (Air National Guard Green Mountain Boys) Defense Systems Evaluation Squadron based at Burlington, Vermont, and the 17th DSES based at Malmstrom AFB, Great Falls, Montana. Both squadrons flew the Martin EB-57 Canberra 'Night Intruder' aircraft. It was a multi-role (bomber, reconnaissance) British-designed aircraft built under licence in the USA by the Martin aircraft company and adapted to the electronic warfare role.

It had a more powerful suite of electronic jammers than the CF-100. Captain Bland, the EWO in Chapter Nine, was fortunate to get an exchange posting with the USAF at Malmstrom AFB. He remembered the EB-57 had three Delta, two Echo Fox, one Golf and two India band jammers. In addition it had communication jammers and chaff dispensers. The aircraft had a unique engine starting device: a starter cartridge. The cartridge explosion was powerful enough to cause the engine to rotate and to send a plume of black smoke skywards, a sensational sight for an onlooker!

Warrant Officer Barrie Laycock. (Courtesy of Barrie Laycock)

USAF Martin EB-57 Canberra. (Courtesy of Gerald Vernon)

The USAF had other aircraft that were utilised as target aircraft. The Boeing B-52 Stratofortress was probably the best known. A subsonic, nuclear-weapon-capable bomber, it had a range of defensive jammers making it a suitable radar training aircraft. Another less-known but spectacular aircraft was the Convair B-58 Hustler. A supersonic strategic bomber, it could fly at twice the speed of sound and presented a tremendous interception challenge to the air weapon controllers and fighter interceptor aircrew. Bob Keith had experience of working with the B-58 during his posting with the 23rd NORAD Region in Duluth, Minnesota. When asked about the B-58, his eyes clouded over with the memories. 'Fast, very fast, extremely fast!'

What were all these target aircraft trying to replicate in the late 1960s and early 1970s? The Soviet standard bombers of the period, including the long-range, subsonic, turboprop Tupolev Tu-95, code name 'Bear', and the supersonic jet TU-22M, code name 'Backfire'.

The 'Backfire' was the subject of a great intelligence debate during the Cold War. Was the bomber's mission a peripheral or intercontinental attack one? Did it or did it not have inflight refuelling capability? Was there really a concealed refuelling probe, to be used to change attack modes? The dominant view of the American intelligence agencies was that it was a peripheral weapon because of its restricted range. Press reports in the late 1980s reported that a Russian defector had in fact confirmed that the Backfire was a supersonic intercontinental bomber, with a stockpiled and hidden 'screw in' refuelling probe, which regularly exercised at intercontinental range.

The CAF CF-101 Voodoos flew missions against supersonic targets, other CF-101s and USAF Convair F-102 Delta Daggers and Convair F-106 Delta Darts, to maintain proficiency. So if the Backfire bombers had come, albeit on a one-way supersonic bombing run, NORAD was ready, willing, and able to meet the threat. The regular training missions would pay off and the bombers would meet with determined resistance. History records that during the Cold War no Soviet bomber came close to Canadian airspace without being intercepted. The NORAD motto stood, and still stands, the test of time – Deter, Detect, Defend.

The Soviet Tupolev TU-95 Bear, on the other hand, became well known to CAF and USAF interceptor crews. It started, for Canada, with the first intercept during 1968, which is related in Chapter Two, and continues to this day, 2011, in the High Arctic. The development of the TU-95 was initiated from a 1943 requirement for a long-range bomber to strike at the heart of Germany. It was fortuitous that three Boeing B-29 Superfortress aircraft which had been bombing Japan had landed in Siberia and were seized by the Soviets.

By mid-1945 one aircraft was at a flight test facility, one was dismantled to study its design and the last one was kept as an example. The engines were replaced by Soviet ASH-73TK engines, but with the B-29 turbocompressor. The Tupolev TU-4, code name 'Bull', was created with two bomb bays, four gun turrets, and a few models had in-flight refuelling capabilities and could carry nuclear bombs. It was still a one-way bombing mission to reach the USA, so by 1956 the next stage of development led to the intercontinental Tupolev TU-95 Bear.

The deciding factors in the TU-95 Bear development were range and speed. These requirements were met by using turboprop engines with contra-rotating propellers to increase range over the pure turbine engine and sweeping the wings back to give a higher cruise speed. It was probably the most successful bomber ever built by the Soviets. It enjoyed a long and valuable service life in a variety of models, which varied from delivery of conventional bombs, nuclear bombs and air-to-surface missiles, to gathering of electronic intelligence and maritime surveillance, a definite threat to North America. Hence the need to have target squadrons simulate Soviet Bear penetration of Canadian airspace to ensure the defence forces were fully trained and ready to respond to any attack.

The Tupolev TU-95, known to US and NATO intelligence services by its original name, the TU-20, had each variant identified with the alphabetical designation from A to J. The Bear A was the initial model and the Bear D was the electronic intelligence version. Bear D was easily distinguished from Bear A by the in-flight refuelling probe, new enlarged chin radome, and a much larger Big Bulge India-band search radar in place of the former weapons bay. It had a 23-mm tail-turret gun as defensive armament, which the fighter interceptor crews always liked to see in a stowed position, pointed skyward!

The Annual Historic Report of 1973 listed the flying hours flown during the year for 414 Squadron. The number of hours flown by the squadron, CF-100 and T-33 aircraft, totalled 9,399.4 hours. To put this in some sort of perspective, it is 5,185,600 km flown using 300 knots as an average speed, the total equates to 130 times around the earth. It was not surprising that 409 Squadron at CFB Comox on the west coast showed the highest number of hours allocated, 452.4. The total would have included the ten hours of positioning time from, and to, the home base of CFB North Bay, Ontario. The exercise that year in Alaska took 128.9 hours. The squadron was also tasked with flying the Queen's Mail to Charlottetown, Prince Edward Island, as was customary for a Royal Visit.

On 31 December 1973 there were forty-nine officers and two other ranks on squadron strength, which included one exchange USAF Electronic Warfare Officer. The squadron operational call sign was 'Yogi', the author

Captain Garry Hunt's grave marker, North Bay, Ontario. (Courtesy of Author)

being 'Yogi 20', which was used everywhere accept for exercise designated call signs. Unfortunately, as mentioned elsewhere, this was also the year of two squadron fatalities during a 22nd NORAD Region exercise. The Annual Historic Report stated: 'Although the Board of Enquiry reached a number of conclusions concerning the accident, the main cause could only be surmised, making it even more difficult for both squadron and family.'

Captain Garry Hunt and Captain Tom Campbell – we will remember you.

On 14 June 1975, the squadron received its Queen's Colours for twenty-five years active service with the RCAF and CAF. Prior to the ceremony, a CF-100 flown by Captain Don Hollington and Captain, later Lt-Col., Rob Dunlop flew a mission testing the long-range radars from Vancouver Island to Newfoundland. The flight covered 5,206 km and took 6.4 hours. It was a fitting flight for a fitting occasion.

CHAPTER NINE

Sparks in the Night Sky

The Amalgam Mute Exercise, 10 May 1973

Bill looked out his office window and noticed the first quarter moon provided some illumination of the carpet of clouds. It was past midnight and the glow from the front office reflected in his window. Everything was quiet, for now, during these early morning hours. Bill pondered the events that led him to be in his office at these 'ungodly hours' when he should have been at home with his family. Bill's office was the rear cockpit of the Avro CF-100, number 100779, assigned to 414 Electronic Warfare Squadron, known as the 'Black Knights'. He was an Electronic Warfare Officer with the squadron and, very shortly, the stillness would end and he would become very busy indeed. He would need all his training and experience as his aircraft, call sign Mute 104, took part in the Amalgam Mute NORAD exercise on 10 May 1973.

His partner this night, Doug, was the pilot in the 'front office' and, together, they would play the 'bad guys' and test the defences of North America. Doug was single, twenty years younger than Bill at the time, and on his first operational squadron tour. He was anxious to get plenty of flying experience and did not mind the early hour as much as Bill. Besides, this exercise was early Thursday morning and the chances were that he would then be off duty Friday night to attend the traditional beer call in the Officers' Mess.

Matter of fact, Doug and Bill shared the same office, sitting in tandem under the cockpit canopy looking out at the night sky. Their roles were very different, Doug was a pilot and Bill an Electronic Warfare Officer, but they came together this night to form a formidable team to test the defences of North America as the population slept. This particular mission was part of a series of exercises that were designed to keep the NORAD defence network operating at peak efficiency – failure was not an option.

Captain Peter Maunsell of the 'exercise shop' said that 'it helped to have a devious mind' when you were designing these exercises. Criss-crossing target tracks and having one low target and one high target on the same track, at the same time, in the hope that some confusion would result, were some of the 'dirty tricks' used. In addition, many different types of aircraft were used – from the USAF Martin EB-57 Canberra and Boeing B-52 Stratofortress to the CAF Canadair T-33. Peter had flown both in the CF-101 Voodoo fighter interceptor and the CF-100 Canuck target aircraft; as a result of his varied flying experience, he had many ideas on how to test the NORAD system to its maximum efficiency.

The Amalgam Mute exercise had been planned earlier in the year to test the 22nd NORAD Region. The 'exercise shop' staff were now down in 'the Hole', the underground NORAD headquarters in North Bay, Ontario, observing the reaction of the whole system as it became apparent that an exercise was underway. The staff had three main purposes at this stage: to ensure that the exercise progressed safely, as planned, to be available as the only authority who knew the big picture of what was devised and to evaluate the progress of the region response. Anyone who had prior knowledge of the exercise details was known as a 'Trusted Agent'.

Lieutenant D. 'Doug' W. Fitzpatrick and Captain W. 'Bill' Bland knew about the exercise a week before it took place. The squadron, 414 Electronic Warfare Squadron based at Canadian Forces Base North Bay, Ontario, had been tasked much earlier by the NORAD exercise shop to provide target aircraft for the exercise on 9 and 10 May 1973. Co-ordination with Squadron Maintenance ensued to ensure that the requested number of aircraft would be available on that date. In 1973, 414 Electronic Warfare Squadron was the last squadron in the Canadian Armed Forces to operate the Avro CF-100. The maintenance organisation had to deal with an aging aircraft and limited spare parts available.

Corporal, later Warrant Officer, L. B. 'Barrie' Laycock was a member of the maintenance team in 1973 that looked after preparing the Avro CF-100 Canucks for their NORAD duties. The CF-100s were not getting any younger as they had started life as front-line fighter aircraft and had now assumed the role of electronic warfare target aircraft. Barry related that 'it took extensive scheduling and late night work in the hanger' to ensure the aircraft were available for various flying duties.

Doug and Bill's aircraft, number 100779, entered the inventory of the Royal Canadian Air Force on 6 November 1958 as a fighter aircraft with 416 Squadron, St Hubert, Quebec. It was subsequently converted by Avro to a CF-100 MK5C for electronic warfare duties on 23 June 1960. It was taken off the inventory on 26 April 1976 and donated, for permanent display, at Peterson Air Force Base (AFB), Colorado Springs, Colorado. This was a fitting tribute by NORAD Headquarters to an aircraft that played an important role in the defence of North America.

There were three types of CF-100 aircraft available and, based on the exercise requirements and serviceability, the specific aircraft would be assigned and notification of aircraft numbers were 'sent upstairs' to the squadron planning office. The three types were the MK5C, the MK5D, with an enhanced jamming capability, and one aircraft, a MK 5 number 100757, which did not have electronic jammers, but could have been outfitted with chaff dispensers.

The planning office assigned flight crew to the exercise as well as a specific aircraft. At any time the flight crew could visit the planning office and look at a Plexiglass board that covered one wall. All scheduled missions were displayed and crew names were assigned to meet the requirements. Past assignments and flying time was tracked to give everyone a fair share of the work. Tracking crew flights and exercises was necessary, as a week during the winter in Goose Bay, Labrador, did not compare with a week in Bermuda flying against the NATO navies.

Earlier in the week, Bill had been in the squadron planning office and picked up the Altitude Reservation. It was the route that he would fly on the exercise and which would be filed with Air Traffic Control to ensure separation of aircraft in the crowded skies. That was the good news. The bad news was that most exercises were run after midnight, when there was less civilian traffic in the skies. The Altitude Reservation had been created by the exercise shop, remember the 'dirty tricks' guys, and now had to be checked by the squadron planning office, and, finally, Bill. Of course, this was all accomplished without the knowledge of the NORAD Region that was about to be tested.

The exercise would involve many aircraft, at different times of the day and night, on different routes trying to penetrate the defences of the 22nd NORAD Region of North America. Many of these exercises involved aircraft from the United States Air Force, so the preparation and organisation of such an immense task took skill, planning, and huge resources. A variety of targets would present themselves to the fighter interceptor aircraft. Some would be at high altitudes, some at low altitudes. Some would fly alone and others in groups. To add to the challenge, there would also be supersonic targets flying through the exercise area.

The Amalgam Mute exercise also involved the men and women of CFB Bagotville, Quebec. The base is 168 kms (105 miles) north of Quebec City. It was home to 425 All Weather Fighter Squadron. Known as the 'Alouettes', the squadron protected the northern and north-eastern approaches of the

22nd NORAD region. The squadron fighter interceptor was the McDonnell CF-101 Voodoo, a two-crew aircraft with a pilot and AI Navigator. During the week of 7 May 1973, 'exercise intelligence reports' came in to the squadron disclosing Soviet unrest in Eastern Europe and increased Soviet bomber flight activity. These reports were generated by the NORAD exercise shop to give some realism to the war games. Exercise intelligence reports increased in number and severity until the NORAD region was put on exercise alert to coincide with the beginning of the exercise.

These reports were also sent to the CADIN/Pinetree radar sites. The radar techs at CFS Ramore near Kirkland Lake, Ontario, CFS Senneterre north-east of Val D'Or (the 425 Squadron deployment base), Quebec, and CFS Chibougamau near Chapais, Quebec, worked on their search and height finder radars to make sure they were performing at their peak. It was almost a professional competition to see how far out each site could 'paint' a radar target. The normal limit of the search radar was 200 nm (370 km). These radar sites are an integral part of our story as they cover the route of Mute 104, the target aircraft, through the 22nd NORAD region.

The week had started out fairly routine for Major E. (Gene) Lukan, later Colonel, and Major, later Lt-Col., Ronald (Tiny) McDonald, members of 425 All Weather Fighter Squadron in CFB Bagotville, Quebec. The 'exercise intelligence reports' had been increasing in number and severity during the week. All indications, from their experience, pointed towards an upcoming exercise. So it was no surprise that on Tuesday there was a Base Recall, requiring all personnel to report to the base for duty. Exercise Amalgam Mute was underway and NORAD was being tested for its response to an aerial threat.

All aircrew members of 425 (AW) Squadron had assembled in the Squadron Flight Operations (Ops) room in the hangar on the flight line. The time was 2300 hours (11:00 PM) on Wednesday. The Ops Officer briefed the assembled aircrew on the nature of the threat, anticipated response, surrounding area weather and aircraft status. The aircraft status indicated which aircraft were serviceable, which aircraft were anticipated to be serviceable and those out of service at the time of the briefing. Gene and Tiny were assigned Voodoo number 101003. They went out to the flight line and placed their parachutes and flying helmets in the aircraft to be ready for a fast departure. Gene also prepared the cockpit for an immediate engine start. There would be no delay in Kilo November 04 getting airborne if this crew could help it. They grabbed some warm food and a coffee in anticipation of departing shortly.

Gene and Tiny's aircraft, 101003, started life as a McDonnell F-101B-65-MC, number 56-262, with the United States Air Force. It was part of the

Operation Peace Wings programme and was transferred to the Canadian Armed Forces by way of Bristol Aerospace Ltd, Winnipeg, Manitoba, on 30 June 1970. It was a dual-control equipment aircraft and was re-designated a CF-101F by the CAF. On 3 August 1971, it was transferred to 410 Operational Training Squadron, also located at CFB Bagotville. The aircraft had dual-flying controls, front and rear cockpits, and the AI Navigator standard rear cockpit, so it could be used for training pilots and AI Navigators. It ended its flying life on 7 January 1985 and is fittingly displayed at the Labrador Air Museum, Goose Bay, Labrador.

It was midnight when the 414 Electronic Warfare Squadron Operations Officer, assigned this exercise, started his briefing in the operations office of Canadian Forces Base North Bay, Ontario. The crew had already been assigned their aircraft and were briefed on the weather expected over their route, the weather at their destination, and alternate landing airport, if needed. Doug and Bill's route this night, or more correctly early morning, would take them north of North Bay and just to the east of James Bay. They would then turn east for a short time before heading south in a zigzag pattern to ultimately arrive over their target – Ottawa, Ontario. The nation's capital was going to be under attack this night. Mission completed, they would then recover to their home base of CFB North Bay. Other squadron crews would fly different routes, from different airports, attacking different targets, and would recover at other airports.

The Ops Officer continued his briefing with information on other conflicting target aircraft, expected fighter activity and which ground radar sites would be trying to present a radar image of their target aircraft so that the ground controllers could vector the fighter interceptor towards them. Radar frequencies were reviewed, with careful attention being given to the best methods of jamming the signals of the ground radar sites and fighter interceptors. The rules of engagement were reviewed with safety in mind, such as how much evasive manoeuvres were permitted.

Bill had 'plugged in' the winds to their flight plan to work out their departure time from North Bay to arrive at the start of their target run, the Initial Point, many miles to the north, at the allotted time. He had calculated that they needed to be airborne at 0054. That allowed just enough time for a coffee and to finish the sandwich and apple in the 'box lunch' that had been provided. The other crews would be departing later and did not have to rush. Doug and Bill had agreed that off the chocks, leaving the flight line, at 0047 would get them to the end of the runway in time. They grabbed their publications bag and flying jackets and headed down the stairs to the Safety Equipment Room.

There they picked up their individually fitted flying helmet with oxygen mask attached. It was affectionately known as the 'bone dome'. Doug and

Bill tested their masks for leaks and correct functioning of the inhalation and exhalation valves. The mask would keep them alive in the rarefied cockpit atmosphere. The CF-100 had been designed in the late 1940s, with the first flight on 19 January 1950. Pressurisation was not a high priority to military aircraft at that time. The primary concern was the adverse effect of taking compressor air off the engine, thereby reducing thrust; the solution was to put the crew on oxygen. At an aircraft altitude of 41,000 feet above sea level the altitude in the cockpit was 26,000 feet, nearly the height of Mt Everest, requiring the crew to have oxygen functioning. In comparison, an airliner at 41,000 feet today would have a cabin altitude of 5,400 feet, allowing the passengers to enjoy the flight without supplemental oxygen.

Oxygen mask and helmet, 'Bone Dome'. (Courtesy of Author)

A few steps down the corridor brought the crew into the maintenance line servicing blister. This building was attached to the hangar and had a view of the flight line. It was a hive of activity as the maintenance team readied the aircraft and paperwork for the upcoming departures. The room was dominated by a squadron aircraft status board on the wall. A quick glance by Doug indicated that their aircraft was serviceable and ready for the exercise. He proceeded to the desk to check the L-14, which was the travelling maintenance documents, to show that all maintenance checks had been done on the aircraft. It also indicated that the fuel, oil, hydraulics and oxygen quantities had been checked as per the Operations Order for the exercise.

Doug signed out the aircraft and turned to leave the blister. 'All set Sir?' Barrie Laycock called out.

'Yes, it's about that time.'

'I will be starting you tonight' said Barrie. Doug and Barrie lived in the same apartment block near Trout Lake and would often see each other at work and at home. Both men played their important roles in 414 Electronic Warfare Squadron. Bill lived with his wife and children on the base. The weather was cloudy with a temperature of 8 °C (46 °F) as they walked out to aircraft 779. The forecast was for rain and fog upon their return, hours later. The fog was always a concern at North Bay, as the airport was situated on the top of a hill and was very conducive to upslope fog during moist conditions.

The flight line was unusually quiet as Doug and Bill walked towards 779. They were the first target aircraft to leave, so the only noise was the power unit that Barrie had hooked up to their aircraft. Bill went up the ladder to his cockpit while Doug started his walk-around inspection. The ladder was positioned on the front cockpit, because of the engine, and Bill had a few precarious steps to walk on the canopy ledge to get to his seat. Not too bad tonight, but it could be quite a challenge during very cold or snowy conditions. It was a familiar routine as Doug looked for leaks, airframe damage (hangar rash, as it was sometimes called), checked external pressure gauges and removed the landing gear safety pins. The chaff pods hung on the wings, ready to do their work as part of the aircraft's electronic jamming package.

Barrie knew the aircraft was ready for flight; he had prepared it, but recognised that it was part of Doug's duty to do a walk-around. Bill had closed the cockpit canopy to Doug's shoulders. This prevented Bill inadvertently catching Doug's arms in the canopy. Barrie unhooked the ladder and Doug completely closed the canopy to cut down the noise of the ground power unit, or energiser as it was called. An exchange of thumbs-up with Barrie and Doug and Bill prepared 779 for the engine start.

Close by, Lt Dennis Kelleher, later Lt-Col., settled into his seat as part of Team 1 in the Weapons Room of the NORAD Underground Complex in Canadian Forces Base North Bay. His team was curtained off from the rest of the Weapons Teams and Senior Director in 'The Blue Room'. His job was to monitor the activity of the target aircraft and keep the air environment safe. Some exercises had fifty to sixty aircraft acting as hostile targets. Dennis remarked that, 'I knew who the bad guy was and where he was coming from'. His personal call sign was 'Irradiate 49', which he used when communicating with the target aircraft.

His first targets had already departed Goose Bay, Labrador and Gander, Newfoundland, and he expected the activity in the Weapons Room to suddenly increase. Intelligence reports throughout the week had suggested that there would be an exercise shortly and rumours had it that it would be tonight! Doug and Bill's aircraft, Mute 104, would not be at the Initial Point for just over an hour and its track would be to the west of the first two targets. They were part of the first wave of targets, with a second wave two hours later.

Doug and Bill fastened themselves into their parachutes and then did up the seat harness of the English Martin-Baker ejection seat. The rocket powered ejection seat could blast the seat and occupant out of the aircraft if necessary. They also threaded the straps through their leg stirrups. These straps pulled their legs tight against the seat in the event of an ejection to prevent injury. Barrie had already pulled the hard-to-reach safety pins and put them in a pouch on the side of the seats. The remaining pins were pulled and now the seats were 'hot' – armed for use. It was possible to eject on the runway with a minimum speed of 80 knots. The eighty knots minimum was necessary to ensure that there was enough wind to fully deploy the drogue chute, then allow enough time for the occupant to separate from the seat and the personal chute to fully deploy. The occupant would then float safely to the ground.

Doug and Bill scanned their dark cockpits with the aid of flashlights and checked all the switches and gauges were indicating correctly. It was time to bring 779 to life – Doug moved the Flight/Ground switch to the Ground position. They were now able to adjust their cockpit lights for the night flight.

'Time is 44 now, Doug,' said Bill. That would allow three minutes for the start and ground crew checks. Doug held up his finger and made the rotary signal to Barrie for permission to start the left engine. Thumbs up from Barrie indicated all clear with the ground start crew in place. Doug placed the Flight/Ground switch to Flight, turned on the anti-collision light ON, switched the Left Fuselage Fuel Booster pump ON, and the Engine Start Switch LEFT.

A muffled whine could be heard inside the cockpit as the starter spooled up the left engine. Fuel was added by opening the High Pressure Cock (HPC) at 10 per cent minimum. The engine accelerated to its idle speed of 35 per cent RPM. A check of the engine instruments revealed all was normal. Doug similarly started the right engine and then commenced the Pre-Taxi check. Barrie signalled for 25 degrees of flap and confirmed they were symmetrical. He signalled for speed brake extension and retraction, confirmed the speed brakes were flush with the upper and lower surfaces of the wing and checked for any obvious fuel, oil or hydraulic leaks. Bill was busy balancing generators and turning all navigation and electronic jamming equipment on. All the circuit breakers for the CF-100 were in the rear cockpit. Doug completed the checklist and called North Bay Air Traffic Control – 'North Bay Ground, Mute 104 taxi, airborne time 54'. Air Traffic Control replied, 'Roger, Mute 104, time check 47, taxi unrestricted runway 08, altimeter 28.37, wind 140 at 10 knots.'

Thumbs up from Barrie, Doug released the brakes and Mute 104 was on its way to attack Ottawa. Now was the time to do the Taxi/Pre–Takeoff Checklist as 779 proceeded down the long parallel taxiway to the departure end of the easterly runway 08. With Bill calling and Doug responding they proceeded through the checklist. For example, Bill, 'Generators', Doug, 'lights out', Bill, 'charging', until they came to Navigation Instruments 'Set'. These instruments and the checklist were completed on the runway.

'North Bay Tower, Mute 104 is ready for 54 departure.'

'Mute 104, taxi to position and hold runway 08, time is 53.'

'Roger Tower, Mute 104 to position and hold runway 08.'

Doug turned on the landing lights and swung 779 onto runway 08. He was now looking down a 10,000 foot black strip of pavement between two rows of lights penetrating the darkness. Doug and Bill checked their compasses were reading correctly with the published runway heading for runway 08 – 083 degrees magnetic. 'Mute 104, time is 54, cleared takeoff runway 08, contact departure on 258.4, Happy Jamming, Good Night'

Doug responded, 'Mute 104, cleared takeoff 08, terminal 258.4, Good Night' as he advanced the throttles to 85 per cent power and checked the engine instruments.

The twin Orenda engines transformed the night with a dull roar which was further increased in volume as Doug pushed the throttles fully forward for maximum power and released the brakes. The engines had been designed in the late 1940s, when noise had not been a consideration; this was comparable to a car with a straight-through exhaust. Except that this was 7,200 pounds of thrust. The citizens of North Bay would, by now, be fully aware that there was night flying and that the Air Force was at work.

CF-100 windshield view. (Courtesy of Canadian Warplane Museum)

The fully laden CF-100, at a weight just over 40,000 lbs, which included a full fuel load of 14,600 lbs, electronic jammers and full chaff load of 384 bundles, accelerated slowly at first. Doug steered the aircraft with his feet on the rudder pedals to maintain the runway centreline. He could feel the controls becoming more effective as the airspeed increased, 779 accelerating more rapidly now as the engines became more efficient at the higher speed. Easing back on the control column until the nose-wheel lifted, Doug then checked forward to avoid an excessive nose-up attitude. At 140 knots (260 km/h) and about 4,000 feet (1,219 metres) down the runway, 779 lifted off the surface; Doug and Bill were airborne and heading for the electronic battle, the 'Sparks in the Night Sky'.

Landing gear and flaps, once selected up, allowed the aircraft to accelerate to 200 knots (370 kmh) before easing the nose up. 'Post-Takeoff Checklist please, Bill'. Bill read 'Landing gear' and Doug responded 'Up' and once again, using the challenge and response method the checklist was completed. Doug let the speed further increase to 325 knots (602 km/h) and now 779 really started to climb. Doug called on the radio, 'North Bay departure, Mute 104 off 08, 3,000 [feet] for 10,000 [feet]'. Air Traffic Control replied, 'Mute 104 radar identified, left turn 330 (degrees), intercept the on course, cleared flight level 200.' Doug read back the clearance and rolled 779 into a left turn.

CF-100 winter twilight takeoff. (Courtesy of AWFA)

At the same time, the first two targets started to show up on the north-eastern edge of the 22nd NORAD region. Unannounced, with no flight plan, the two target aircraft started to penetrate the NORAD system. Gene and Tiny were enjoying their coffee when the scramble order came over the Public Address system for two designated aircraft, not their aircraft, not this time. The other crews ran out of operations to their aircraft and Gene remarked, 'I guess it has started Tiny, it could be a long night.' It certainly would be, and unbeknown to them, their target, Mute 104, was turning northbound from North Bay on course.

'Mute 104, check that you're on course, contact Irradiate on 324.7, Good Night.'

Dennis and his Intercept Director Technician partner had been sitting for a few hours since the briefing. More than a few coffees had been consumed and Dennis mentioned that 'this was 1973 and most people smoked, a blue haze hung throughout the room'.

'Irradiate, this is Mute 104 on frequency, 14,000 feet climbing Angels 20 [20,000 feet], requesting Angels 41'. Dennis turned to his scope partner, the Interceptor Director Technician, and said, 'Here we go, good, Mute 104 is on time'.

'Mute 104, Irradiate 49, radar contact, cleared Angels 41, call level'. The target Weapons Team had a discreet Identification Friend or Foe/ Selective Identification Feature squawk, transponder code, so they could keep track of the entire target aircraft without the Weapons Teams seeing the secondary radar squawk displayed on their screens. Dennis, at the same time, was talking with a USAF Martin EB-57 at Angels 35 [35,000 feet] that was approaching its Initial Point. This was a formidable aircraft, with an array of electronic jammers which would test the ability of the fighter interceptor AI Navigators' ability to avoid radar jamming. Dennis mentioned that 'at the target monitor briefing he had been assigned a sheet containing the call signs and Initial Point times of perhaps five or six targets to monitor'.

At 0102 Mute 104 was levelling at Angels 41 approximately 167 km north of North Bay, just north-east of Kirkland Lake, Ontario. Doug reviewed his Altitude Reservation flight plan route and did a Ground Speed/Fuel check. 'Irradiate Mute 104 level Angels 41 [41,000 feet]', was called by Doug, 'Roger Mute 104'. All temperatures and pressures were correct; Mute 104 and crew were ready for the ensuing air battle. Bill, meanwhile, as the Electronic Warfare Officer, readied his equipment for the task ahead. First of all, he checked the left and right MX900-A chaff dispensers. Chaff was tiny strips of aluminium foil tied together in bundles which were released from 779. These strips were cut to specific lengths to interfere with the fighter interceptor radar and the ground radar sites. When these bundles left 779 they exploded into a cloud of metal strips which, hopefully, the fighter and ground radar would 'lock on' to and not 779. The chaff dispensers hung, bomb-shaped, under each wing. The bundles contained two types: 003 chaff for fighters and 002 chaff for ground radar sites.

Bill turned his attention next to his AN/ALT-4 I Band radar transmitter and his AN/APR-9 India Band receiver. These were the tools of the trade to look for the fighter interceptor's telltale radar signal as he tried to 'lock on' to Mute 104. Bill's transmitter would attempt to overcome the fighter's signal and make it 'break lock'. Without a 'lock-on', the fighter would be unable to use its fire control system to fire its weapons. However, the Voodoo had two weapons in its arsenal: the rocket-powered, nuclear-capable Genie rocket normally used for frontal attacks, as well as the Falcon heat-seeking missile for stern attacks. Keeping in mind that this was an exercise and, although no weapons would actually be fired, the Voodoo had devices on board to record the performance of the fire control system, as if a weapon had been fired.

Doug and Bill's route took them over Rouyn, Quebec, and west of Matagami, Quebec. About 15 minutes past the town of Matagami, Bill expected the last radar site to stop 'painting' them and Mute 104 would disappear off all the radar screens. For the purpose of the exercise CFS Moosonee, in the 23rd NORAD Region, was excluded from active participation and assumed a passive observation role. Mute 104 was going to be invisible to the CADIN/Pinetree Line. The plan was for Mute 104 to remain at Angels 41 and turn southbound just north of the Cree community of Waskaganish, which is located on the south-east shore of James Bay. Mute 104 would then proceed on a zigzag track to the 'bombs away' point of Ottawa, Ontario – the nation's capital.

Doug turned 779 southbound on the new target track and very soon would call 'hot, active target', to Dennis, sitting underground at North Bay in Irradiate Control. Up until this point, Mute 104 was positioning itself for the attacking target track.

'All set, Bill?'

'Yes, everything is ready back here!' replied Bill. Doug's job was to look after the aircraft, follow the Altitude Reservation routing and be the safety eyes for the crew as the fighter interceptors came to 'shoot them down'. Bill's job was to prevent the fighter interceptor from doing that by jamming the fighter's radar as Gene and Tiny took over the attack. Jamming was a skilful combination of electronic jamming, dispensing chaff and evasive manoeuvres.

Speeding southbound at 420 knots in the night sky, Mute 104 was about to start its target route. 'Mute 104 is Initial Point inbound'. 'Roger Mute 104, no chicks (fighters) your vicinity,' Dennis replied, thinking that it would not last for too long. Bill had unlatched the AN/APR-9 Receiver scope again, tilted it towards him and was watching the screen intently for the telltale sign of a fighter interceptor India Band radar looking at him.

On the ground at Canadian Forces Station Ramore, Ontario, Sergeant L. (Larry) S. Wilson, later Master Warrant Officer, worked hard as a Radar Tech to ensure the Westinghouse FPS-27 Search Radar was at maximum efficiency. The radar was designed to have a maximum range of 407 km, but required some tweaking to maintain that distance. The FPS-27 was later converted to solid-state circuitry, but on 10 May 1973 it was still primarily vacuum tubes. Larry was determined that CFS Ramore would play its part in the exercise and be the first to get the radar information into the Semi-Automatic Ground Environment system in North Bay, Ontario.

East of CFS Ramore, a Radar Tech was tuning the Bendix FPS-508 Search Radar at CFS Senneterre, Quebec to make sure it was sending its radar signal out to at least 370 km. The tech was determined that the radar sets, both search and height finder, would continue to operate at maximum efficiency. Along with CFS Chibougamau, Quebec that portion of the 22nd NORAD Region near Waskaganish was well covered with the overlapping search radars. The CADIN/Pinetree Line was on alert, as it always was 24/365, and ready to forward any information to the

22nd NORAD Region Identification Section in the Underground Complex, many kilometres to the south at CFB North Bay.

In North Bay, Lt M. (Marty) Schlosser, later Lt-Col., prepared himself for the ensuing aerial battle which he suspected was about to start. He had picked up a coffee just after 0100 and proceeded back along the corridor to the Identification Section, which was deep underground in 22nd NORAD Region Headquarters. Would 10 May 1973 be a quiet night? He suspected not! There it was – a small dot had appeared on the Surveillance Team's scope that was assigned to the area just south of James Bay. Was it just radar noise or was it something else? Another sweep of the CFS Ramore search radar and there it was – the dot again. By now CFS Senneterre search radar was also picking up the target and had a dot on its screen.

The Radar Input Counter Measures Officer, Marty, was working with his technicians, the Radar Input Counter Measure Technicians, to get the best possible data on the target for the SAGE computer. They, in turn, worked directly with the Air Defence Technicians in the Data Management Control Center at the radar sites. The Air Defence Technicians would coordinate the requests with the relevant sections, for example, height finder, radar, or data processing section. Keep in mind that the year was 1973 and that they were dealing with vacuum tube-driven computers, ferrite core memory, and data drum storage. It was a constant battle to get good data, and then the target aircraft would start electronic jamming – a nightmare for the Air Defence Technicians.

Information from the search radars was processed at the radar sites by the Common Digitiser and the data was then transmitted over phone lines to the SAGE computer in North Bay. It compared the two sets of data and displayed the resulting target dot on the Identification Officer's screen. The surveillance tech would line up the target track, in this case 172 degrees magnetic, punch in the estimated speed in knots and 'initiate a track'. The track would be initiated as 'pending' and the Identification Officer had two minutes to identify the track by declaring it friendly, special, fighter, search and rescue or 'unknown'. This was done by comparing the unidentified track with the flight plans that Transport Canada, Air Traffic Control, continuously sent to SAGE by teletype. The information was then placed on eighty-hole punch cards by the Manual Input Section and read into the SAGE computer. Mute 104 had not filed a flight plan, but an Altitude Reservation registered with Air Traffic Control.

To ensure that the operation of NORAD was not compromised during an exercise there were special procedures to be followed. All air traffic would be tagged with a track number and observed by the Identification Team 'Trusted Agent'. Then the Trusted Agent would communicate with the Identification Team and say 'Track Mike 1274 does not have a flight plan because he is one of our 'players' and is on an Altitude Reservation for target aircraft'. So for the purposes of the exercise, Track Mike 1274 would become an unknown.

The Identification Officer announced on the Public Address system so all in the 'Blue Room' could hear. 'Control Center, this is Identification, Track Mike 1274 Pending at 0602 Zulu Identification, out.' The 'clock' was started with a two minute limit to identify Mike 1274 track. In that time Mute 104 would be 25 km closer to Ottawa. The Senior Weapons Director, Captain Jim Graham this night, was by now well aware of a possible unknown entering the system and he checked the board for the resources at his disposal. Since the phase-out of the Bomarc missile program in 1972, the fighter interceptor was the only Canadian weapon available. The weather was operational at CFB Bagotville and there were 425 Squadron Voodoo interceptors available. He gave the intercept to Team 3 Weapons Director, who contacted the squadron's Operations Officer to prepare for a possible scramble of two aircraft.

'Control Center, this is Identification, Track Mike 1274 Unknown at 0604 Zulu, Identification out.' The air battle had begun. Mute 104 had become Track Mike 1274 and a threat to Canadian airspace. Jim made the decision to scramble two fighters out of CFB Bagotville for the intercept. He passed the request to his Team 3 Weapons Director. The Team 3 Weapons Director, with the assistance of Cpl Bob Keith, the Weapons Director Technician, checked that 425 Squadron had serviceable aircraft at the ready. The Weapons Director then assigned the intercept to Intercept Director 2, call sign controller 26, part of his team. He, in turn, had his Interceptor Director Technician call Squadron Operations at CFB Bagotville and scramble Kilo November 04 and Kilo November 07. These aircraft were showing ready status, refuelled, crewed and armed, in this case, with the simulated recording weapons.

'Scramble Kilo November 04 and ...' Gene and Tiny heard no more. They were the crew of Kilo November 04 and, emptying their coffees, they ran out of the Operations Room into the darkness of the flight line. They quickly climbed up their ladder to their cockpits and started to strap into their parachutes and Weber ejection seats. The line maintenance crew removed the ladders and stood by the energiser, air compressor and fire extinguisher for the engine start. Gene simultaneously started the engines as he continued his strap-in. 'Hands Clear?' An affirmative from Tiny and Gene closed the canopy.

External power and air disconnected, 'Speed Brakes – In' and 'Flaps – Recycle Check and Down', 'Chocks – Removed' followed by the visual confirmation and wave off by the ground crew and Kilo November 04 was heading for the runway.

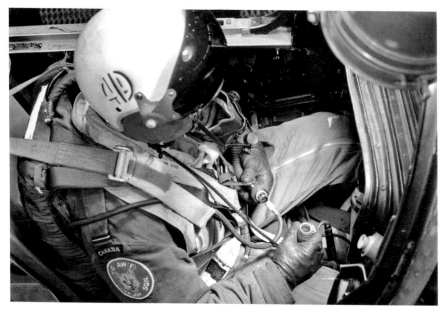

Voodoo crew strapping in, connecting oxygen mask hose. (Courtesy of Canadian Forces Joint Imagery Centre, Department of National Defence)

'Bagotville Tower, Kilo November 04, Scramble.'

'Roger, Kilo November 04, Taxi Runway 29, altimeter 29.93 inches, wind 270 at 10 knots, cleared takeoff, contact departure on 356.0.' Tiny called out the Pre-Takeoff Checklist, Gene responded and checked and responded to the items called as they continued their fast taxi. Gene adjusted his taxi speed to stay away from the airframe shimmy speed which the Voodoo was prone to. Kilo November 04 turned out on to the runway for departure. 'Hang on, Tiny', and Gene pushed the throttles forward and called, 'Tower, Kilo November 04 rolling'.

Gene advanced the throttles to approximately 80 per cent RPM, checking that the engine instruments were normal and, for now, that the afterburner nozzles were closed. Pushing the throttles fully forward, he checked the Engine Pressure Ratio gauges for correct thrust output. Kilo November 04, aircraft 101003, 003 for our purposes, accelerated fast under full military power, but that was nothing compared to what happened next. Gene moved the throttles to the full afterburner power position. The engines responded with a muffled bang as raw fuel was added to the exhaust to give extra thrust. The crew experienced a slight aircraft veer as the afterburners did not 'light off' together, which caused a slight yaw, easily corrected with nose-wheel steering and rudder. An outside observer would have seen the telltale cone of flame trailing from

416 squadron Voodoos formation takeoff. (Courtesy of Canadian Forces Joint Imagery Centre, Department of National Defence)

each engine, together with the earth-shattering roar; it was an impressive sight in the early morning darkness.

Gene raised the nose wheel at 155 knots and Kilo November became airborne at 175 knots. 'Gear – UP', immediately followed by 'Flaps – Up', at 200 knots occurred as Kilo November 04 accelerated rapidly to its climb speed of 370 knots. At 250 knots, Gene terminated the afterburners to conserve fuel and maintained full military power. A vector heading and a clearance altitude were provided by departure control and then Gene switched to frequency 245.5, All Intercept Control Common, and talked to Team 3 in North Bay, who had been assigned the intercept. 'Kilo November 04, Irradiate 26, maintain heading 280, climb Angels 39, target one thirty, 500 (nautical miles) Be advised you are on your own, Kilo November 07 did not get airborne.'

Mute 104's track was very close to the western boundary of the 22nd NORAD Region. It was a good test for the fighter interceptors based at CFB Bagotville to do intercepts at the region extremities. In reality there were fighter interceptors based at Val D'Or, Quebec, which were much nearer to Mute 104. However, the exercise planners had temporarily closed the runway at CFB Val D'Or due to 'an accident', which forced Jim Graham, the Senior Weapons Director, to select Kilo November 04 to respond to the hostile threat. The air battle, like a game of chess where a target moves and a fighter interceptor counter-moves, had begun. Amalgam Mute was doing its job, testing the system.

'Kilo November 04, Irradiate 26, Follow Dolly'.

All future communication commands for the intercept would be received by datalink as a result of the command to 'Follow Dolly'. Commands for intercept were typed in by the Intercept Director Technician on the radar scope at North Bay and displayed on an instrument in the cockpit. It gave steering commands to the crew of Kilo November 04 until they could see the target, Mute 104, on their radar screen and take over the intercept. Mute 104 was not going to make their task easy; electronic jammers, chaff and evasive manoeuvres were its tools for the air battle.

It was not easy for the Intercept Director to see Mute 104 on the radar screen. The exercise planners had organised an USAF EB-57 to simultaneously pass through the same area and it had the capability of jamming the ground radar sites on the Delta and Echo Band frequencies. Marty, the Radar Input Counter Measures Officer, had his challenges to give the Intercept Director the best scope presentation possible in the face of the massive jamming from the EB-57. The jamming affected CFS Ramore, Senneterre and Chibougamau. So the Radar Input Counter Measures Technician at North Bay got the radar sites connected on a communications network. 'Meet me on the loop' was the request, so that all involved could address the problem, namely the EB-57 radar jamming.

Everything that could be changed, altered and modified would be attempted to avoid the jamming and get a clear radar target picture to the Team Weapons Director and the Intercept Director. The radar sites could try changing the radar transmitter and receiver frequencies, jumping around radar frequencies to avoid the jamming, and clipping data. The Radar Input Counter Measures Officer could also triangulate, using Ramore, Senneterre and Chibougamau, the jamming signal if the target aircraft made the mistake of continuous jamming. Triangulation could give the position of the target aircraft, which could be used by the Intercept Director to get the fighter interceptor within range of its own radar.

The raw search radar data at the sites was processed by an AN/FST-2 computer, containing 7,100 tubes, which sent the resulting data by phone line to the AN/FSQ-7 SAGE computer at North Bay. The SAGE computer would look at the data from the three sites in our story and average out, or discard as necessary, the position data to give the most accurate target position. Once the position had been established, the Radar Input Counter Measure Officer would attempt to get the target height. The 2.5-ton height finder antenna could swing 180 degrees in two seconds. A Radar Tech, Master Corporal Pierre Parent, says: 'he still has the scars to prove it!' Doing some routine maintenance someone swung the antenna and Pierre could not get out of the way quick enough. This request would be handled by the Air Defence Technician, who would run the cursor on the Range Height Indicator to the centre of the sweep and then punch a send button to send the height data to the FSQ-7 computer in North Bay.

When asked what it was like during an exercise at a CADIN/Pinetree radar site, Pierre responded,

> The radar site would be locked down to ensure security during the exercise. An officer, the senior telecom officer, advised by an NCO would be the link between the site and the sector, the Air Defence technicians would respond to height requests, the Radar Techs would make sure the machinery ran as it should, the cooks down the hill would feed us, the MSE section would transport us, the power plant guys would make sure the lights were on, the Air Conditioning guys would make sure that the equipment didn't fry, the Supply section would action any requests usually at a code 1 level and last but not least the (Meatheads) military police would bring us coffee and doughnuts. Bottom line ... there were lots of people involved'.

Jim continued to watch as other 'unknown' targets appeared in the 22nd NORAD Region. Working closely with his teams and assistant tech, he assigned Weapon Directors and resources to meet the growing threat. In turn, the Weapons Directors would assign targets to the Intercept Directors in their Team. He was observed and guided by the presence of the 'Battle Staff'. The Battle Staff was comprised of senior officers and other advisors from every component of Air Defence Command. The Battle Staff was present on this night as this Amalgam Mute exercise required their attendance; they would not attend for smaller exercises.

The Intercept Director turned Kilo November 04 slightly left, to heading 275 degrees magnetic. In Kilo November 04, Gene noted the slight turn as 101003, on autopilot, responded to the datalink instruction. It had been thirty minutes since Gene had left CFB Bagotville and he was now 445 km to the west. In that time Mute 104 was 389 km further south and closer to its target – Ottawa. The two were about to meet in the dark skies over the Province of Quebec near Senneterre, which coincidentally was one of the radar sites looking for Mute 104. During this mission there was also a practice nuclear weapon release authority exercise. This was simulated as the CAF never flew in peacetime with live nuclear weapons. The authority was firstly to release the American nuclear weapons to Canada and then secondly to upload the weapons, if on the ground, or to launch if airborne.

'Kilo November 04, Irradiate 26, we have Antler Elk at 0611 Zulu.'

'Irradiate Zero Four, authenticate Charlie Whiskey at 0614 Zulu.'

'Kilo November 04, standby.'

The Intercept Director would now contact the Weapons Director for the reply applicable to the 0614 Zulu challenge.

'Kilo November 04, Irradiate 26 authenticates Charlie Whiskey at 0614 Zulu as Hotel Bravo.'

'Zero Four.'

Gene armed his weapon for the frontal attack, the Genie rocket. The nuclear Genie rocket would only be onboard an aircraft during wartime, so instead Kilo November 04 had an electronic recorder, the McDonnell Simulator Rocket, which duplicated the firing of the weapons system.

'Kilo November 04 disregard Dolly, left 270 degrees, your target is 290 at 50'. Gene and Tiny's target was on a bearing of 290 degrees, westerly direction, and fifty nautical miles (ninety-three kilometres) distant.

Tiny was hunched over his radar, manoeuvring the antenna to try and see the target. He had the radar height so he knew that the target was close to their altitude. 'I may have him Gene, standby' said Tiny, peering at his scope. It was like looking for a white spot on a TV screen where the station had gone off the air.

There it was again, the telltale spike, like the shape of Mt Everest, of an India Band radar on his APR-9 receiver. Bill spotted Tiny's radar signal and immediately started to jam the fighter interceptor's signal. 'Sparks in the Night Sky' had truly begun. Bill planned his counter measures with a combination of jamming and sporadic clouds of chaff hoping to confuse the fighter interceptor radar and, more importantly, the AI Navigator operating it – Tiny.

Gene disengaged the autopilot as he preferred to manually fly the intercept. 'Kilo November 04 right 310, target one o'clock, 30 miles [56 km]', said the Intercept Director. Marty, the Radar Input Counter Measures Officer, had delivered. The Intercept Director had a good radar picture on his scope and was able to continue vectoring Gene and Tiny towards the unknown target, Mute 104. 'Mute 104, Irradiate 49, you have a chick paired, eleven o'clock, 30 miles (56 km)', the Target Director called. He would continue to call the fighter position during the intercept to assist Doug to find him visually in the night sky. Safety of both aircrew and aircraft was of the utmost importance. Tiny stared at his scope. He could see the radar noise, white spots, all over his scope but he knew that in there somewhere was the target, Mute 104. 'See anything yet, Tiny?' Gene knew that events were going to happen rapidly. Two aircraft approaching each other at a closing speed of 920 knots would pass each other in just over two minutes.

Tiny was changing frequency rapidly to stay away from Bill's jamming. He carefully avoided 'locking-on' his radar to the clouds of chaff Bill was

CF-101 Voodoo armament panel. (Courtesy of Andy McGraw)

dispensing. An inexperienced AI Navigator may have been tricked to 'lock-on' his radar to the chaff instead of the aircraft. It seemed an eternity, but finally Gene heard, 'I am locked-on, Gene', and Tiny immediately called 'Judy' to the Intercept Director. Tiny said, 'Your dot, Gene'. This meant that the fighter interceptor was in position with its radar locked and could continue the attack using only the onboard radar, no vectors or further information required. Gene looked at his scope – there was the steering dot, slightly up and to the right. It was his job to follow the dot and fire the weapon. The Fire Control System would do the rest as it calculated the time to fire the weapon based on closure rates and other parameters. It was Tiny's job to make sure that he kept the radar locked on so that Gene could 'follow the dot' to put the Voodoo in the correct position for the Genie rocket release.

The Fire Control System was built using tubes, or valves as they are called in England. It was 1973 and solid-state electronic circuitry was not installed in the Voodoo. The tubes were susceptible to heat, cold, moisture and vibration; in the face of electronic jamming they had to work at peak efficiency to maintain radar 'lock-on'. Sometimes the dot jumped around and it was the pilot's experience that allowed him to average out the gyrations until the dot became more stable.

This night the dot was particularly challenging for Gene to steer. Tiny was having trouble maintaining radar 'lock-on' and, notwithstanding the electronic jamming, began to suspect that the Fire Control System was not operating up to standard.

'Mute 104, (with Doug and Bill) chick (fighter) is eleven thirty, 10 miles (19 km)', said the Intercept Director assigned to target monitoring duties for the exercise. The fighter, with Gene and Tiny, was drifting slightly to Doug's left. 'Kilo November 04, target eleven thirty, 10 miles (19 km)', the Intercept Director called as he became aware of the fighter interceptor drifting right of the intercept track. There was now only 40 seconds before Mute 104, the target, and Kilo November 04, the fighter, passed in the night sky.

Then it happened. The radar on Kilo November broke lock and the dot disappeared from Gene's scope. Both Gene and Tiny saw it at the same time. 'Break right, Gene'. Gene had already started the evasive manoeuvre by rolling the aircraft about 150 degrees inverted and pulling the control column towards him to start the fighter interceptor down and away from Mute 104. Simultaneously, Doug saw Kilo November 04's flashing red anti-collision lights slightly low and to the left.

'He is passing clear on our left side, Bill'.

'Mute 104, the fighter is passing on your left side and in a right turn, so is probably setting up for the stern re-attack', Dennis, the Intercept (Target) Director, informed Mute 104.

A temporary glitch in the fighter interceptor radar system had brought about the Missed Intercept, every fighter interceptor crew's nightmare if they had been the cause. The Intercept Director in Team 3 briefed his Team Weapons Director on the Missed Intercept and the re-attack in progress. The Weapons Director, in turn, informed the Senior Director of the progress on track Mike 1274, the unknown. Mute 104 was getting closer to Ottawa every minute and Jim's, the Senior Director, options were now limited. It all rested with the crew of Kilo November 04.

'Continue the turn, Kilo November 04, to 160 degrees, target will be 12 'o' clock at 10 miles [19 km]', controller 26 instructed.

'Mute 104, the fighter is five thirty for 10 miles (19 km), closing', Dennis informed the crew. The electronic battle continued. Gene switched weapons systems to the Falcon heat-seeking missile to shoot down Mute 104. The missile used the heat of the metal in the engine to lock on to the target aircraft. In modern warfare, the target would dispense burning flares to trick the heat-seeking missile, but this was 1973 and, barring shutting down both engines, Mute 104 was now on borrowed time. The EB-57 was no longer a factor in jamming the ground radar, so controller 26 had a good scope picture to vector Kilo November 04 until Gene and Tiny took over the intercept.

Bill dispensed some clouds of chaff to interfere with the ground and airborne radar, but the 384 bundles were nearly all gone. He hoped that the chaff and jamming had been responsible for the fighter interceptor breaking lock on the frontal attack and causing the need for a re-attack. Maybe Mute 104 would get really lucky and avoid the usual outcome – shot down.

'Mute 104, fighter is 5 miles [9 km], six o'clock', Dennis transmitted as he scanned his scope. The re-attack using the Infrared Search and Track system was a difficult and somewhat dangerous manoeuvre normally, only used when the rocket, the nuclear Genie, had failed.

Gene banked the aircraft and tightened the turn to begin the re-attack. He increased his speed to Mach 0.9, which he figured would give him an overtake speed of 2 miles per minute (3 km), about 90 seconds to weapon release. He could live with Mute 104 being 10 miles (19 km) closer to Ottawa. His eyes constantly scanned the flight instruments as he manoeuvred the aircraft in cloud to begin the chase of Mute 104. He selected the infrared position on the weapons selector panel. Keeping in mind that this was peacetime and a Weapons System Evaluation Missile, instead of a pair of Hughes AIM-4D Falcon missiles, would be the only device triggered and fired. It would record if Kilo November 04 had the right geometry and parameters to have successfully shot down Mute 104.

Tiny was busy on the radar trying to avoid Bill's electronic and mechanical jamming. He could get a lock-on for a few seconds, only to have it break lock again. He was trying to provide Gene with range to target and closing speeds. On a dark night, flying in and out of cloud, this information was invaluable, both for the attack and, most important, safety. Kilo November's effectiveness as a fighter interceptor was now downgraded, due to the performance of its radar and having to use the infrared Falcon missiles. It was all up to Gene and Tiny now, the Kilo November team. Gene initiated a slight climb to see if he could get above the cloud tops. The infrared sensor did not work well without a cloud-free path to the target.

Switching radar mode to infrared 'A Scope', Tiny was looking for the telltale pip or spike on his scope to show a heat source from Mute 104.

'Left 10 degree, Gene', Tiny instructed. Now Tiny had Kilo November pointed straight at Mute 104. The infrared bulb-type sensor on the Voodoo nose was picking up the CF-100 heat signature. Tiny had been timing since the last range estimate. 'One mile (2 km), in the range window now, Gene', said Tiny. It was time for Gene to squeeze the trigger to the first detent, Trigger 1 position. This action would activate the missile battery and the nitrogen coolant would be released at this time in the nose of the Falcon missiles. This allowed the missile seeker head to pick up Mute 104. A further squeeze to the full detent, Trigger 2, would cause small charges to separate the missiles from the launcher rails. The rocket motors would fire and the Falcon missiles, travelling at Mach 3, would fly up the engine tailpipe of Mute 104. 'Irradiate, Mike Alpha', Gene called. This meant that the Mission had been Accomplished, target destroyed. But this was an exercise, so the Weapons System Evaluator Missile would tell the story when Kilo November returned to base – Mission Accomplished or Missed Intercept. It was safe to say that on this occasion, Mute 104 had been successfully shot down south-east of Senneterre, Quebec, many miles from Ottawa. That night and the following day, the whole NORAD organisation would continue at full alert, from the cooks providing the human fuel to the generals providing the human guidance, as many targets and fighter interceptors played out their part in 'Sparks in the Night Sky'.

'Mute 104, Irradiate 49, chick requests vis ident (visual identification fly by)'. The fighter was requesting to come alongside Mute 104 and shine a brilliant spotlight on it to 'visually identify' the aircraft.

'Irradiate 49, vis ident approved, ceased buzzer [turned off electronic jammers], heading 165 Angels 41'. Doug and Bill sat back and waited. Tiny now had a good picture on his scope and locked on to the target. 'One mile (2 kilometres) Gene, overtake 30 knots (35 mph) (56 km/h)'. Tiny started to call out the distance and overtake to Gene as they approached Mute 104 on the right side. Gene had been watching the flashing red anti-collision lights ahead, but it was impossible to judge the distance in the dark. The Hughes MG-13 Fire Control System would give commands to the Voodoo pilot to bring the interceptor 200 feet to the right and 600 feet slant range from the target. Very carefully, Gene inched up on the right side of Mute 104 and then moved closer until he was flying formation just off Doug's right wing. Things looked awfully close in night formation.

Gene really enjoyed the next event. Doug and Bill not so much – they both shielded their eyes. Tiny turned on the identification light, a 600-watt

Adversaries, CF-100 & CF-101 tails. (Courtesy of Author)

quartz halogen lamp, which lit up Mute 104 so you could see every detail, including 'the maker's name', said Gene.

'Irradiate, Kilo November Identified CAF CF-100 number 100779' Tiny transmitted and then turned off the light, plunging the night into darkness. Not for long. Gene put the throttles into full afterburner, illuminating Mute 104 with twin streaks of bright orange afterburner exhaust as Kilo November pulled up and away from Mute 104. Doug and Bill never tired of this spectacular sight, even though they had just lost the aerial joust.

'Irradiate, Kilo November 04 Bingo (minimum fuel to return to CFB Bagotville) Fuel'.

'Kilo November, left 080 Angels 37'. Gene and Tiny were on their way home.

'Mute 104, you have been splashed (neutralised as a target), right 235'. It would be a short night for Doug and Bill. Their Altitude Reservation route had intended to have them fly to their Ottawa target and then back to CFB North Bay, but now they were heading straight home. The good and bad dichotomy of the exercise was now evident. The 'bad', for Mute 104, was that they had been shot down, but also 'good' as they had been shot down by Kilo November 04. NORAD was awake, sleep tight!

'Mute 104, Irradiate 49, contact North Bay terminal on 258.4, thanks for the good jamming, good night.' Dennis transmitted and then turned to his Intercept Director Technician, 'time for a coffee before the next one?'

'Thanks for keeping us safe Irradiate 49, Mute 104 switching to terminal,' Doug said and prepared for the approach and landing in North Bay.

'North Bay Terminal, Mute 104, Flight Level 410'.

'Roger, Mute 104, Squawk 3236 and ident'.

'Mute 104, identified, cleared direct the North Bay Tacan, descend 9,000, your discretion, altimeter is 28.36'. Tacan – TACtical Air Navigation – is an accurate military navigational beacon that gives both bearing and distance information to the aircraft from the beacon. Bill had called the Squadron Operations, Yogi Ops, and got the latest weather for North Bay. Doug and Bill went through the challenge and response of the Pre-Letdown/ Circuit Entry Check. At 167 km from North Bay Doug pulled back the throttles to idle and Mute 104 began its return to home base. The weather was a cloudy night with some light rain. Doug and Bill continued their descent through the clouds, Doug now hand flying and Bill monitoring the aircraft's heading, altitude and speed.

'Mute 104, what kind of approach are you requesting at North Bay?'

'Terminal, Mute 104 is requesting precision approach, runway 26'.

Ground Controlled Approach, precision approach, is an approach aid to land an aircraft in bad weather conditions. It consisted of a controller sitting in front of two radar screens. The position of the runway extended centreline was on one screen and the three degree slope to the runway was on the other screen. The controller observed the position of the aircraft on his radar screens and 'talked it down' to put the aircraft on the runway centre line and glide slope. A very valuable approach aid in the 1970s before an instrument landing system was installed in some aircraft.

'Roger, turn right, heading 240, maintain 4,000 contact radar on 287.6. If no joy return my frequency, Good Night'.

'Roger, Good Night'.

'Radar, Mute 104 heading 240, 4,000'.

'Mute 104, Final Controller 35, altimeter 28.38'.

'Precision approach 1,420 feet, no transmission for a period of five seconds on final approach, overshoot 260 to 5,000 feet, acknowledge'.

'Mute 104'.

'Mute 104, further right 250 for right hand precision approach, runway 26 North Bay'.

'Mute 104 slightly right of on course, correcting slowly'.

'Mute 104, right 260 on course, 10 mile final, 1 mile, to glidepath intercept'.

'Now established on final approach, do not acknowledge further transmissions except if requested'.

'Eight miles from touchdown, standby for descent'.

Ground-controlled approach trailer. (Courtesy of Wayne Ralph)

'Intersecting glide path, commence descent *now*'.

Doug started a standard descent rate, extended the landing gear, selected full flaps and called 'Pre-Landing Checklist'. Bill responded by calling the checklist and checking Doug's responses. Controller 35 gave continuous instructions to Doug regarding descent rate, to maintain him on the glide path and heading, to keep him on the runway centreline. In this way Mute 104 was talked back to earth, specifically Runway 26 at Canadian Forces Base North Bay, descending in the gloom of the night stratus clouds.

'Five miles to touchdown'.

Controller 35 checked with North Bay Tower if the runway was clear and Mute 104 had clearance to land.

'Mute 104, cleared full stop runway 26, wind 260/10'.

Doug scanned his flight instruments and made continuous corrections to heading and descent rate to stay on the glidepath slope so he would be in a position to land.

'On course on glidepath,' controller 35 droned.

'One mile until touchdown (wind) 260/10'.

The runway approach lights cast a hazy light through the clouds on the cockpit canopy. Suddenly, there was home – the runway stretched like two ribbons of light into the foggy murk. Simultaneously, Controller 35 said, 'Precision minimums look up if visual, land straight ahead'. Doug's eyes quickly adjusted outside to the outside world, he turned on the landing light to give a better view of the runway, and he positioned Mute 104 for a smooth landing back home. Deploying speed brakes to destroy the lift on the wings and gently applying brakes, 100779 slowed to a safe speed and taxied off the runway. Mute 104 had accomplished its task of keeping NORAD on its toes this night.

'Mute 104, next left, cleared taxi to the ramp, Good Night'.

'Good Night'. Bill was glad that his night was finished as the Air Traffic Controller was on shift until 0700. Post-Landing checks were completed on the taxi in and they were looking for the ground crew to marshal them in to the parking position. Turning off the landing light, Doug approached the flight line. Then he saw Barrie in the floodlights, giving him directions to his parking spot. Obeying his signals, he pulled 100779 into its spot and set the parking brake.

Shutting down the left engine, Doug tested the right hydraulic pump by selecting the flaps down. All normal, he shut down the right engine and opened the canopy. Ah, fresh air and silence, for now. Mute 105 was still an hour away. Cockpit 'Shut Down Check' and now 100779 was in darkness; the fifteen-year-old aircraft proved with proper maintenance that it still 'could do the job'. Barrie put the ladder up to the left side of the aircraft and the crew descended to terra firma.

'How is the bird, Sir?' inquired Barrie.

'No problems, she is ready to go again Barrie'.

'OK, we will do a post-flight inspection and gas her up for her next flight'. It would be a long night for Barrie and line maintenance. Some of the squadron aircraft would continue to arrive back hours later and each one would have to be attended to. A squadron was a 24-hour operation and during an exercise that was what the ground crew worked. Also, remember that this was an all-weather operation. The aircraft would be fixed or serviced on the hangar line outside in Goose Bay, Labrador, in the middle of winter, in -40 °C (-40 °F), or Bermuda in +30 °C (86 °F) during the summer. Both could be unpleasant for the ground crew.

Doug and Bill had completed their mission and were now on their way home through the dark and quiet streets of North Bay. What of Kilo November 04? Gene and Tiny had landed in CFB Bagotville, Quebec, and had grabbed some food in operations while their aircraft was being serviced. The radar was repaired and 101003 sat on the hangar line, ready to take to the skies again. Gene checked his log book and he noted that 'we were subsequently scrambled again at dawn for another target'. Three hours and forty-two minutes of very intense time airborne on the two successful missions. Gene mentioned that after landing from the second mission, 'Tiny and I would have to take care of our administrative duties before heading home'.

Weeks later, Captain Peter Maunsell and the exercise team would meet to correlate the results of the Amalgam Mute exercise before disseminating the information throughout the NORAD Region. It would confirm that Mute 104 had been on track and on time. It would confirm that Kilo November 04 had 'shot down' two targets, the second target at dawn, hours after shooting down Mute 104. It would confirm that 100779 and 101003 were serviceable and completed their airborne tasks, as assigned by Peter. It would prove that Doug, Bill, Gene and Tiny were capable of their assigned duties, and confirmed that Marty, Jim, Dennis, and Bob could respond to any unidentified aircraft entering Canadian airspace. It would establish that Ottawa, the nation's capital, could be protected against the Soviet bomber threat. Finally, it would confirm that during the Cold War and into the twenty-first century, NORAD was capable of living up to its motto – Deter, Detect, and Destroy.

Epilogue

It has been over twenty years since the end of the Cold War. North America, the USA and Canada, have been involved with 'ideological difference' skirmishes in various parts of the world far from our shores. Canada's troops have been in Kosovo and are in Afghanistan supporting a North Atlantic Treaty Organisation initiative. Limited forces were involved in the 1991 Gulf War and the United Nations campaign in Croatia and Bosnia and Herzegovina. The Cold War became actual combat wars where Canadian citizens died in the pursuit of preserving democracy and freedom of choice overseas.

What of NORAD now that it is more than fifty years since the first agreement was signed? It still exists and meets the requirements of the defence of North America in the twenty-first century. In 2006, it added a maritime warning division, which included inland waterways. 'The Hole' in North Bay, Ontario, is closed and there has been some thought of using it as a secure storage area. Colorado Springs has also mothballed its underground facilities and moved them to the surface, at Peterson AFB, Colorado.

In this day and age of medals, perhaps it is remiss that there was not a NORAD medal issued, like the one awarded for NATO service? The defence of the 'home front' is just as, or more, important as Canada's commitment overseas as a member of NATO. Perhaps the unique agreement between Canada and the USA was politically and militarily expected and thus became the norm. It was not worthy of special recognition.

The numbered regions have been replaced with three regions, the Alaskan Region, the Canadian Region and the Continental Region. The Canadian NORAD Region is headquartered with the 1st Canadian Air Division in Winnipeg, Manitoba. It is divided into two sectors, Canada East and Canada West. Both sectors have their Operations Control Centers in North Bay, Ontario. The Canadian NORAD Region covers Canada geographically.

The North Warning radar system had replaced the DEW Line radar sites by 1992. It Canada it consists of forty-seven unmanned radar sites supported by five maintenance centres. It is comprised of eleven long-range and thirty-six short-range radars. The CADIN/Pinetree Line closed its final sites in 1990.

What happened to the Voodoo replacement, the Hornet? The multi-role aircraft holds NORAD Alert at two bases, 425 Tactical Fighter Squadron at CFB Bagotville, Quebec, and 409 Tactical Fighter Squadron at CFB Cold Lake, Alberta. The training is still done by 410 Squadron, now called Tactical Fighter (Operational Training). There is provision to move the fighters further north to Forward Operating Locations such as Inuvik and Yellowknife in the Northwest Territories. Similar to the initial batch of Voodoos, it has in-flight refuelling capability. It is now nearly thirty years old and it is approaching the end of its service life.

Author Wayne Ralph completed his MA thesis on the procurement of Canada's CP-140 Aurora and CF-18 Hornet as a Department of National Defence Strategic Studies Scholar at the University of Calgary. He showed that those two programmes completed in the 1980s were the last complex aircraft weapon systems acquired by Canada. Though still capable, they are aging systems and will ultimately need replacement. However, the cost is many times greater than Canada has ever faced. In 1977, the Aurora and the Hornet acquisitions were each over one billion dollars, an unprecedented budgetary cost for the times, but nothing compared to 2017 dollars. For about half as many fighters as were bought so long ago, the government's current choice, the Lockheed-Martin F35 Lightning II, may eventually cost $12 to 15 billion. Ralph observed:

> The true cost over the 40-year-life of any weapon system is always higher and hidden. The history of fighter acquisition in Canada is buy what you think you need, then run out of operating budget to fly them. Several dozen fighters are stored away, sometimes cycled into and out of service to extend the airframe life of the fleet as a whole, while squadrons are disbanded due to inadequate funds. The RCAF in the 1950s had more than 20 operational fighter squadrons, but the CAF today has three. Having the budget to buy 60 state-of-the-art fighters does not guarantee the significant annual increases to pay for operations, maintenance and modernization. There will always be competing financial demands – other weapon systems needing replacing, other operational challenges on land or at sea, new wars demanding weaponry not in the inventory. The industrial benefits promised by the purchase of each new weapon system are never fully realized. In fact, employment benefits and offsetting sales

Lockheed Martin F-35A Lightning.

of Canadian products are rarely tallied up some 20 years into a program if, indeed, they can be clearly recollected.

Aircraft such as the Hercules, the Cormorant, the Chinook have high hourly operating costs; sometimes much higher than was anticipated when first acquired. Can we know what the hourly cost will be for an advanced fighter such as the F35 in 2021? History shows that it is usually much more than we ever imagined. Cost overruns and operational shortfalls are not new in weapons design and procurement. It is just the number of zeroes at the end that have changed; little new has been learned.

United States President Dwight D. Eisenhower delivered his famous cautionary "military-industrial complex" speech when he left office in January 1961. A military man who understood both the military's insatiable demands and its limitations, Eisenhower said, "... partly because of the huge costs involved, a government contract becomes virtually a substitute for intellectual curiosity ... [and] public policy could itself become the captive of a scientific-technological elite ..."

The present target aircraft for the CAF are supplied by a contracted airborne training services company called Top Aces. The aircraft is a Dassault-Breguet-Dornier Alpha jet equipped with jammers and has a crew of two, a civilian pilot and, since 2009, a CAF Electronic Warfare

Officer in the rear seat. In January 2009, 414 Squadron reformed as an Electronic Warfare Support Squadron to support the Top Aces Company in Gatineau, Quebec.

NORAD exercises are still going on, although there appear to be more notification exercises than surprise no-notice ones.

The Canadian press reported on Thursday 17 February 2011 that:

> NORAD holds exercises over Eastern Canada. People in Eastern Ontario and Southern Quebec shouldn't worry Thursday if they see fighter jets chasing a small plane. NORAD says it is just conducting exercise flights from mid-to-late morning. It said people west of Montreal and east of Ottawa may hear or see fighters quite close to what looks like a Lear jet. NORAD (North American Aerospace Defense Command) said the exercise is designed to practice intercept and identification procedures. It has been conducting similar exercise flights throughout Canada and the U.S. for years.

What happened to the exercise aircraft in Chapter Nine, 'Sparks in the Night Sky'? The Voodoo, number 101003, is displayed at the Goose Bay airport, Happy Valley Goose Bay, Labrador, Canada.

The Canuck, number 100779, is displayed at Peterson Air and Space Museum, Peterson AFB (Colorado Springs), Colorado, USA.

CF-101 Voodoo, 101003, Goose Bay, Labrador. (Courtesy of Michael Charters)

CF-100 Canuck, 100779, Peterson AFB, Colorado. (Courtesy of Malcolm Nason)

It is a fitting tribute to these two great aircraft and the part they played in the defence of North America. It is very appropriate that the American aircraft is displayed in Canada and the Canadian aircraft is displayed in the USA, two independent nations, one mission – to maintain the defence of North America.

What of the people who took part, or were otherwise involved with NORAD and its resources, in the Amalgam Mute exercise in May 1973? What did life hold for them after the mission?

The Voodoo Crew

Gene Lukan took over command of 410 Squadron, the Voodoo OTU, in 1976. Following a ground tour in Europe, which included a checkout on the CF-104 Starfighter, he returned to National Defence Headquarters in Ottawa. NORAD operations training and CF-18 procurement duties completed his posting. The commanding officer of AETE at CFB Cold Lake and Director of Air Plans completed his career. His engineering background took him to the Canadian Space Agency and work on the robotic arm for the space station. Gene lives in Alberta and enjoys skiing and building his own aircraft.

Tiny McDonald continued his military career with NORAD postings to CFB Goose Bay, Labrador, North Bay, Ontario, and NORAD Headquarters at Colorado Springs. In civilian life, after military retirement in 1981, he operated his own flight schools in North Bay, Ontario. Among many things, Tiny is remembered for his caricatures. He passed away in 2007.

The Canuck Crew

Doug Fitzpatrick left 414 (EW) Squadron in 1973 to become a flight instructor on the Tutor aircraft at CFB Moose Jaw, Saskatchewan. Doug left the military in 1974 to join Pacific Western Airlines, which became Canadian Airlines and finally Air Canada. Doug retired as an airline captain. He lives in Alberta and volunteers in his church and the hospital.

Bill Bland was posted as an exchange Electronic Warfare Officer to the USAF in 1974. He flew the Martin EB-57 at Malmstrom Air Force Base, Montana. Returning to North Bay, Ontario, he had further NORAD postings, in exercise planning and 414 (EW) Squadron. He retired from the military in 1985 and worked for Canadair/Bombardier on the Challenger electronic warfare aircraft. Bill is now his own head gardener on Vancouver Island.

NORAD Exercise Shop

Peter Maunsell continued to work with NORAD, in North Bay, Ontario, both down 'the Hole', in the exercise shop, and with 414 (EW) Squadron. Peter retired in 1985 and volunteers his time as a hospital chaplain.

Air Weapons Controllers

Jim Graham worked in NORAD at the BUIC site in St Margarets, New Brunswick, before returning to North Bay, Ontario. He had a position in NORAD, standards and evaluation, and assisted in the transition from SAGE to the new ROCC radar system. Jim enjoys trailering trips in his retirement.

Dennis Kelleher continued his career with NORAD, serving as an instructor at the Air Weapons Control and Countermeasures School, CFB North Bay and at CFS Falconbridge radar site, eventually becoming commander of the school in 1985. A posting to Europe to oversee NATO Airborne Warning and Control System aircraft operations, Alaska, as Canadian Forces detachment commander, and senior liaison officer with the RCMP completed a thirty-two year career. The past sixteen years have been involved with Human Factors Engineering, aspects of different military applications with CMC Electronics, General Dynamics Canada and CAE. Dennis lives in Ontario and says he is getting closer to retiring to the lake.

Marty Schlosser's operational experiences were predominantly in the area of aerospace control, both aboard Airborne Warning and Control System platforms and ground-based command. He was an operationally qualified Aerospace Controller and Systems Analyst. Commanding Officer of 21 Aerospace and Control Squadron, directing CF Fighter Group operations and acquiring new defence capabilities completed his thirty-seven years with the CAF. Marty is an avid woodworker who both designs and builds furniture. He lives in Ontario.

Air Defence Technicians

Bob Keith spent twenty years as a NORAD fighter control operator, serving on four radar sites and two combat centres – Duluth, Minnesota and North Bay, Ontario. In 1974, he left the military and moved west and worked for B.C. Hydro railway, retiring in 1997. His hobby is landscape photography and international travel. Bob lives in British Columbia.

Radar Technicians

Pierre Parent was a radar technician on the CADIN/Pinetree radar line for twenty years and worked on many radar sites from Quebec to Saskatchewan. Retiring from the military in 1974, he continued his interest with electronics by working for Transport Canada. After eighteen years travelling in Northern Manitoba, Eastern Nunavut and the Eastern High Arctic maintaining sites, he decided to retire in 1996. Well not quite – he operates a cable network for a 1,000 customers and is active in the local theatre. Pierre lives in Manitoba. We have never met but have spent many hours on the phone.

Larry Wilson joined the RCAF in September 1961 and after training, worked as a RCAF/CAF Radar Technician in various radar sites in the NORAD system. He retired in 1987 to take a position as a Life Cycle Maintenance Manager, first with Directorate Electronics Engineering and Maintenance, then in the North Warning System Office, retiring in 1996. From 1987 until 2001 he worked as a technician in the University of Ottawa, Physics Department, Electronic Shop. Larry lives in Ontario.

First Bear Intercept

Ron Neeve was posted to Colorado Springs in 1974 as DEW Line liaison officer. Later, in 1976, he was part of Prime Minister Trudeau's welcoming committee at Colorado Springs. Trudeau was the only Prime Minister to visit NORAD headquarters in the mountain at Colorado Springs. A 409 Squadron tour preceded nine years at National Defence Headquarters in Ottawa on the military co-operation committee and officer's promotions. He was the recipient of the Queen's Jubilee Medal in 1977. He retired in 1990 and took some time to travel. Ron lives on Vancouver Island.

1972 Top Gun

Lowell Butters went on to serve in units across Canada and in Europe. He retired in 2001 after thirty-five years' service in the RCAF/CAF. He continues to work as an aviation and market research consultant for CIRRUS Research Associates Inc. He is often seen on the golf course. Lowell lives in Ontario.

Douglas Danko, the 1972 Top Gun AI Navigator, later cross-trained as a pilot. He was subsequently killed in a military flying accident in Europe in 1977.

Bristol Aerospace

Bob Moore retired from Bristol Aerospace in 1991 and went travelling from one end of Canada to the other. In 2007, his peers persuaded him to take over the restoration department of the Western Canadian Aviation Museum. Bob lives in Manitoba.

Line Maintenance

Barrie Laycock was posted to Europe to work with the CF-104 Starfighter. He had a tour with 409 Squadron on the CF-101 and retired from the military in 1989. Barrie then worked as a supervisor with Spar Aerospace and Canadian Helicopters. In 1993, he started a new career as an ISO auditor. Barrie lives in British Columbia.

Larry Lundquist continued to serve the CAF in various engineering capacities, which included a Master's Degree in engine propulsion. On leaving the CAF, he joined IMP Aerospace (a company that specializes in military aircraft depot level maintenance). While there, he held a variety of executive-level positions in production, engineering, contracts, and product support over a period of twenty years. He likes to play golf. Larry lives in Nova Scotia.

Gordon Wilson, the author, embarked on an airline career after his military service, until it was cut short by multiple sclerosis. He medically retired as an airline captain and has started a writing career. Gordon lives in British Columbia.

The Air Force in Canada has gone through many name changes since early 1968 when it was known as the Royal Canadian Air Force (RCAF). The Minister of National Defence Paul Hellyer decided to unify the three Canadian services, Army, Navy and Air Force, on 1 February 1968 under the title of the Canadian Armed Forces (CAF). The CAF adopted army ranks for all personnel and the author spent his career as a Lieutenant and subsequently Captain instead of the more common sense descriptive Flying Officer and Flight Lieutenant. Effective of 16 August 2011, the Air Force will once again be known as the Royal Canadian Air Force; the rank structure remains the same.

The Amalgam Mute exercise and the memories of those days are now committed to this book and reside in libraries and aviation museums. Hopefully, the words and photos have stirred emotion with some readers who are reading about these events for the first time and also for those readers who were there and contributed to the NORAD effort. Unsung heroes and tales of heroic 'above and beyond the call of duty' events which did not get recorded abound by the thousands. These events in the book did happen and are now consigned to memories and history. Today's and tomorrow's events will continue to happen and keep NORAD alive and well through the efforts of the unseen army of men and women.

DETER DETECT DESTROY

Conversion Table

Standard Metric Units
Metre, Kilometre, Kilogram

Metres to feet	multiply by 0.30
Kilometres to miles	multiply by 0.62
Kilogram to pounds	multiply by 2.2

Aviation Units
Feet (Altitude), Knots (Speed), Pounds (Weight)

Feet to metres	multiply by 3.28
Knots to mph	multiply by 1.15
Knots to km/h	multiply by 1.85
Pounds to kilograms	multiply by 0.45

Sources

Airforce Magazine: Canada's Air Force Heritage Voice (multiple issues)
Annual Historical Report: 409 (AW) Fighter Squadron (1970–1974)
Annual Historical Report: 410 (OTU) Squadron (1970–1974)
Annual Historical Report: 416 (AW) Fighter Squadron (1970–1974)
Annual Historical Report: 425 (AW) Fighter Squadron (1970–1974)
Annual Historical Report: 414 Electronic Warfare Unit (1959–1967)
Annual Historical Report: 414 Electronic Warfare Squadron (1970–1974)
AVRO Arrow: The Arrowheads (1980)
Baglow, Bob, *Canucks Unlimited: Royal Canadian Air Force CF-100 Squadrons and Aircraft, 1952–1963* (1985)
Bishop, Arthur, *True Canadian Heroes in the Air* (2004)
Boyne, Walter & Philip Handleman, *Brassey's Air Combat Reader: Historic Facts and Aviation Legend* (1999)
Brodie, Bernard, *Strategy in the Missile Age* (1959)
Brown, Louis, *A Radar History of World War 11* (1999)
Campagna, Palmiro, *Storms of Controversy: The Secret Avro Arrow Files Revealed* (1993)
Canadian Forces Sentinel, April 1971, Volume 7 Number 3 (1971)
CF-100 Aircraft Operating Instructions: Canadian Forces (1975)
CF-101 Aircraft Operating Instructions: National Defence (1979)
Clarke, Bob, *The Illustrated Guide to Armageddon: Britain's Cold War* (2009)
Clearwater, John, *Canadian Nuclear Weapons: The Untold Story of Canada's Cold War Arsenal* (1998)
Continental Air Defense: A Dedicated Force is no Longer Needed – Report to Congressional Committees (1994)
Defunct Clunk Club of Canada Newsletter (1980)
Dempsey, Daniel, *A Tradition of Excellence* (2002)

Dorr, Robert, *McDonnell F-101 Voodoo* (1987)

Dose, Daniel, *NORAD a New Look: National Security Series* (1983)

Dow, James, *The Arrow* (1997)

Drendel, Lou and Paul Stevens, *F-101 Voodoo: Modern Military Aircraft Series (5002)* (1986)

Dwyer, Gwynne, *Ignorant Armies* (2003)

Electronic Warfare Principles and Radar and Communication Principles: Canadian Forces Aerospace & Navigation School (1984)

Ellis, Frank, *In Canadian Skies* (1959)

Flying September 1951

Forces Development Objective: FDO A-2/72 Aerospace Defence 1972–1984 DND (1972)

Fighting Jets: The Epic of Flight (1983)

Fitts, Richard, *The Strategy of Electromagnetic Conflict* (1980)

Freedman, Lawrence, *The Cold War* (2001)

Fundamentals of ECM Technology: Association of Old Crows (unknown)

Gaddis, Lewis, *The Cold War: The Deals. The Spies. The Lies. The Truth* (2005)

Gordon, Doug, *USAF Tactical Reconnaissance in the Cold War: 1945 to Korea, Cuba, Vietnam to the Iron Curtain* (2006)

Gray, Colin, *Canadian Defence Priorities: A Question of Relevance* (1972)

Griffin, John, *Canadian Military Aircraft: Aircraft of the Canadian Air Force* (2006)

Hamilton-Paterson, James, *Empire of the Clouds* (2010)

Hellyer, Paul, *Minister of National Defence* (1964)

Hitchins, Frank & Richard Hovey, Don Schmidt, Harold McNamee, *416 Squadron: Complete History* (1974)

Holmes, Harry, *Avro: The History of an Aircraft Company* (1994)

Hurtig, Mel, *Rushing to Armageddon* (2004)

Jackson, Roger, *Avro Aircraft* (1998)

Jockel, Joseph, *Canada in NORAD 1957–2007: A History* (2007)

Jockel, Joseph, *No Boundaries Upstairs: Canada, the United States, and the Origins of North American Air Defence 1945–1958* (1987)

Jones, Barry, *English Electra Canberra and Martin B-57* (1999)

Keenan, Patrick, *Canadian Warplane Heritage* (2001)

Lashmar, Paul, *Spy Flights of the Cold War* (1996)

Leslie, Robert, *There Shall be Wings: A History of the Royal Canadian Air Force* (1959)

Library of Nations, *The Soviet Union* (1985)

Lucas, Edward, *The New Cold War: Putin's Russia and the Threat to the West* (2008)

Lyzun, Jim, *Canadian Profile: CF-100 Canuck* (1985)

MacMillan, James, *CF-100* (1981)

McIntyre, Robert, *Canadian Profile: CF-101 Voodoo* (1984)

Milberry, Larry, *Aviation in Canada* 1979

Milberry, Larry, *Canadian Air Force Today* (1987)

Milberry, Larry, *Sixty years: The RCAF and CF Air Command 1924–1984* (1984)

Milberry, Larry, *The Avro CF-100* (1981)

Millar, George, *The Bruneval Raid: Flashpoint of the Radar War* (1974)

Moore, Robert, *The Voodoo and I* (2010)

Morse, Stan and David Donald, *Wings of Fame: Volume 18, The Journal of Classic Combat Aircraft* (2000)

Nicks, Don, *A History of the Air Service in Canada articles* (1997)

Nijboer, Donald, *Cockpits of the Cold War* (2003)

Niyiri, Nicolas A, *An Integrated Defense Strategy for Canada and the US in NORAD* (2003)

Pace, Steve, *Air Force Legends Number 205: McDonnell XF-88 Voodoo* (1999)

Page, Ron, *Canuck: CF-100 All Weather Fighter* (1981)

Peden, Murray, *Fall of an Arrow* (1978)

Pilot's Check List CF-100: Canadian Forces (1973)

Pilot's Check List CF-101: Canadian Forces (1977)

Povejsil, Donald & Robert Raven & Peter Waterman, *Airborne Radar* (1965)

Price, Alfred, *Instruments of Darkness: The History of Electronic Warfare* (1977)

Price, Alfred, *The History of U.S. Electronic Warfare* (2000)

Ralph, Wayne, *Aces, Warriors and Wingmen* (2005)

Reed, Thomas, *At the Abyss: An insider's History of the Cold War* (2004)

Regehr, Ernie, *Canada and the Nuclear Arms Race* (1983)

Regehr, Ernie & Simon Rosenblum, *The Road to Peace* (1988)

Rossiter, Sean, *The Chosen Ones: Test Pilots in Action* (2003)

SAGE Goes Underground: Information Booklet DND (1964)

Salter, James, *Gods of Tin: The Flying Years* (2004)

Sgarlato,Nico, *Soviet Aircraft of Today (1978)*

Spick, Mike, *An Illustrated Guide to Modern Attack Aircraft* (1987)

Stewart, Greig, *Shutting Down the National Dream: A. V. Roe and the Tragedy of the Avro Arrow* (2008)

Streetly, Martin, *Airborne Electronic Warfare: History, Techniques and Tactics* (1988)

Streetly, Martin, *World Electronic Warfare Aircraft* (1983)

Talmadge,Marian & Iris Gilmore, *NORAD The North American Air Defense Command* (1967)

Taylor, John, *Jane's Pocket Book of Major Combat Aircraft* (1974)
The Emerging Shield: The Air Force and the Evolution of Continental Air Defence 1945–1960
Thompson, Terry, *Warriors and the Battle Within* (2004)
Yenne, Bill, *The Great Warplanes of the 1980s* (1986)
Van Brunt, Leroy, *Applied ECM* (1982)
Van Brunt, Leroy, *The Glossary of Electronic Warfare: EW Primer* (1984)
Vargas-Caba, Miguel, *Bear: Flight to Liberty* (2007)
Veale, Thomas, *Guarding what you Most Value: North American Defense Command Celebrating 50 years* (2008)
Wade, Harold, *Cold War Fighter Pilot* (2004)
Walpole, Nigel, *Voodoo Warriors: The story of the McDonnell Voodoo Fast-jets* (2007)
West, Julian, *Electronic Counter Measures: Lecture 19 January 1949*
Wheeler, Barry, *An Illustrated Guide to Modern American Fighters and Attack Aircraft* (1987)
Whitaker, Reg & Steve Hewitt, *Canada and the Cold War* (2003)
Whitcomb, Randall, *Avro Aircraft and Cold War Aviation* (2004)
Whitcomb, Randall, *Cold War Tech War: The Politics of America's Air Defense* (2008)
White Paper on Defence, Government of Canada March 1964
Wings Magazine, Volume 23, No. 1 February 1993
Zuk, Bill, Janusz Zurakowski, *Legend in the Skies* (2004)
Zuk, Bill, *The Avro Arrow Story: The Revolutionary Airplane and its Courageous Test Pilots* (2004)

INTERVIEWEES

CF-100 CANUCK& CF-101 VOODOO

Ron Bell, Bill Bland, Lowell Butters, Nick Chester, Rob Dunlop, Dan Farrell,
Randy Faulkner, Doug Fitzpatrick, Rick Hovey, Gene Lukan, Peter Maunsell,
George McAffer, Robert Merrick, Gordon Moore, Ron Neeve, Grant Nicholls, Ken Penny, Jim Pocklington, Richard Sopczak, David Trotter, Lew Twambley, John Wiggin

CF-100, CF-101 MAINTENANCE, WEAPONS

Barrie Laycock, Larry Lundquist, Bob Moore, Roy Roch, Gary Wiffen

CF-100, CF-101 COCKPIT MOCKUPS, SIMULATORS

Andy McGraw, Wayne Scott

RADAR & RADAR SITES

Malcolm Dewar, Jack Donnelly, Jim Graham, Bob Keith, Dennis Kelleher, Pierre Parent, Ken Peacock, Marty Schlosser

TOP GUN

Lowell Butters

FIRST SOVIET BEAR INTERCEPT

Ron Neeve

BOMARC

Maurice Hanberg

HISTORICAL RESEARCH, WRITING ADVICE

Richard Girouard, Wayne Ralph, Jerry Vernon, Dr Stephen Harris

Index